"With new insight and informed theological rigor, Belcher advances the now decades-long effort to appreciate and promote the human symbolic activity of sacraments as experiences of sharing in the very life of God. True to the wisdom and knowledge she has gleaned from the field of ritual studies, she delves into the particulars of one rite, infant baptism, to demonstrate how its personal, bodily, cultural, communal, and spiritual dynamics make the sacrament such a prevalent and formative practice for the real-life church in its members."

—*Bruce T. Morrill, S.J.*
Vanderbilt Divinity School

Efficacious Engagement
Sacramental Participation in the Trinitarian Mystery

Kimberly Hope Belcher

Mrs. Lewis —
Thanks for your vocation.
Kimberly Hope Belcher

A Michael Glazier Book

LITURGICAL PRESS
Collegeville, Minnesota

www.litpress.org

A Michael Glazier Book published by Liturgical Press

Cover design by David Manahan, OSB.
Illustration of the Trinity by Frank Kacmarcik, OblSB.

Library of Congress Cataloging-in-Publication Data

Belcher, Kimberly Hope.
    Efficacious engagement : sacramental participation in the Trinitarian mystery / Kimberly Hope Belcher.
        p. cm.
    "A Michael Glazier book."
    Includes bibliographical references (p.   ) and index.
    ISBN 978-0-8146-5763-8 -- ISBN 978-0-8146-8041-4 (ebook)
    1. Sacraments—Catholic Church.   2. Catholic Church—Doctrines.   3. Infant baptism.   4. Trinity.   I. Title.
BX2203.B45   2011
231'.044—dc23   2011029230

For Matt
for your gift of self

Contents

Foreword   ix

Acknowledgments   xi

Chapter One   The Sacramental Plan of Salvation   1

Chapter Two   Efficacious Engagement:
                  Ritual Formation of Dynamic Persons   32

Chapter Three   Initiating Infants   60

Chapter Four   Folds   93

Chapter Five   Threefold:
                  The Trinitarian Dynamic of Infant Baptism   128

Chapter Six   The Spirit: Unfolding the Gift   156

Bibliography   182

Index of Names   194

Index of Subjects   196

Foreword

I n Flannery O'Connor's short story "A Temple of the Holy Ghost," a child is the only person that seems to make sense of all the gibberish that resounds around her. The child, who remains nameless throughout the story, is the younger cousin of two other girls who keep calling each other Temple One and Temple Two. When asked why, the two foolish girls, giggling, tell about Sister Perpetua's advice to say, "Stop sir! I am a Temple of the Holy Ghost!" if a man should "behave in an ungentlemanly manner with them in the back of an automobile." It is the child, however, who "was pleased with the phrase," and it "made her feel as if somebody had given her a present." Later on, when told about the freak, "a man and woman both," whom the other two girls had seen at the fair, the child once again is able to figure out the "riddle that was more puzzling that the riddle itself" by picturing in her mind the freak saying, "God made me thisaway and I don't dispute hit," and making this truth her own by offering herself in her prayers, "I don't dispute hit. This is the way He wants me to be." As the story comes to a close, it is the same child who unexpectedly perceives God's sacramental presence. After accompanying the two foolish cousins back to the convent school, "the child's round face was lost in thought. She turned it toward the window and looked out over a stretch of pasture land that rose and fell with a gathering greenness until it touched the dark woods. The sun was a huge red ball like an elevated Host drenched in blood and when it sank out of sight, it left a line in the sky like a red clay road hanging over the trees."

The mysterious life of the child in "A Temple of the Holy Ghost" seems to me the best way to introduce this engaging and efficacious book which primarily focuses on the idea that the effectiveness of the sacraments comes from the integration of the Holy Spirit into the natural ritual patterns of human life.

I have known Kimberly Belcher first as a brilliant doctoral student and now as a talented scholar, first-class liturgical theologian, and loving mother of two beautiful children. In the following pages, she lucidly argues that the sacraments are an embodied, trinitarian part of salvation history and form identity by shaping the bodies of participants. She also thoroughly examines the rite of baptism from the point of view of the infant as a participant who can use ritual for self-development, and cogently suggests that the postconciliar Roman rite of baptism for infants is a ritual process that allows infants to engage in Christian world-building through embodied participation. By unfolding the trinitarian nature of infant baptism, she finally, and perhaps most importantly, argues, in the final chapter, that the Spirit is the principle that allows symbol to reveal the divine reality; that the Spirit is the basis for the "givenness" of the divine gift; and that from the Spirit ritual creates a space, a *temple* for freedom where "a person can be transformed into the self-gift that, being human, he or she longs to be, and find in it joy." As the French theologian Louis-Marie Chauvet beautifully writes about the Spirit in *Symbol and Sacrament*, "fire, which no one can seize without being consumed, is the symbol of the absolute otherness of God. . . . Fire is thus a particularly expressive symbol for the paradoxical twofold function of the Holy Spirit: it is simultaneously the agent of God's *recession* from the world in God's absolute holiness, and of God's *procession* into the world through the communication of God's holiness to humans." We thank Kimberly for this beautiful book.

Nathan D. Mitchell

Acknowledgments

I am thankful for the help of all those who contributed to the development of this work. Many thanks to my classmates at Notre Dame, especially Melanie Ross, Andrew Casad, and Noel Terranova, who gave me encouragement, critiques, and suggestions. Maxwell E. Johnson and Cyril O'Regan were especially helpful in integrating the interdisciplinary methods incorporated in the work, and I remember their unwavering support with deep gratitude. Without the confidence, feedback, and friendship of my dissertation director, Nathan D. Mitchell, this work could not have been written. I fondly remember many cups of tea in his office that began in perplexity and ended in laughter.

At Saint John's University, I am grateful for Martin Connell's advice as I made revisions and for the support of my other colleagues. I give thanks for the vision of Hans Christoffersen and the expertise of the rest of the staff at Liturgical Press, who have helped bring this work to a swifter completion. David Hwang provided invaluable assistance with the cover.

Without the constant support of my friend Erin Wolf Chambers, this project would have taken much longer, if it were ever to get done at all. I am sure she has learned more about baptism than she ever needed to know in these last few years.

Without the love, friendship, and faith of my husband Matt, there would have been nothing to say. I thank him for the most beautiful gifts: our children, Thomas and Juliana, who were born during the writing of this work.

Thanks be to God.

Chapter One

The Sacramental Plan of Salvation

W hat is a sacrament? The definition of a sacrament shapes what acts of worship we consider essential or normative, how these acts of worship should be structured, and who should partici- pate in them. Definitions of sacrament, like other theological concepts, have been shaped by questions about the church's experience and reflections upon its biblical roots. The heart of sacramentality is the belief that when Christians worship, they participate in God's life, and this belief must be the backdrop for any sacramental theology.

Contemporary Western sacramental theology has tried to correct the neoscholastic understanding of sacraments as "signs and causes of grace." While Thomas Aquinas treated the sacraments as signs first and foremost, the neoscholastic understanding privileged sacraments as causes of grace; their sign quality was almost forgotten.[1] Because the symbolic aspects of sacramental worship were neglected, theologians and practitioners struggled against magical or palliative misunder- standings of liturgical prayer. Modern and postmodern commentary on the sacraments has emphasized instead the ongoing conversion of humanity and the symbolic quality of rites, encouraging full, rich sig- nification in sacramental liturgies. Contemporary sacramental theology emphasizes the human subjects of liturgical action and their reliance on culture and symbols to mediate their relationships with God.

---

[1] Thomas Aquinas, *Summa Theologiae*, III, q. 60. In quoting the *Summa* (hereafter ST), Latin texts have been taken from the Blackfriars edition: Thomas Gilby and T. C. O'Brien, eds. (New York: Cambridge, 2006). English translations are those of the Benziger Bros. 1947 edition, trans. Fathers of the English Dominican Province, unless otherwise noted. This translation is available online at http://www.op.org/summa/ and elsewhere.

The original context of the medieval definition can provide a more accurate picture of the relationship between sacramental signification and sacramental causality. In the medieval interpretations, both signification and causality were permeated by reference to God's work in the world. For example, when Thomas considers why the sacraments are a kind of sign, he is careful to contextualize this in salvation history. The sacraments follow Christ's incarnation in the *Summa Theologiae* because incarnation and sacraments are the path that leads humanity back to God.[2] Thomas defines sacraments as signs in this salvific context: the sacraments are "ordained to signify our sanctification . . . [including] the very cause of our sanctification, which is Christ's passion; the form of our sanctification, which is grace and the virtues; and the ultimate end of our sanctification, which is eternal life."[3] The sacraments signify God's work sanctifying people in the world because God has ordained them to sanctify people in the world.[4]

When speaking of the sacraments in general, Thomas does not try to distinguish sacraments from other kinds of prayer but to discern how sacraments connect Christians to Jesus Christ.[5] Thomas defines sacrament from human needs: "signs are given to human beings," so a sacrament is "a sign of a sacred thing as it is sanctifying human persons."[6] To understand sacraments as a category—generalizing from baptism and eucharist to sacrament—we must see them as part of the structure of salvation history. In sacrament, the trinitarian God, through the missions of the incarnate Word and the Holy Spirit, invites and enables human persons to participate in the eternal happiness of the Godhead. This happens through ritual signs addressed to human beings, who are sanctified by those signs.

---

[2] The treatise on the incarnation occupies ST, III, qq. 1-59, and that on the sacraments takes up III, qq. 60-90. See Jean-Pierre Torrell, *Aquinas's* Summa: *Background, Structure, and Reception,* trans. Benedict M. Guevin, OSB (Washington, DC: Catholic University of America, 2005), 48–62.

[3] ST, III, q. 60, a. 3. The sacraments were traditionally considered as sign and cause by Thomas's time. In the *Summa,* however, Thomas argues that they belong in the category of sign and that their causality can be deduced from this definition. This allows him to affirm certain rites in the Hebrew Bible as sacraments, although they do not cause grace; see III, q. 62, a. 6.

[4] ST, III, q. 62, a. 1.

[5] See the preface to III, q. 60, which turns from the treatise on the incarnation to that on the sacraments in general (*"[D]e sacramentis in communi . . ."*, ST, III, qq. 60-65).

[6] ST, III, q. 60, a. 2. My translation.

In the *Summa Theologiae*, then, sacraments are ecclesial celebrations that are part of the economy of salvation. Although Thomas does eventually treat them as signs and causes, they are more basically the ritual component of salvation history, the evidence that God uses culture to bring human beings into God's own life.[7] Thomas acknowledges that sacraments can be considered according to a number of different patterns but argues that the category of sign reveals the sacraments most broadly, in their largest application.[8] What is distinctive about a sacrament, for Thomas, is the fact that in it God's work is embedded in human culture, so that in the sacraments, God speaks human language. Human beings are changed by signs, so the sacraments—as a general category—are best considered under the category of sign.[9]

The question, What is a sacrament? is best answered not from premature attention to the categories of sign and cause but from the church's conviction that God is at work for us in the sacraments. It is right to see significance and causality as cooperative, as contemporary commentators have noted, but, more deeply, the sign function and causality of the sacraments are always secondary to their salvific importance.

During the twentieth century, the Trinity was recognized as central in soteriology and sacramental theology. Karl Rahner argued that the Trinity was the one mystery of human salvation: participation in the trinitarian love of God is the deeply mysterious way that human beings can attain happiness.[10] If sacraments are part of the way of salvation, the sacramental economy must have a trinitarian shape, because the life of the Trinity is the gift of grace given to human persons in sacrament. Only by considering this trinitarian dimension can the sacraments' integral place in salvation history be appreciated. Sacraments are the ongoing and existential availability of God's salvation to human persons. Human life in the world is organized partially by symbols, but there are other ways human life is organized as well: human habits and discipline, "meaningless" ritual behaviors, and unexamined sensory experiences, for example. These aspects, while not "signs" strictly speaking, can be part of the sacramental economy.

---

[7] *Economy* comes from Greek, *oikonomia* (see, e.g., Eph 1:10), which means "householding" but is usually translated "plan."

[8] ST, IIIa, q. 60, a. 1.

[9] See ST, IIIa, q. 60, a. 4.

[10] See Karl Rahner, *The Trinity* (New York: Crossroad, 1999).

Sacraments are effective in two ways: culturally effective in organizing human life and theologically effective in integrating human persons into the life of God. Cultural efficacy is not divine power, but human beings encounter the Trinity in human culture, through the incarnation and through sacrament. The church's experience includes rich reflections on the relationship between these two kinds of efficacy. In this chapter I begin by considering the plan of salvation scripturally, through the lens of the Gospel of John. Later, I turn to the modern *ressourcement* of the trinitarian theologies of Rahner and Hans Urs von Balthasar. Third, I explore the roles of liturgical and sacramental practice in allowing human beings to enter the trinitarian life. I highlight the tradition that treats sacraments as the epitome of human participation in God's life in order to reinterpret sacraments as the ritual formation of the Christian self through the self-gift of the Trinity.

Section 1.1
Ritual Experience and Trinitarian Relationships in the Gospel of John

In the New Testament, the communal celebrations of baptism and eucharist are not set off from the rest of the liturgical life of the early believers—or, indeed, from their secular, economic, and domestic lives. New Testament writers offer reflections on a faith that is fully lived out in the body, even as they caution against reliance on ritual alone for salvation. For example, the Gospel of John unites a focus on the trinitarian relationships with a narrative presentation of the events by which salvation became manifest.

Scholars disagree on whether the community reflected in John's gospel practiced "sacramental" worship (i.e., baptism and eucharist recognizable by later Christian practices).[11] The historical background for the gospel's many references to water, bread, fish, and wine is disputed, but the encounter with Jesus in word and body strongly relies on ritual imagery. In this gospel, participation in Christ is presented as worship in the Spirit, the proclamation of the good news, and the work of God. Jesus' body is the center of trinitarian activity in the world and

---

[11] See Raymond E. Brown, *Introduction to the New Testament* (New York: Doubleday, 1997), 377–78 for an introduction to this discussion. In this section I am more interested in the Gospel of John as a foundation for sacramental and trinitarian thought than as a reflection of that thought.

the font of salvation, which believers experience in their own bodies. The Jewish ritual practices of the first century are presented as the necessary structures against which Jesus' body can be recognized as God's Word and Wisdom in the world. Worship is "in the Spirit" when believers participate in Christ's body and, by this, in the trinitarian life.

Raymond E. Brown notes that in the book of signs (John 1:18–12:50), Jesus replaces key Jewish times and places for worship.[12] This theme developed as a reflection on the destruction of the Jerusalem temple in 70 CE. At this time, both Judaism and nascent Christianity were adapting to the loss of the temple. The theme of replacement should be seen as one among many Jewish strategies for reinterpreting temple imagery in the face of disaster, rather than as evidence of Gentile hostility to Judaism in the gospel.[13] In fact, Jewish ritual practice is crucial to recognizing the role of Jesus' body as the wellspring of participation in the Trinity for believers. Jesus' body as temple, Sabbath, and festival cycle structure the Gospel of John's insistence on faith and participation in the sonship of Christ through the Holy Spirit.

In John 2, Jesus' body is the new temple and the Father's house (John 2:16-22). When the authorities demand that Jesus provide an authority for the prophetic act of cleansing the temple, Jesus refers to an authorizing sign that is yet to occur: his death and resurrection. For the author of John, the crucifixion relativizes the temple because it reveals Jesus as the ultimate place of God's presence on earth. The crucifixion is thus a true sign of Christ's authority to critique and eventually replace the temple. Jesus' body is the place where the glory of the Lord can be seen on earth, and this is visible in the crucifixion above all (3:14). His body becomes a ritual site for encounter with God.

Similarly, in the conversation with the Samaritan woman, Jesus' body is the origin of the gift of "water gushing up to eternal life." This gift leads one to "worship the Father in spirit and truth" rather than in the house of God in Jerusalem (4:14, 23). Jesus' body is the temple where the Spirit of God dwells and humanity is engaged in true worship of the Father. Jesus' body localizes the trinitarian dynamic in a way that can be shared with those who encounter him in faith.

---

[12] Ibid., 338–51. I am indebted to Brown's interpretation throughout this section. All biblical quotations are taken from the New Revised Standard Version found in *The New Oxford Annotated Bible* (2001).

[13] See, for example, Oskar Skarsaune, *In the Shadow of the Temple: Jewish Influences on Early Christianity* (Downers Grove, IL: InterVarsity, 2002).

These two stories enclose the scene with Nicodemus (3:1-21), where the relationship Jesus enjoys with the Father (being "begotten of God") explains his knowledge of divine realities and can be shared with others, but only when one is born "of water and Spirit." This introduction of a theme of ritual water associated with the Holy Spirit exemplifies the way embodied ritual (drinking, eating, washing) is connected to participation in the trinitarian relationships, expressed here as worship of the Father in the Spirit, who is given by Christ.

The next section of John's book of signs is introduced and concluded by two healings on the Sabbath. The first, in John 5, is concerned with Jesus' lordship over the Sabbath but treats this theme differently than the similar stories in Matthew, Mark, and Luke. The healing of the blind man in John 9 reprises the theme of Jesus' authority to heal on the Sabbath but adds a uniquely Johannine element in the treatment of Jesus as the source of light. The story in John 5, like those treating Sabbath healings in the other gospels, evokes conflicts between Jesus and the Jewish authorities about the interpretation of the law. While in the other gospels Jesus' defense is a proof of his messianic authority (Mark 2:1-13 and parallels) or of the purpose of the Sabbath as God's care for human beings (Mark 3:1-6 and parallels), in John it is a revelation of the relationship between the Father and the Son. The Father works, even on the Sabbath, raising the dead and giving them life, and the Son follows the Father's example (John 5:17, 19-21). The Sabbath, the completion of creation (Exod 20:8-11), is found in Jesus' body, which "has passed from death to life"; because of him, believers may also have eternal life (John 5:24).

The Sabbath, as manifestation of God's care for humanity and of Israel's special relationship with the creator, is replaced by Jesus' body, which is the manifestation of life even in death. By participating in this body, readers too may be healed, the story suggests, becoming a part of God's liberating works. This image is repeated in John 9, where Jesus as life is supplemented with Jesus as light (as in 1:3-5).

Bracketed within these treatments of the Sabbath are narratives in which the annual festal cycle is replaced by Christ's body. John 6 gives the fullest treatment of Jesus' body replacing the Passover, whereas John 7–9 is set during the feast of Booths. Passover recurs throughout the book, as the setting for John 2, 6, 11–20. The treatment of Booths is more unusual, since it was not universally associated with Jesus' death in the New Testament. Jesus' actions during this festival in John serve to explain and develop the themes of living water and enlightenment, which were so dramatically rendered in John 3 and 4.

The feast of Booths was named after the tents the Hebrews lived in during the exodus period and celebrated the giving of the law at Mount Sinai. Its imagery was first suggested by the prologue, when the Word of God "became flesh and lived among us" (John 1:14). For the Word to "pitch his tent" (*eskēnōsen*) among human beings recalls Sirach 24:8 and grounds Jesus' witness at the feast of Booths (*skēnopēgia*, John 7:2). The narrative reinterprets the festival symbols of light and water. In the gospel, on the final and greatest day of the feast, Jesus "cried out, 'Let anyone who is thirsty come to me, and let the one who believes in me drink. As the scripture has said, "Out of the believer's heart shall flow rivers of living water"'" (7:37-38). This call reveals the incarnation of the Word (1:14) as the liberating presence that echoes and replaces the deeds ("works") of the Torah, especially Genesis and Exodus (e.g., 1:51; 3:14; 4:10; 6). The alternate reading for 7:38, "Out of his [Jesus'] belly shall flow rivers of living water," strengthens this interpretation by casting Jesus as the rock of Exodus, a typology common among early Christian writers (1 Cor 10:4).[14] The evangelist's parenthetical note interprets the "living water" as the Spirit that is the gift of the glorified Son of God, identified with the water flowing from the temple in Ezekiel 37.

In John it is clear that the relationship between Father and Son is in the foreground; a consideration of the role of the Spirit, however, shows that the Spirit is introduced into the Johannine discourses of the book of signs in order to explain how the relationship between Father and Son can be shared by other human beings. In John 3, for example, birth of water and the Spirit enables a human person to be "born of God," as the Word is and as the prologue insists others can be through him (John 1:12-13). In John 4, the Spirit enables the human person to engage in true worship in the new site (Christ's body), freed from the need for the temple (since this is not an option after 70 CE). In John 7, Jesus, crucified and glorified, is the source of the Spirit that marks the new temple. These two themes, the recognition of the relationship between Father and Son and the need for the Spirit of Christ in order to participate in that relationship, continue in the farewell discourses (14–16).

In chapter 9, implicitly included in the feast of Booths and explicitly designated as the Sabbath, Jesus unites these themes through the

---

[14] Raymond E. Brown argues that this should be the preferred reading; see Brown, *Introduction to the New Testament*, 347.

symbolism of sight and himself as light. The story begins with Jesus warning his disciples, lest they misinterpret the action (as in 11:4, 9-15). The works of God, the manifestation of God's glory, can happen only through Jesus, the light of the world (9:4-5). The healing is simple: Jesus makes mud and anoints the man's eyes, telling him to wash in the pool of Siloam ("Sent"); he does so and can see. The rest of the narrative of the chapter is concerned with the meaning of the healing: the Sabbath, the Pharisees, and Moses are invoked as authorities who conclusively prove that Jesus is not from God, but the light the man sees demands another explanation. "Here is an astonishing thing! You do not know where he comes from, and yet he opened my eyes. We know that God does not listen to sinners, but he does listen to one who worships him and obeys his will. . . . If this man were not from God, he could do nothing" (9:30-31, 33). The blind man's perception indicates that with the light of the world he has received also the living water, and so Jesus, finding him, says, "You have seen him . . ." (9:37). The embodied experience of sight, of healing, becomes the grounds for spiritual recognition. The early church's experience of the Spirit both confirmed faith and thrust it out into the regular rhythms of life, where it confronted the authorities: ritual, Scripture, and interpretations. In John, it is not enough to recognize Jesus as Messiah (as Nathanael does already in 1:49); believers must participate in him not only to "see greater things than these" but also to "do greater works than these" because of Jesus' oneness with the Father (1:50; 14:12).

The use of Passover provides the strongest example. Jesus' body as replacement for the Passover, foreshadowed in his title "Lamb of God" in John 1:29, attains increased clarity in John 6, when Jesus feeds the masses, recollecting the manna in the desert, and walks on water, alluding to the crossing of the Red Sea. Jesus' signs here echo God's revelatory works during the exodus that not only liberated the Israelites from slavery and established the covenant but also revealed God's glory to them and to the nations.[15] The power of Jesus' signs to glorify God becomes, in John, one of the primary arguments for Jesus' authenticity as Son of God.[16]

In the discourse that follows these signs, Jesus first reveals himself, as Word, as the revelation of God's glory (6:35-51a) and divine Wisdom (cf. Prov 8–9). When the focus switches from Jesus' word to his body

---

[15] See, e.g., Exod 10:1; 14:18; 34:10; Deut 3:24; 7:13; 11:3.
[16] John 1:14; 2:11; 8:54; 9:24; 11:4.

("the bread that I will give for the life of the world is my flesh," John 6:51b), the rejection of Jesus' body is tantamount to the rejection of his wisdom teaching.[17] The crucified body, the one "given up" for the life of the world, is at once the "sign" requested and, as divine Wisdom, the "bread" of the faith: "What sign are you going to give us then, so that we may see it and believe you? . . . Our ancestors ate the manna in the wilderness . . ." (John 6:30-31). Jesus' body, crucified and glorified, is the sign, the content, and the Word of revelation.

How can the Passover bread, the Lamb of God, be a human body? How can one find, in a body, Wisdom, or in water, Spirit? How can the glory of the Father rest in a human person rather than in a temple? These are the eternal questions of Christianity. The testimony of the Gospel of John does not minimize these questions, but it marks that the answers are available only through embodied experience read against a horizon of ritual practice. The blind man sees, but it is not sight alone that informs the narrative but the torches of the temple while the water is poured out to celebrate the harvest of grapes and pray for rain.[18] Only against the light of those torches can Jesus be recognized as the true vine and the source of living water, the ultimate manifestation of God's glory and liberating will for humanity.

The Gospel of John shows that it is embodied experience, especially ritual experience, that lets human beings recognize the Word in the flesh and, by the gift of the Spirit, participate in the Son's love of the Father. We recognize Jesus as the author of creation and giver of salvation against the horizon of the human body landscaped by ritual. Seeing the body of Christ as the site of salvation, the church has transmitted ritual disciplines for landscaping personal and social bodies so that the blind can continue to receive sight. The sacramental rites of the church are so designated because, in the church's experience over time, they are those in which humanity can come nearest to the body of Christ, and thus to participating in the trinitarian mystery that abides in the person of the Word.

In John 14–16, Jesus' gift of the Spirit is finally linked to his return to the Father: not only does Jesus "abide with" humanity but the Spirit "dwells in" those who "abide in" Christ (14:17; 14:4). Jesus prays, "The glory that you [Father] have given me I have given them, so that they may be one, as we are one, I in them and you in me, that they may

---

[17] Brown, *Introduction to the New Testament*, 346–47. Cf. 1 John 4:2; 5:6; 2 John 7.
[18] Brown, *Introduction to the New Testament*, 347.

become completely one, so that the world may know that you have sent me and have loved them even as you have loved me" (17:22-23). This trinitarian love, in which believers dwell, is in the body of Christ, but the divine love can only be seen against the horizon of ritual embodied experience.

Section 1.2
The Trinitarian Dynamic of Salvation History in Modern Theology

In the *ressourcement* of twentieth-century theology, the Trinity and salvation history were recognized as the foundation of all theological treatises. The doctrine of the Trinity developed from the early Christian experience of salvation through the work of Jesus, his Father, and the Spirit of God. By the middle of the twentieth century, however, the Trinity was so divorced from the vitality of Christian life that Karl Rahner proclaimed, "should the doctrine of the Trinity have to be dropped as false, the major part of religious literature could well remain virtually unchanged."[19] Rahner feared that the church clung to dogmatic trinitarian language that did not manifest the trinitarian reality to the hearts and lives of believers, particularly Roman Catholics.

Rahner, like the author of John, believed the Trinity manifests a truth about the economy—the way God comes to be known and felt in human experience. In *The Trinity*, Rahner's starting point is grace, which is the existential participation of each particular human person in the divine life. Rahner's description of the Trinity spans the economy from the divine will and plan to its realization in the life of one human person. The human person is created "in the image of God," able to receive the communication of the trinitarian mystery; grace is the actualization of this potential as the Trinity reaches human beings.[20] In Rahner's analysis in *The Trinity*, the emphasis falls on the constitution of human persons as recipients of grace and the trinitarian form of that grace.

Rahner's exposition of trinitarian grace in this work proceeds from three basic premises. First, God's self-communication is free not because God made an arbitrary choice of how to communicate but because God acts freely in communicating God's self. Because God communicates God's self, grace must be trinitarian, but this does not

---

[19] Rahner, *Trinity*, 10–11.
[20] Ibid., 89–90.

jeopardize its free character.[21] In the attempt to preserve God's absolute sovereignty, it is not necessary to assert, as the scholastics did, that God could have become incarnate as any kind of creature, nor to assert that any one of the Persons of the Trinity could have taken on a human nature; these assertions, Rahner argues, would make nonsense of our teaching about the Trinity and the incarnation.[22] If God is Trinity, God need not choose to communicate God's self to any created being; however, if God does so choose, the communication will be shaped by trinitarian reality, because it is a communication of God's self by God's self.[23] God's freedom already has a trinitarian character, so it is not necessary to suppose that the missions of the Son and the Spirit in salvation history (whether proper or appropriated) are independent. On the contrary, Rahner supposes that the missions are closely integrated with one another, dependent on one another.[24] This premise opens the possibility for Rahner to make ontological claims about the trinitarian character of the economy of salvation.

Rahner's second premise, closely connected to the first, is that God's self-communication is a real communication: it must have an addressee, and that addressee must be capable of receiving the communication of God. Both the incarnation and grace, in different ways, are self-communications in which God "really arrives at" humanity, "really enters into" the human condition.[25] The incarnation and the advent of grace in human life form one economy of salvation. The Word takes on the fullness of the human condition while remaining God because human nature is by creation the realization of God's self-communication. Human nature is "the condition of the possibility of constituting an addressee" for free extra-trinitarian communication and the necessary condition for the Word's entrance into the created order, for "Christ's human nature . . . is precisely that which comes into being when God's Logos 'utters' himself outwards."[26] In other words, Rahner's second premise is that human persons are created in such a way that the Word can become human and that other human beings may receive the communication offered by incarnation and

---

[21] Ibid., 86.

[22] Ibid., 28–30, 89–90.

[23] See ibid., 86–87.

[24] Ibid., 85.

[25] Ibid., 88–89. Italics in this work appear in the referenced text unless otherwise noted.

[26] Ibid., 89.

grace. Both facts about human nature—its suitability as exteriorization of the Logos and as addressee of revelation—are to be attributed to the order of creation.

This leads to Rahner's third premise, that observing the realm of grace leads to real conclusions about the economy of salvation, precisely because grace is particular, concrete, and human. The self-communication of God is addressed not to humanity in general but to this human being in his or her particularity, including cultural particularity. The starting point for analysis of the economy of salvation, according to Rahner, is the individual human person who is constituted as the recipient of the mystery of God's self-communication, rather than the unity of the Godhead or the historicity of the incarnation.

Salvation history, from creation to the salvation of this specific human being, reveals the interrelated missions of Christ and of the Holy Spirit. In accordance with his famous axiom, "The 'economic' Trinity is the 'immanent' Trinity and the 'immanent' Trinity is the 'economic' Trinity," Rahner takes the experience of these missions in the life of the human person seeking salvation to reveal the relations of the Persons to one another.[27] Grace, for Rahner, is directed to complementary aspects of human existence: history or truth and spirit or love.

Rahner begins by laying out four opposed moments of human existence: origin and future, history and transcendence, offer and acceptance, and knowledge and love. The four pairs of concepts and the interrelatedness of each characterize the missions of Son and Spirit in salvation history. Rahner is guided by the events of revelation rather than by philosophical reflection or speculative theology: his primary data are the incarnation and its purposes, revealing the Father and giving the Spirit.

The mission of the Son is characterized as origin, history, offer, and truth in creation and incarnation. The work of the Logos originates and offers the self-communication of God the Father by creating human nature, made in the image of the Word, which can enter into the divine love.[28] This offer takes place in history because the Word, by creation, initiates history, and by the incarnation takes it up and makes the offer of God's self-communication a historical fact.[29] This mission is "truth" because the offer means "letting [God's] own personal essence come

---

[27] Ibid., 22. Italics of original text have been suppressed.
[28] Ibid., 91, 94.
[29] Ibid., 94–95.

to the fore, positing [God's self] without dissimulation,"[30] which is the core of truth. "Divine self-communication, as a 'revelation' of God's nature, is truth for us."[31] The Word's mission is truth because the Word is the faithful showing forth of the Father, which allows the Father to communicate God's self to the world. This is true in three ways: in the intratrinitarian realm, in the realm of creation of the human nature, and in the historical event of the incarnation.

The mission of the Spirit, on the other hand, is characterized by future, transcendence, acceptance, and love. Rahner acknowledges that this mission is more difficult to see and comprehend. One of his concerns is to argue, against Pelagianism, that the acceptance of God's self-communication and its voluntary aspect is itself the work of God the Holy Spirit. Affirming this without evacuating human free will is of course a perpetual problem in theology. Part of Rahner's solution is the interdependent dynamic of the two missions: the acceptance of the offer flows naturally out of the offer itself, just as in human existence openness to the future flows naturally out of the individual's history and experience.[32] Briefly, then, the work of the Spirit is to arise out of the offer, both in the created freedom of the creature and in the gift of the strictly divine freedom, so that God may become the future and the transcendence of the human person.[33] Rahner admits that the relationship of these aspects to "love" remains rather obscure but argues that accepting the historical manifestation of God's self-communication into a personal and appropriated relationship is the consummation of love between God and humanity.[34]

God's "self-communication, insofar as it occurs as 'truth,' happens in history; . . . insofar as it happens as love, it opens this history in transcendence towards the absolute future."[35] Creation and incarnation— and we can include here the sacramental extension of the incarnation

[30] Ibid., 96.

[31] Ibid.

[32] Ibid., 97; cf. 91–92.

[33] Ibid., 98.

[34] "It is more difficult to explain how [this aspect of the divine self-communication] must be characterized as love. Yet the self-communication which wills itself absolutely and creates the possibility of its acceptance and this acceptance itself, is precisely what is meant by love. It is the specifically divine 'case' of love, because it creates its own acceptance and because this love is the freely offered and accepted self-communication of the 'person'" (ibid., 97–98).

[35] Ibid., 98.

through the ministry of the church—are understood in continuity, as together revealing the triune nature of God. Our understanding of the divine nature is grounded in the observed inseparability of the missions of Son and Spirit. Perhaps the best measure of this model's explanatory power comes from a comparison with a few verses of John 14–16, which characterize the relationships between Father, Son, Paraclete, and disciples with a similar fluidity and dynamism. For example, the mission of the Son as offer and truth (faithful presentation of the Father) is a good exposition of John 14:10: "Do you not believe that I am in the Father and the Father is in me? The words that I say to you I do not speak on my own; but the Father who dwells in me does his works." Likewise, the interrelationship of the two missions clarifies how "the Spirit of truth" (14:17) becomes the agent of recognition of Christ's ongoing presence even after his return to the Father (14:18-24) and is also recognized as love for Christ. Finally, Rahner's choice to locate the fundamental evidence for the economy in the human person's experience of grace can provide interpretation for how the testimony of the disciples of Christ and that of the Spirit can be considered to be interchangeable or complementary (15:26-27).

The telescopic gaze of Rahner's trinitarian economy of salvation has its limits. Clearly, the ministry of the Word in creation and in incarnation (and perhaps also in sacraments) is distinct in some ways even though coherent in others. Similarly, the work of the Spirit in prophecy and inspiration before the incarnation and in recognition and sacrament after it cannot be assumed to be the same. The history of salvation must, in fact, be historical; even if one can affirm that the whole history of salvation is present in the salvific experience of one particular person, this cannot mean in an undifferentiated way but rather as the full presence of an entire process contained in a point. The whole dynamic change must be made present in the compression, with real distinctions in the economy preserved.

This drawback of Rahner's work can be minimized by conversation with the work of Balthasar, whose rendering of the trinitarian economy of salvation is quite profoundly historical—so much so that historicity itself becomes a reflection of the "theo-drama" that is characteristic of the intratrinitarian relations. For Balthasar, the ontological gap between creation and God, while infinite, is relativized by the incarnation event, which changes the meaning of power and of distance in the world, transforming both into love.

According to Balthasar's understanding, God is best described neither by the term *being*, since such is most easily associated with the existence that finite creatures have, nor by *becoming*, because that in turn may be confused with earthly change. Instead, Balthasar suggests that the immanent Trinity's mode of existence may best be imaged as an eternal "happening," which is "the coming-to-be, not of something that once was not (that would be Arianism), but, evidently, of something that grounds the idea, the inner possibility and reality of a becoming."[36] This divine "Event," the processions of Son and Spirit from God the Father, is a timeless dynamism that grounds the incarnation as well as creation. In fact, earthly change is possible because God's eternal existence is marked by Event, which is beauty, goodness, and truth.[37]

The divine Event is also the foundation for the economy, the extratrinitarian missions of love in the world. "The immanent Trinity must be understood to be that eternal, absolute self-surrender whereby God is seen to be, in [God's self], absolute love; this in turn explains [God's] free self-giving to the world as love, without suggesting that God 'needed' the world process and the Cross in order to become [God's self]."[38] The idea that the central mystery of God can be considered "Event" is the reason why the events of time, according to Balthasar, can be considered "theo-drama," that is, a working out in time of the essential mystery that is the immanent Trinity. What makes it "drama" is, of course, a plot, and the center of this plot is the self-sacrifice of the incarnate Word, or Jesus' "hour." Balthasar's use of the Johannine language (cf. John 4:21-23; 12:23-27; 13:1, etc.) is noteworthy: his explication of the theo-drama rests on the sense, present especially in this gospel, that Jesus' ministry has a decisive turning point, which is both the goal and the overthrow of everything that has come before it (law and incarnation), both the ultimate tragedy and the ultimate victory.[39]

The self-sacrifice of the Son, according to Balthasar, has this paradoxical quality because it is the moment at which the historical drama of the created universe becomes transparent to the eternal drama of

---

[36] Hans Urs von Balthasar, *The Last Act*, Theo-Drama vol. 5 (San Francisco: Ignatius, 1998), 67 (hereafter abbreviated as TD5).

[37] See, e.g., Balthasar, *Epilogue* (San Francisco: Ignatius, 2004).

[38] Balthasar, *The Action*, Theo-Drama vol. 4 (San Francisco: Ignatius, 1994), 323 (hereafter TD4).

[39] Ibid., 231–44.

the Trinity. This is the reason why Jesus' death can have significance within the created order in the past as well as the future.[40] Crucial to this paradox, moreover, is the unity within the hour of passive and active potentiality in Jesus' mission, of power and powerlessness: "He *allows* himself to be handed over. But, at the heart of this obedient letting-things-happen, there is an active consent, deliberate action: 'I lay down my life' (Jn 10:17) 'of my own accord' (18)."[41]

This paradoxical passivity is a revelatory flash of the intratrinitarian dynamic. It is not only a revelation of the Word within the Trinity but actually a manifestation of the whole intratrinitarian dynamic, which Balthasar explains using the overarching language of self-giving and love. Divine love is enacted through two kinds of divine power, an active and a passive power.[42] The divine nature is ultimate love and self-gift; thus, the Father, because he gives over everything without reservation, "does not lose what he gives, that is, himself."[43] Meanwhile, the Son plays an indispensable role in his own generation: "The Son even cooperates in his begetting by *letting* himself be begotten, by holding himself in readiness to be begotten."[44] Passive power is not limited to the Word, because the Father receives his "Fatherhood" when the Son and Spirit willingly proceed forth.[45] Active and passive powers mark the whole trinitarian dynamic.

The Trinity's perfect power can accommodate a kind of cooperative passivity even within the Godhead, and this is crucial to understanding sacramental grace offered to a fully dynamic human person. God "wishes to be almighty not solely by creating: by begetting and breathing forth, and allowing himself to be begotten and breathed forth, he hands over his power to the Other—whoever that Other may be—without ever seeking to take it back."[46] Balthasar concludes, "absolute self-giving is beyond 'power' and 'powerlessness': its ability

---

[40] The term "hour," in Balthasar's work as well as in John, already incorporates Christ's resurrection, glorification, and ability to send the Spirit (ibid., 238).

[41] Ibid., 241; cf. 237.

[42] In the tradition of trinitarian reflection, divine power originates with and is appropriated to the Father. Wisdom is appropriated to the Son and love to the Holy Spirit. "Appropriated" terms are those that can be rightly said of all three Persons but fit human experience of one Person in salvation history particularly well.

[43] Balthasar, *TD5*, 85.

[44] Ibid., 87.

[45] Ibid., 245.

[46] Ibid., 66.

to 'let be' embraces both."[47] For Balthasar, salvation history becomes the drama by which God draws human beings (and the whole cosmos, time, and space) into this trinitarian love.[48] Since Father and Son are constituted by their opposed relationships (begetting, being begotten), the infinite distance between them is the basis for the possibility of all other distinctions. This distance is maintained and bridged by the Spirit.[49] This distance is performed on the stage of the world in the hour of Christ, because in Jesus' death, the Son's obedient love for the Father appears in history. Every finite distance (of sin) between God and the world is embraced by the ultimate distance on the cross. The Father "made him to be sin who knew no sin" (1 Cor 5:21) so that the Spirit can become the bridge between the alienated cosmos and God the Father even at the height of the world's alienation, that is, "while we were sinners" (Rom 5:8).[50] This is the ultimate soteriological import of Jesus' hour, which transforms the world historically and not merely subjectively for each believer.

For the purpose of creating a broad background image of the trinitarian dimensions of salvation history before considering how the sacraments fit into that history, it is possible to explore these two visions together. It is worth noting that both Rahner and Balthasar are attempting retrieval—Rahner in the immediate context of magisterial statements on the Trinity, Balthasar using spiritual writers. Both are influenced by contemporary philosophy, and both recognize the sheer variety, as well as the depth, of traditional thinking on the economic Trinity. Both constructions can thus be labeled traditional in outline, and there is a fair amount of overlap between their depictions.

In brief, then, the immanent Trinity is the foundation for the economy of salvation. There are at least three concrete moments of this economy that have revelatory potential in opening human beings toward participation in the relationality of God: the cosmic order, created humanity, and the history of the incarnate Word. These are by no means independent moments; in fact, they are ordered to one another. They are dependent on one another and together manifest the Trinity in the

---

[47] Ibid., 74.

[48] Ibid., 87.

[49] Balthasar, *TD4*, 323–24. For more on the Spirit as distance, see the work of Sarah Morice-Brubaker, "Place of the Spirit: A Trinitarian Theology of Location," (PhD diss., University of Notre Dame, 2009).

[50] See esp. Balthasar, *TD5*, 256–65.

world. Furthermore, although the dynamic of the immanent Trinity is not accessible to the created intellect, whatever can be known about the Trinity through God's free self-gift in the economy is true; the mystery does not preclude that anything can be said about God but rather assures that all that can be said about God does not exhaust God's nature.

One of the more interesting areas of agreement, then, between Rahner and Balthasar is that the manifestation of God in the world is neither an arbitrary external manipulation of the created order by a God who remains essentially unknowable (or only reveals purely verbal formulations about God's self) nor a revelation of particular Persons acting in particular instances. In other words, their analyses allow for understanding God's nature through the economy without abandoning the notion that when the Trinity acts *ad extra* (in the world), all the Persons are acting. In Rahner's understanding of the trinitarian constitution of the human person as a recipient of God's self-communication, humans are not merely made in the image of Christ but are codetermined by history and freedom so they are able to enter into the trinitarian mystery in truth and spirit. Similarly, for Balthasar Christ's "hour" does not merely reveal Christ's place in the trinitarian mystery but in fact dramatizes in time the whole mystery of the Father's self-emptying love, including Christ's obedient gratitude and the infinite gap and bridge of the Spirit.

There are two images by which sacraments have traditionally been seen as part of the economy of salvation: as means of grace and as extensions of the efficacious salvific power of the incarnation, passion, death, and resurrection of Christ. Rahner and Balthasar's visions of salvation history, in different ways, address the implicit trinitarian structure of these images. Their work strongly suggests that as the sacraments are means of grace and the work of Christ incarnate in his church, they cannot be considered otherwise than in a trinitarian context; moreover, they provide some initial lines for recognizing the trinitarian dynamic within the sacramental economy. Presuming for the moment that there is traditional support for considering the sacraments as a fourth (not independent) moment of the manifestation of the Trinity in the world, the sacramental economy will be marked by history (remembrance or anamnesis), which is to be traced to the mission, in creation and incarnation, of the Word of truth. That history, however, will realize itself in freedom as the human person turns toward God as his or her future. In this free cooperation of the human will with God's plan of salvation, the Holy Spirit's work of love can be recognized. From Balthasar's understanding of the economy, sacrament is the means of the *admirabile commercium* ("wonderful exchange") by which Christ, through his self-emptying love, gives to his people his own place in the trinitarian economy.[51] This is accomplished by immersing the distance of sin in the infinite distance of the Spirit, which bridges the moral and ontological gaps between humanity and God.

Section 1.3
The Sacramental Economy of Salvation

The analysis of trinitarian language in sacramental ritual is not enough for liturgical and sacramental theology to take account of the trinitarian shape of salvation history, because the missions of Son and Holy Spirit in sacrament are as interdependent as in the rest of the economy of salvation. Instead, a different model of sacramental efficacy is needed, one that integrates the trinitarian missions in the whole understanding of what sacrament is. If the testimony of the Gospel of John, Rahner, and Balthasar are any indication, a full exposition of the sacramental life of the church will encompass the embodied (physical and cultural) dynamic of worshipers and how the rite helps them enter into the trinitarian mystery.

In trinitarian theology, Catherine Mowry LaCugna has recognized the need for a deeper integration of the methods of trinitarian and liturgical theology. She sees the liturgy as a theological source for trinitarian spirituality. *God for Us* includes a chapter on the historical testimony of the liturgy to trinitarian theology.[52] LaCugna also refers to the importance of the liturgy in her essay "Can Liturgy Ever Again Become a Source for Theology?" Trinitarian spirituality in the liturgy does not come from the number three or from hearing the names of the Trinity. Rather, the liturgy is trinitarian because it is "the ritual celebration of redemption by God through Christ in the power of the Spirit."[53] Liturgy is a source for trinitarian reflection because liturgical

---

[51] See Balthasar, *TD4*, 241–42, 244–54.

[52] LaCugna, *God for Us* (San Francisco: HarperCollins, 1993), 111–42. More recent liturgical scholarship has called into question some of the assumptions about date and provenance that are critical to her argument in this chapter, especially with regard to church orders. See Paul Bradshaw, *Search for the Origins of Christian Worship* (New York: Oxford, 2002), 73–97.

[53] LaCugna, "Can Liturgy Ever Again Become a Source for Theology?" *Studia Liturgica* 19, no. 1 (1989): 5.

practice is how Christians participate in the Trinity; it is part of the manifestation of the Trinity in the economy.

As LaCugna suggests, a verbal analysis of rites can take one only so far toward a full recognition of the trinitarian nature of Christian liturgy. Robert Taft, likewise, argues that "eastern prayer is explicitly and consciously trinitarian" in a way that goes beyond any verbal analysis: "I am not talking about phrases, the repetition of trinitarian formulae like doxologies, but about the *liturgie profonde*," which results in an Eastern "piety that remains trinitarian through and through."[54] Taft's "*liturgie profonde*" comes from the experience of the regular celebration of a liturgy, from the words, actions, and things of the liturgical rite, but cannot be reduced to them by a facile analysis.

Both LaCugna and Taft recognize that even where trinitarian language and trinitarian redemption are both present in liturgical practice,[55] description of the trinitarian language is not enough to account for the fullness of the communication of trinitarian life that happens in the liturgical act. Gheevargese Panicker's analysis of the trinitarian dimension of the Anaphora of St. James provides a clear example.[56] Panicker quotes Rahner's concern that the Western church lacks a real trinitarian spirituality and argues that the Syro-Malankara rite, of which he is a practitioner, can provide insight. He describes the Liturgy of St. James and argues that the anaphora is "full of trinitarian expressions" and "conspicuous by the clarity of its trinitarian schema."[57]

Still, Panicker is unsatisfied with his analysis of language as a demonstration of the real "trinitarian dimension" of the liturgy. He admits that "it is the epiclesis which has become almost exclusively the pneumatological moment par excellence indicating the intervention of the Holy Spirit," but maintains, "in reality the role of the Holy Spirit in the eucharist surpasses the design of a pointed formula. The eucharist of the Church and the eucharistic Church is entirely the epiclesis invocation, as it is entirely a memorial."[58] The eucharistic rite has a pneumatological character that *transcends* the Spirit language of the epiclesis because the church, as a eucharistic body, is identifiable

---

[54] Robert Taft, "'Eastern Presuppositions' and Western Liturgical Reform," *Antiphon* 5:1 (2000): 11.

[55] LaCugna, "Can Liturgy Ever Again Become," 4.

[56] Gheevargese Panicker, "The Liturgy of St James and Theology of the Trinity," *Studia Liturgica* 30:1 (2000): 112–28.

[57] Ibid., 121.

[58] Ibid., 125.

by its pneumatic and epicletic life (as well as its memorial and thus christological life).

The trinitarian language of the rite reflects the trinitarian identity of the particular church that practices it, but it does not exhaust that identity, because the trinitarian identity of the church is not simply the internalization of many repetitions of trinitarian names but is rather the result of the Trinity working within the rite to establish the church. "In the same way as in the time of incarnation of the Word, the Holy Spirit did not incarnate himself, but penetrated the human nature of the Lord from whom he is eternally inseparable; so in the same way in the time of the Church, the Holy Spirit is not the object of a festive or eucharistic memorial, but he constitutes the power, the very grace of the memorial and of the presence of Christ in the Church."[59] The deeply trinitarian dimension of the West Syrian Anaphora of St. James, then, according to Panicker, is revealed in a trinitarian dynamic that grounds the "christocentric but not christomonic" language: Christ is always at the center of the liturgy, but the liturgy does not glorify Christ alone.[60] This dynamic is most clearly revealed when it is concealed: the role of the Holy Spirit, who "is at the same time the ineffable person and the divine gift which hides his visage and his name,"[61] is the fulfillment and completion of Christ's presence for his people in the eucharist. The Spirit is always present where Christ is present, but the Spirit's presence is sometimes camouflaged by the ritual action.

The epiclesis of the Anaphora of St. James is the point at which that liturgy's pneumatic dimension comes into clear focus, although in fact the whole anaphora is equally pneumatic with that epiclesis. According to Panicker, the very "hiddenness" of the Spirit, in the tendency of liturgical language to emphasize Christ's action rather than the Spirit's, is a manifestation of the trinitarian dynamic. The work of the Holy Spirit is to make Christ visible, not to be visible. The tendency to see a pneumatic dimension of the liturgy in a relative lack of pneumatological language is clearly an indication of Panicker's deep trinitarian identity and spirituality.

If the sacraments shape Christian identity, sacramental theology must find a way of exploring the trinitarian depth dimension of liturgical practice. But even in the strongest case, a verbal exploration of

---

[59] Ibid.
[60] Ibid., 123.
[61] Ibid., 126.

the names of the Persons of the Trinity in the liturgy fails to disclose the fullness of the manifestation of the Persons in the mysteries of the church. If even in the East, the Holy Spirit "hides his visage and his name,"[62] what can be said for the liturgy, spirituality, and Christian identity of the Latin rite Roman Catholic Church, whose traditional anaphora's "epiclesis" has no reference to the Holy Spirit?[63]

Panicker has already intimated the direction of an answer to this question. The Holy Spirit in the West Syrian liturgy, he reflects, "constitutes the power, the very grace of the memorial and of the presence of Christ in the Church."[64] It is the activity of God, traditionally the "efficacy" of the sacrament, that is trinitarian. Trinitarian liturgical language is a partial reflection of this sacramental economy but does not exhaust it. Christian identity too reflects the liturgical language that forms it but is not exhausted by it. Edward Kilmartin's work provides some indications of how this may be so. He observes that the law of prayer provides its practitioners with "a comprehensive, and, in some measure a pre-reflective, perception of the life of faith."[65] In other words, the adage "the law of prayer founds the law of faith"[66] applies most perfectly at the level of prereflective identity of the believer: the practice of liturgical prayer is the basis for Christian identity, out of which springs explicit reflective belief.[67]

The "law of prayer," then, is the foundation of the trinitarian dimension of Christian identity because liturgical practice plants Christians within the trinitarian activity of the economy of salvation. The sacraments are the rites recognized as particularly important for that practice, economy, and identity. This in turn suggests a methodological revision: instead of a merely linguistic analysis, what is necessary here is an examination of *the trinitarian efficacy*, linguistic, symbolic, performative, embodied, by which the sacraments become the manifestation of the trinitarian enactment of salvation for human persons.

---

[62] Ibid., 126.

[63] "Supplices te rogamus, omnipotens Deus, iube haec perferri per manus sancti Angeli tui in sublime altare tuum, in conspectu divinae maiestatis tuae; ut quotquot ex hac altaris participatione sacrosanctum Filii tui Corpus et Sanguinem sumpserimus, omni benedictione caelesti et gratia repleamur."

[64] Panicker, "Liturgy of St James," 125.

[65] Edward Kilmartin, *Christian Liturgy: Theology and Practice* (Franklin, WI: Sheed and Ward, 1988), 97.

[66] Prosper of Aquitaine, *De vocatione omnium gentium*, I, 12. See, e.g., discussion, ibid., 96–97.

[67] Cf. Aidan Kavanagh's *On Liturgical Theology* (Collegeville, MN: Liturgical Press, 1992).

The disciplines of the social sciences, particularly those implicated in the cross-disciplinary field of ritual studies, have a set of methods for exploring the cultural efficacy of ritual practices. As said above, trinitarian efficacy and cultural efficacy are not the same. Divine power, unlike cultural power, cannot fail or misfire (Isa 55:10-11); it does not have its ultimate foundation in the human realm. There are two problems with confusing these types of efficacy: one is a fear of conceptually "trapping" God's power in human action and thus failing to do justice to God's absolute sovereignty (the "magic" critique), and the other is the concern of attributing oppressive social constructs to God (for example, medieval pogroms that were motivated by eucharistic worship). Both concerns are about respecting God's radical otherness, and any attempt to take account of the sacraments as culturally efficacious instruments must rule out these misinterpretations. Despite these concerns, though, cultural efficacy is an indispensable element in the theological consideration of any divine efficacy of the sacraments.

Section 1.4
Liturgy and Embodied Christian Identity

Sacraments can be considered "in common," that is, as a genre or integrated set of practices, only within the structure of salvation history, which is marked by the Trinity. This implies that the efficacy of the sacraments, which are "economic," is likewise trinitarian. What is the basis for the connection between the cultural efficacy of the sacraments and their salvific power? This connection is at the heart of how sacraments can be thought to make Christian people, how they can be the "law" or "rule" of prayer. It is also the foundation for any trinitarian theology of sacrament.

"Sacrament" is a theological concept that developed gradually in order to account for the church's early and abiding experience, in which certain rituals were a particularly significant participation in the economy of salvation, the great plan by which God the Father was reconciling human beings to himself through the work of Christ in the Holy Spirit. Like the Trinity itself and other concepts later understood to be indispensable to Christian faith, sacramentality is rooted in the New Testament texts, develops in patristic exegesis and reflection, and continues to be the subject of theological analysis thereafter. Only a concise presentation of examples from these first two periods is possible here, but a very few examples will suffice to show that the later understanding of sacrament grew out of a widespread conviction that Christians could participate in God's economy of salvation through their ritual life.[68]

The body of Paul's letter to the Romans, written between 55 and 58 CE,[69] makes an argument for the consideration of baptism as a sacrament because of its place within the economy of salvation. The context of Paul's well-known discussion of baptism is Romans 5–8, a soteriological explanation for how God's economy of salvation has been extended to Gentiles, who stand outside the revelation of the Torah. Baptism holds a central role in the economic bestowal of salvation in Christ.

Paul sees the problem of humanity as sin, a problem that is not resolved by the giving of the law because the law itself creates a more powerful desire to sin (Rom 7). In other words, the problem is not merely one of knowledge of the good but also of ability to do the good. By the death of Jesus Christ, God solves this problem: "For God has done what the law, weakened by the flesh, could not do: by sending his own Son in the likeness of sinful flesh, and to deal with sin, he condemned sin in the flesh, so that the just requirement of the law might be fulfilled in us, who walk not according to the flesh but according to the Spirit" (8:3-4). Baptism is essential to this transition, although circumcision is not (1 Cor 7), because those who are dead are free from the law and from sin (Rom 7:1-3). Christ is dead and free, but those who are alive are still subject to the commands of the law and the deception of sin (7:7-25). But Christians have died through their participation in Christ's death, because of their baptism: "Do you not know that all of us who have been baptized into Christ Jesus were baptized into his death? Therefore we have been buried with him by baptism into death, so that, just as Christ was raised from the dead by the glory of the Father, so we too might walk in newness of life. For if we have been united with him in a death like his, we will certainly be united with him in a resurrection like his" (6:3-4). For Paul, baptism is an essential element of salvation history because it is the economic

---

[68] Sacraments were narrowed to seven rituals only in the Western church late in the medieval period. Hugh of St. Victor's *On the Sacraments of the Christian Faith* treats as sacraments many things that would be considered sacramentals later in the history of the Roman Catholic Church (see, e.g., II:9.1). Similarly, in many Eastern churches today, there are more than seven sacraments.

[69] Brown, *Introduction to the New Testament*, 560. In the discussion that follows my reading is partially influenced by Brown's discussion of Romans in this text.

completion of Christ's mission; it is what allows both Jews and Gentiles to be "reconciled to God through the death of his Son" (5:10)—or, to put it differently, what allows the death of the Son to touch others. By baptism human persons enter into God's economy as it is enacted by the death and resurrection of Jesus. This is why the memorial effected by baptism is not mere recollection but a living anticipation of our resurrection. Baptism is a trinitarian event, because participation in Christ's death also entails a particular share in the Holy Spirit: living in "newness of life" is parallel to walking "according to the Spirit" (8:4-5). In Romans 6, then, baptism is already recognized as (somehow) participation in the trinitarian plan (economy) of God through both Christ and the Holy Spirit.

The sacramental narratives of the gospels may not have represented a liturgical tradition in the New Testament period.[70] Although the liturgical practice of the New Testament period is unclear, it is clear that these passages became inextricably linked to sacramental rituals in later commentary, shaping ritual practice, ritual access, and interpretation. For example, the Johannine passages introduce the motif of the necessity of the sacramental acts for participation in the salvific mystery. This idea is pronounced in the discussion of birth by water and the Spirit (John 3:5), eating the bread of Christ's flesh and drinking his blood (6:53), and the footwashing (13:8).[71] These scriptural injunctions of necessity were attached to initiatory practice and to the eucharistic meal. They eventually provided an argument that all should be able to access initiation and eucharist, including infants, the ill, and the aged. They also affected interpretation of these rites as essential aspects of Christ's mediation of salvation to human beings. In this sense they contributed to the conviction that baptism and the eucharist were part of salvation history.

Typological interpretation of the sacramental rites in the early church also demonstrates early recognition of the role of initiation and eucharist within salvation history. Patristic exegetes expanded

---

[70] See Maxwell E. Johnson, *The Rites of Christian Initiation: Their Evolution and Interpretation* (Collegeville, MN: Liturgical Press, 2007), 23–39. The sacramental narratives include the accounts of baptism in all four gospels, including the peculiar testimonies of John 1:29-34; 3:22; 4:1-2; the synoptic accounts of the Last Supper and the feedings of the multitude; and John 3; 6; and 13.

[71] For an example of a reconstruction of the distinctive qualities of this community that assumes these passages reflect liturgical practice, see Brown, *The Community of the Beloved Disciple* (New York: Paulist, 1979), e.g., 78–79, n. 145.

the New Testament interpretation of Hebrew Scriptures, using typological exegesis to explore the unity of God's overarching plan for
the salvation of the world. Typology used Old Testament imagery to
establish a continuum between the preincarnational workings of God
on behalf of God's people and the work of Christ and the church and
to extol the new covenant for its accessibility to Gentiles. Similar ex-
egetical styles are applied to liturgical practice, especially baptism and
eucharist, from the early period.[72] For example, Origen's typological
readings of baptism emphasize the crossing of the Red Sea and of the
Jordan River as types.[73] Baptism can be interpreted by the metaphor
of Israel's exodus experience, for Origen, because Christian baptism is
the ultimate referent of the saving experiences offered by God in the
Old Testament.[74] Origen, reading the exodus story cycles in the light
of John 3:5, argues that the exodus was fulfilled by baptismal practice
because the exodus was already in essence baptismal.[75]

In the West, baptism's integral role in the scope of salvation history
gave weight to the continuity between the Old Testament and the New
Testament. Tertullian used widespread agreement about the purpose
of baptism, which was "the remission of sins, deliverance from death,
regeneration, and the bestowal of the Holy Spirit," to underscore the
centrality of the doctrine of the fall to Christian soteriology.[76] On this
basis, he ridiculed Marcion's dualism and the rejection of the Old
Testament.[77] Tertullian's argument for the integrity of the Christian
canon rested on the conviction that Christian initiation was an essential
element of the economy of salvation.

---

[72] See Jean Daniélou, *From Shadows to Reality: Studies in the Typology of the Fathers*
(London: Burns & Oates, 1960), cited in Everett Ferguson, "Baptism According to
Origen," *Evangelical Quarterly* 78, no. 2 (2006): 118. By the fourth century, chrono-
logical typological readings of the actions of the initiatory rites have become a genre
for the rhetoric of mystagogical catechesis, with established tropes and dynamics: see
Hugh M. Riley, *Christian Initiation: A Comparative Study of the Interpretation of the
Baptismal Liturgy in the Mystagogical Writings of Cyril of Jerusalem, John Chrysostom,
Theodore of Mopsuestia, and Ambrose of Milan* (Washington, DC: Catholic University
of America, 1974).

[73] Everett Ferguson argues that these readings reflect liturgical practice, not merely
textual exegesis: "Baptism According to Origen," 117–35.

[74] Ibid., 119.

[75] Ibid., 121.

[76] Jaroslav Pelikan, *The Emergence of the Catholic Tradition (100–600)*, The Christian
Tradition, vol. 1 (Chicago: University of Chicago Press, 1971), 163.

[77] Tertullian, *Adv. Marcionem*, I.28.

Soteriologically, then, the sacraments facilitate the formation of an identity that enables their participants to enter into the trinitarian mystery of salvation: to become conformed to Christ and be filled with the Holy Spirit. Consideration of the trinitarian names in sacramental ritual should not camouflage the fact that the whole reality of sacraments is trinitarian; the sacramental regimen alters the fabric of Christians' whole identity. The sacraments, beginning with initiation and eucharist, are seen as efficacious in creating a Christian identity—a project in which the Trinity cooperates with human beings.[78]

Georgia Frank's examination of the fourth-century mystagogues and their liturgical catechesis is an apt guide to the embodied and experiential character of Christian identity in the church fathers.[79] Frank's goal is to consider the functioning of the physical and spiritual senses in the liturgical catechesis of Ambrose of Milan, Cyril (or perhaps John[80]) of Jerusalem, John Chrysostom, and Theodore of Mopsuestia. She is particularly interested in vision as the most trusted of the senses and in the functioning of mental imagery as a guide to physical perception in the eucharistic context. The liturgical exegesis of mystagogy is supposed to make sacramental practice more effective; in other words, the purpose of these homilies is to enhance the identity-forming potential of ritual experience for the auditors. The mystagogues assume in these homilies that there is a unity between the cultural and the personal, the sensory and the spiritual, which uniquely enables the ritual formation of the self.

First of all, Christian identity was *cultural*. It depended on a framework of perception that was sensory but learned. Frank begins by noting that Ambrose tries to forestall his neophytes' confusion about the first experience of the eucharist by pointing out the possibility of another layer of perception: "You have seen what you were able to see with the eyes of your body, with human perception; you have not seen those things which are effected but those which are seen."[81] To learn to perceive this new layer of experience required one to practice discernment,[82] to overlay on liturgical experience "a host of mental

---

[78] Cf. Phil 2:12-13.
[79] Georgia Frank, "'Taste and See': The Eucharist and the Eyes of Faith in the Fourth Century," *Church History* 70:3-4 (2001): 619-43.
[80] For the purposes of this section, the mystagogue will be called Cyril, as the matter of authorship does not affect the argument.
[81] Ambrose, *De sacramentis*, 3.10; cited in Frank, "Taste and See," 620.
[82] See Frank, "Taste and See," 636.

images that would reframe the physical perception of the Eucharist."[83] In other words, the fourth-century mystagogues did not attribute to the sacrament (or to their own words) a miraculous propensity to overcome the debased physical senses but rather helped to shape a *cultural discipline* that allowed their auditors, through practice, to see the unseen.

Frank points out that in the Eastern tradition beginning with Origen and continued in Cyril of Jerusalem's homilies, the "spiritual senses" corresponded to the physical senses on the one hand and to the spiritual exegesis of Scripture on the other. The experienced, well-formed Christian is able to perform "exegesis" on his or her sensory perceptions, so his or her embodied perception "[begins] at the body, but perceive[s] what [i]s beyond it."[84] Cyril, however, transformed the spiritual senses: they were not the privilege of the spiritually advanced but were the gift of baptism; moreover, they transform rather than displace the physical senses. When the liturgical rite touches the physical sensorium, the spiritual senses can discern the spiritual reality.[85] Similarly, the homilies of John Chrysostom emphasized that even though the content of the physical and spiritual senses may sometimes be at odds, spiritual vision "transformed and enhanced bodily sight rather than ignoring it."[86] When the initiand comes "to the sacred initiation, the eyes of the flesh see water; the eyes of faith behold the Spirit."[87] There is no implication here that the physical eyes are superfluous, let alone erroneous; spiritual sight is able to "make the unseen visible from the seen."[88]

This leads to a second observation, closely related to the cultural nature of Christian identity, in the homilies: Christian identity is in and through the physical body. This follows in part from the incorporation of the physical and spiritual sensorium in the teachings of Cyril of Jerusalem and John Chrysostom but can also be seen in their attentiveness to participants' gestures. Part of the cultural conditioning implied in Cyril of Jerusalem's homilies, Frank argues, is the creation of "imaginal bodies" for the worshipers and the cosmos that enabled the participants in the eucharist to create "a space in which to receive

---

[83] Ibid., 621.
[84] Ibid., 626.
[85] Ibid., 627.
[86] Ibid., 636.
[87] John Chrysostom, *Catecheses baptismales*, 3.3.9; quoted ibid., 635.
[88] *Cat.* 2.9; cited in Frank, "Taste and See," 635.

a body," that is, the body of Christ.[89] Frank notes that despite the importance of the biblical locations of Jerusalem in the *Catechetical Lectures* (prebaptismal catecheses), the sacred territory of the Holy Land did not play a role in the sanctifying imagery of the *Mystagogical Catecheses*. Instead, Cyril emphasizes the neophyte's capacity for spiritual sight and spiritual gestures, suggesting that through baptism his or her body has replaced the Holy City as the location of the sacred mysteries of redemption.[90]

John Chrysostom's approach is even more instructive. His homilies emphasized the postural and gestural elements of the baptizands' experiences as integral to the discernment expected of the spiritual sensorium, creating "bodies . . . through which to see the unseen."[91] These spiritual aspects of the neophytes' bodies, moreover, were not perceptible only through the use of the neophytes' own mental imagery but were also sensible to other spiritual agents, especially Satan. They were real, not just mental constructs.[92] Thus Frank concludes that the mystagogues shared "the conviction that the worshiper approached and encountered divine presence in space, and not in some disembodied illusionism. And the body was the starting point for such consideration."[93] Where a modern interpreter would see mere mental imagery, the mystagogues saw disciplines by which the soul of the subject built a "spiritual body" that could perceive the spiritual realm.

This provides an interesting hermeneutic for Augustine's suggestive but vague definition of sacrament in *Tractate 80 on John:* "The word is added to the elemental substance, and it becomes a sacrament, also itself, as it were, a visible word."[94] Augustine's definition is crucially, though not solely, responsible for the tendency to privilege spoken words over embodied ritual action in Western understandings of sacramental theology. Yet the context suggests that Augustine's meaning might have been as soteriological, cultural, sensory, and embodied as his fourth-century predecessors. First, the word Augustine refers to here is not the ritual formula (as it becomes in scholastic theology) but "the word that I have spoken to you" (John 15:3): that is, Christ's

---

[89] Frank, "Taste and See," 629.
[90] Ibid., 630.
[91] Ibid., 631.
[92] Ibid., 631–32.
[93] Ibid., 642.
[94] Augustine, *Tractates on the Gospel of John*, The Fathers of the Church, vol. 90 (Washington, DC: Catholic University of America, 1994), 80.3.1, p. 117.

word, which in the Gospel according to John, is effective "because it is believed."[95] In other words, the word here represents the whole ministry of Christ, the Word. It becomes united with the sacramental element to create the soteriological ritual that Augustine designates as sacrament. As a result, Augustine says, the water of baptism "touches the body and yet washes clean the heart" by the word's effect, "not because it is said, but because it is believed."[96] The soteriological effect of Christ's ministry, then, is incorporated into the bodily act of baptizing in water through the ritual of the sacrament. Support for this reading comes at the end of the homily, when Augustine concludes,

> this word of faith has so much power in the Church of God that, through the very one who believes, offers, blesses, immerses, it cleanses even the tiny infant, not yet having the capacity with its heart to believe in justice and with its mouth to make a profession of faith to salvation [Rom 10:9-10]. All this is done through the word, of which the Lord says: "Now you are clean by reason of the word that I have spoken to you."[97]

Clearly, the word here accepted in faith does not require a cognitive appropriation of the sacrament. The cleansing power of the word refers instead to the culturally and corporeally effected incorporation into the work of Christ, which results in a Christian identity with specific characteristics.

This brings up a third feature of patristic reflection on sacramental Christian identity: it is *corporate*. This is particularly clear in the case of Augustine's reflection on infant baptism above, which depends on the ecclesial context, but it is implicit in any presumption that identity can be culturally formed by ritual and authoritative exegesis. Thus, it is true also in the soteriological understandings of sacrament discussed above in this chapter. This point has been postponed this far, however, in part to preclude the possibility that the corporate character of sacramental Christian identity can be interpreted as excluding its full *personal* character. The cultural and bodily aspects of formation, especially inasmuch as they are determined by rituals and learned through directed practices, presuppose a corporate Christian identity, but at the same time guarantee that the fully developed identity will

---

[95] Augustine, *Tract. on John*, 80.3.2 (117); cf. John 6:60-65.
[96] Ibid.
[97] Ibid., 80.3.3.

be personal inasmuch as its development depends on the initiand's participation in the developmental process and its end is the result of the initiand's own phenomenological experiences.

In sum, Christian sacramental practice entails a participation in the trinitarian mystery by which human persons are reconciled to God because of a mysterious connection between certain rituals in Christian life and the ministry of Christ, the incarnate Word, whose existence is already trinitarian. Despite the mystery of this connection, the establishment of Christian identity by means of sacramental practice is anthropological: it is personal, culturally developed, embodied, and corporate.

The anthropological principle of sacramental interpretation is best understood as springing from a theological and historical principle. As seen in the understanding of Rahner and Balthasar, the trinitarian economy can be seen breaking into the world in at least three ways: in the creation of humanity, which is constituted by an availability to trinitarian completion; in the existential, individual act of this completion, which includes participation in the (historical) ministry of the Word and the (transcendent) mission of the Spirit; and in the drama of the mystery of salvation by which the turning point of history is identified as the moment at which the Word becomes a human being so that the trinitarian love and distance (Spirit) encompass creation and sin as well as the intratrinitarian relationships. In every case, this trinitarian economy implicates the cultural and bodily—the anthropological—by God's free economic action, rather than by necessity. Human persons were created bodily and cultural, they experience realities in an embodied cultural context, and in the incarnation of the Word the triune God irrevocably involved God's self in a human reality that was not only embodied, subject to pain and death, but also fully cultural—exposed to Hellenism and Judaism of various forms, integrated in various ways.

Christian identity that is trinitarian, salvific, embodied, cultural, corporate, and personal will clearly be human, anthropological, but its form and formation might well vary according to the needs and capacities of those to whom the Trinity is bringing salvation. Just as the Word chose to take on the whole range of human embodiment (physical and cultural) and to reveal the Father against the horizon of his own ritual experience, the Christian sacraments initiate human beings into the life of God through the embodied practices that connect them to their world.

Chapter Two

Efficacious Engagement
Ritual Formation of Dynamic Persons

S ince sacraments can be thought of as those human rituals that the church has recognized as part of God's plan to save human beings, the anthropological and cultural character of sacramental worship is part of these rites' salvific quality. Twentieth-century sacramental theology made great strides toward identifying the truly human character of the sacraments in general, but the way human ritual shapes human beings is still not integral to the treatment of the sacraments in general.

Section 2.1
The Contributions of the Symbolic Model

Recent work on sacramental efficacy has depended on the concept of human beings as symbolic and linguistic creatures. This approach to sacramental theology has the advantage of being grounded in the scholastic understanding of sacraments as signs and in contemporary trinitarian theology.[1] In addition, symbolic models for sacraments allow for a phenomenological understanding of human subjectivity, rather than seeing humans as passive recipients of sensory impressions. The symbolic model of sacramental action has helped eliminate "magical" understandings of sacramental efficacy and the failures of so-called "onto-theology," which reifies the divine. More important, it has motivated a

---

[1] See, e.g., Karl Rahner, "Theology of the Symbol," in *More Recent Writings*, Theological Investigations, vol. IV (Baltimore: Helicon Press, 1966), 221–52. For Rahner, the whole concept of symbol is grounded in the Word as image of the Father.

liturgical performance that moves beyond the minimalistic approach associated with a strict "causation" model. Instead, rites influenced by symbolic understandings of sacrament tend to be rich with unsuppressed sensory phenomena and capable of overflowing into abundant existential meaning for participants. Nonetheless, the symbolic model can lead even careful thinkers into excessively cognitive understandings of faith and salvation.

For example, Karl Rahner's essay "The Theology of the Symbol" made several crucial contributions to sacramental theology: seeking an understanding of *symbol* that would fit the sacraments, the human body, and the Logos, Rahner argued that a symbol results when any being constitutes itself by "really projecting its visible figure outside itself as its—symbol, its appearance, which allows it to be there, which brings it out to existence in the world, and in doing so, it retains it— 'possessing itself in the other.' The essence is there for itself and for others precisely through its appearance."[2] The symbol of a thing is the intrinsic self-realization of its essence, not an extrinsic and optional record of its existence for another's information.

According to Rahner's understanding of theological analogy, this is first and foremost true of the trinitarian life of God, and derivatively true of human personhood. The Logos is the perfect symbol of the Father, the self-expression by which the Father possesses himself by opposing to himself another within his essence.[3] By the incarnation this symbol is visible to humanity, making present "what—or rather, who—God wished to be, in free grace, to the world."[4]

In a distant echo of this, human beings are so created that their bodies are a self-expression and self-realization of their souls. The human person goes outward in his or her body and becomes present in the world, so that the actions of the body in the world are really his or her own actions. This description counteracts the division of human activity into "bodily" and "spiritual-intellectual," which privileges the latter. As such, it is a huge step toward understanding sacramental actions, and especially toward a new understanding of eucharistic presence.

Nevertheless, Rahner suggests that human misapprehensions can destroy the proper symbolism of creation: "Every God-given reality, where it has not been degraded to a purely human tool and to merely

---

[2] Ibid., 231.
[3] Ibid., 236.
[4] Ibid., 237.

utilitarian purposes, states much more than itself."[5] This is hard to reconcile with his claims that he is doing an ontology of symbol: if a reality realizes itself as symbol primarily for itself and only secondarily for others, surely no human misunderstandings, no matter how dire, can eliminate the essential symbolism of a being.[6] It also seems anti-thetical to the human experience of symbolism, however, for symbol seems to require utility. Take the act of eating, for example. In the eucharist Christians receive a morsel of bread, which is the foretaste of the heavenly banquet. This is no small matter; it is symbolic, not utilitarian. Suppose, on the other hand, that someone who is starving is given an equally small morsel of bread to keep him or her alive. This is utilitarian, but is it not symbolic? Of course it is symbolic: it not only makes present the love of this person that has offered the bread but also human charity in general. It expresses the life of the human body and human hope. In fact, the "symbolism" of eucharist cannot be divided from this "utilitarian" example; we recognize the eucharist as foretaste of the heavenly banquet on the basis of our own experience of acute hunger. The reception of Christ himself in the eucharistic elements is, to the extent we can recognize it, the most deeply useful experience we can have. Symbols are symbolic to the extent that we recognize their utility.

Louis-Marie Chauvet made a more recent contribution to the symbolic model of sacramental efficacy in his monumental work *Symbol and Sacrament* and the revised edition *The Sacraments*.[7] Chauvet uses a symbolic model to explain sacramental efficacy: human beings attain their identities through symbolic behavior, that is, through language. Therefore, sacramental efficacy is a special case of the efficacy of language; in sacraments, God speaks a grace-filled word to human beings. This model leads to two major contributions to sacramental thought: an explanation for how the "presence in absence" of sacraments is better than physical presence, and a structure that links Scripture, liturgy, and ethical practice in determining Christian identity.

Christian identity, for Chauvet, is expressed paradigmatically in the Emmaus story of Luke 24. If we seek the physical body of Christ,

---

[5] Ibid., 239.

[6] See ibid., 225.

[7] Louis-Marie Chauvet, *Symbol and Sacrament: Sacramental Reinterpretation of Christian Existence* (Collegeville, MN: Liturgical Press, 1995); *The Sacraments: The Word of God at the Mercy of the Body* (Collegeville, MN: Liturgical Press, 1997).

we fail to recognize Jesus' active presence among us; if we consent to the "absence" of Christ—that is, to the mediation of the church—we behold Jesus in the breaking of the bread. Jesus Christ is, after the ascension, absent; it is only through the symbolic mediation of the Scriptures, the sacraments, and the ethical life of the church that he can be experienced as present: even then, it is as a presence of an absence, or of the Absent One. "Absence" is not a negation of presence for Chauvet but an apophatic reminder that the risen Christ is no longer subject to human power. A corpse can be moved at will, but the risen Lord must be sought where he may be found: in the church. The search for a more immediate presence is a temptation to rewrite the story of salvation to fit our own desires: "the two disciples of Emmaus have had to . . . accept something monstrous for any good Jew, a Messiah who would have to go through death. You too must convert your desire for immediacy and *assent to the mediation of the church.*"[8]

"Presence in absence" is echoed by Chauvet's characteristic emphasis that sacramental grace can only be received by an "appropriation . . . through disappropriation."[9] Chauvet introduces the idea of "symbolic value" and "symbolic exchange" to understand the grace effect of the sacraments: sacramental grace is a gift given by God to the human community of the church. This gift has symbolic value, the value that establishes cultural communion, which Chauvet opposes to economic value, associated with "production." Every gift, however, obligates the recipient to a return that acknowledges the gift as gift. Chauvet argues that the ethical life, "agape between brothers and sisters," is the return-gift of the church's sacramental life.[10] In his structure of Christian identity, the proclamation of the Scriptures leads the church to the celebration of the sacraments, by which the church commits itself to the ethical life.

There is an implicit trinitarian structure to Chauvet's account. If sacramental grace is the trinitarian self-communication to a human person, as Rahner suggests, the sacramental gift must include the ethical life, because God's self-communication must contain in itself both offer (sacrament) and acceptance (ethical life).[11] In other words, the

---

[8] Chauvet, *The Sacraments*, 28, emphasis original. Susan Ross has pointed out that this advice is far more perilous to women than to men in *Extravagant Affections: A Feminist Sacramental Theology* (New York: Continuum, 1998), 155–58.

[9] Chauvet, *The Sacraments*, 276. Italics omitted.

[10] Ibid., 277. Italics omitted.

[11] Rahner, *The Trinity* (New York: Crossroad, 1999), 92–93.

return-gift is no extrinsic obligation but is contained in the gift itself as given. If God's gift "really arrives at" humanity, it includes an element of free acceptance that is God's own work.[12] Moreover, the sacramental gift offers a trinitarian identity to the participant. Sacramental grace goes beyond healing the *imago Dei* or *vestigia trinitatis* in the human soul but is the adoption of the human person into the fullness of Christ's filiation (John 1:16). Since the divine life, as Balthasar sees it, is "in essence perfect self-giving,"[13] the appropriation of the gift will of necessity imply a disappropriation: just as the Son's filial obedience means he gives himself up "even unto death," so Christian entry into the trinitarian life consists in becoming a secondary fountain of self-gift.[14] Thus the intratrinitarian generation is the origin of the return-gift that Chauvet describes as *"agape between brothers and sisters."*[15]

Section 2.2
Critiquing the Symbolic Model

Clearly, a symbolic model for the sacraments gives great insight. Why, then, go on beyond—or behind—symbolic models for sacramental action? Because human experience begins before symbolism, and the human experience of salvation is greater than the symbolic. Christian ritual is not just about constructing a symbolic world for the human person to inhabit; it is about constructing a human body that can inhabit the Christian world. We need a language that addresses how human bodies can freely accept the capacity to be secondary fountains of self-gift: in other words, how do sacraments arouse the desire and develop the capabilities to be self-giving love?

There are three basic motivations for examining a ritual foundation for sacramental efficacy: extralinguistic grace (God's gift to prelinguistic children and the developmentally disabled); the importance of the body in human relationships; and the embodied experience of the rite itself, including the participants' ability to subvert and reject their own symbolic and cultural system through ritual behavior.

Despite the depth of Chauvet's approach, the flaws of the symbolic method are revealed in his narrative analysis of Eucharistic Prayer

---

[12] Ibid., 89.
[13] Balthasar, *The Last Act*, Theo-Drama, vol. V (San Francisco: Ignatius, 1998), 82.
[14] Ibid., 88.
[15] Chauvet, *Symbol and Sacrament*, 277.

II (hereafter EPII) of the postconciliar Roman Rite in chapter 8 of *Symbol and Sacrament*. This "case study" establishes the dynamic of sacramental communion between God and human persons, then accepted as characteristic of all sacrament.[16] Chauvet sees the text of the prayer as a symbolic gift exchange between human persons and God. God gives the sacramental body and blood, together with grace, which obligates the assembly to offer a return-gift, motivating the offering clause of EPII.[17] This ritual offering is a symbolic representation of the real ethical return-gift, which is the life of communal love (agape, the ethical life mentioned earlier). The offering clause therefore demonstrates "appropriation through disappropriation," because the gift once received and placed on the altar is immediately offered back to God; it likewise represents the connection between liturgical and ethical practice characteristic of Chauvet's work.[18]

The crucial problem is the isolation of EPII from its ritual and performative context, which leads Chauvet to misread the significance of the eucharistic gift. No doubt influenced by traditional medieval Western understandings of consecration, Chauvet identifies the institution narrative as the moment when the gifts of God, the body and blood of Christ, are received.[19] But the assembly does not receive the body and blood of Christ until the ritual meal, which is at once the *embodied symbol* of the reception of the gift and the *performative enactment* of their communal love. The church offers the eucharistic gift back to God (in the offering clause) even *before* they receive it; or rather, the gift offers *itself* in "an act of oblation, that is, of dispossession" that gives the assembly the ability to "become what they receive."[20] Despite being an advance, Chauvet's tie between liturgical and ethical practice is still too extrinsic. If the eucharistic gift is grace, that is, entry into the trinitarian life, then the *capacity* to become absolute self-giving in the world is *the gift itself*, not an obligatory return-gift. More, this capacity to pour oneself out, kenosis taking on the form of the body of Christ through

---

[16] "All of this process of 'becoming eucharist' expresses all of the process of Christian identity" (ibid., 280). The following page applies the result of the analysis of EPII to "the function of the moment 'Sacrament'" (281).

[17] Ibid., 270–76.

[18] Ibid., 276–78.

[19] "This [sub-program] seeks to obtain Jesus Christ, through the Spirit, under the mode of sacramental body and blood: the anamnesis *declares this realized,* but . . . in an act of oblation, that is, of dispossession" (ibid., 270–71, emphasis added).

[20] Ibid., 271; Augustine, Sermon 227.

the power of the Spirit, is the only form grace can take, because God has no other gift to give than God's own life.

Chauvet's language act model leads to this isolation of text from ritual action. "The word should not be treated," he says, "as merely one example among others but as the very archetype of what happens between subjects and within any subject."[21] And a word obligates the recipient to a return-gift, an acknowledgment of the word.[22] Chauvet introduces the model of language to replace the "sign and cause" model of sacramentality, because "there is an (apparently fundamental) heterogeneity between the language of grace and the instrumental and productionist language of causality."[23] The scholastic tendency to see grace as part of the causal order was a kind of "conceptual idolatry"[24] in which the clarity of the theological method of analogy hides the fact that God is the *"non-other,"*[25] the "unrecognizable,"[26] who can never be known except in a relationship.[27] Chauvet intends the symbolic model of sacrament to be a performative language, altering those who use it even as it allows them to speak.[28]

In order to construct this pole, Chauvet turns to the later work of Martin Heidegger on language. Heidegger believed that in thinking about being, one asked as much about one's own subjectivity as about one's subject.[29] Ontology is intimately connected to epistemology. According to Heidegger, it is the essence of human beings to *ek-sist* ("be outward").[30] Humanity is suffused with potential and risk: the human person "stands out into the openness of Being,"[31] always experiencing the self against the transcendent.[32] Heidegger says that human being,

---

[21] Ibid., 266.

[22] Ibid., 267.

[23] Ibid., 7.

[24] Ibid., 217.

[25] Ibid., 74.

[26] Ibid., 75.

[27] These concerns are quite similar to those motivating the reappropriation of scholastic theology by Edward Schillebeeckx and Rahner. In *The Sacraments*, xiv–xvii, Chauvet seems to exculpate Thomas himself and lay the blame instead on the inflexibility of his followers; cf. *Symbol and Sacrament*, 17–22.

[28] *Symbol and Sacrament*, 65, 72.

[29] Martin Heidegger, "What is Metaphysics?," *Basic Writings*, David Farrell Drell, ed. (New York: Harper & Row, 1977), 93.

[30] See Heidegger, "Letter on Humanism," *Basic Writings*, 230–31.

[31] Ibid., 252.

[32] See also Heidegger, ". . . Poetically Man Dwells . . . ," *Poetry, Language, Thought*, Albert Hofstadter, trans. (New York: Harper, 2001), 220–21.

"being-in-the-world," depends on finding language that can reveal God as the unknown: "God's manifestness—not only he himself—is mysterious."[33] Poetry comes closest to actually fulfilling this ultimate purpose of language, beckoning us toward a thing's nature.[34] Since Heidegger believes language is irreducibly oriented toward the subject and draws humanity toward the unknown while maintaining its mystery, Chauvet concludes that only a model of sacrament formed by language can take account of grace, which "is of an entirely different order from that of value or empirical verifiability."[35]

When Chauvet turns from philosophy to the social sciences, however, he silently introduces a whole new set of presuppositions about language. He compares the symbolic order "to contact lenses which cannot be seen by the wearers since they adhere to their eyes but through which all their vision of the real is filtered. Therefore, the real as such is by definition *unreachable*. What we perceive of it is what is constructed by our culture and desire, what is filtered through our linguistic lens."[36] The symbolic order (his new methodological pole) and linguistic reality are, in all essential respects, equivalent.[37] From something that allows a subject to step out into the transcendent (to "ek-sist"), language becomes a horizon that limits a subject's ability to see outside his or her cultural setting.

It is not surprising that Chauvet should find himself in this position, because Heidegger's "language" is not, strictly speaking, a linguistic reality. In "A Dialogue on Language" Heidegger expresses a hope for a disclosure of a mystery shared by his language, German, and that of his Japanese colleagues. He seeks to be reassured by his bilingual interlocutor that true "language" may transcend cultural specifics: "Some time ago I called language, clumsily enough, the house of Being. If man *by virtue of his language dwells within the claim and call of Being*, then we Europeans presumably dwell in an entirely different house than Eastasian man."[38] The interlocutor expands on his use of the word "presumably": "Assuming that the languages of the two are not merely different but are other in nature, and radically so."[39] Again Heidegger

[33] Ibid., 220.
[34] Ibid., 214.
[35] Ibid., 44–45.
[36] Ibid., 86.
[37] Ibid.
[38] Ibid. Emphasis added.
[39] Ibid.

seeks reassurance: "And so, a dialogue from house to house remains nearly impossible,"[40] provoking this comforting response: "You are right to say 'nearly.' For still it was a dialogue."[41]

Heidegger is trying to find a "language" that goes beyond linguistic limitations, in which "there sings something that wells up from a single source."[42] No single language act really performs the task of "language" for Heidegger: language itself, like Being, continually withdraws from thought. It is not contact lenses but a "house of Being"—a *meeting-place* in which Being and humanity dwell and where their mutual relationship can take place. This relationship is "meaning," or what Heidegger calls "world."[43] When language builds "world"—insight into human existence against transcendence—language functions as a metaphor for "being-in-the-world," but language can also, as the dialogues recognize, be a screen hiding the single source.

For the social sciences, on the other hand, "speech expresses meaning; it does not reveal or disclose it. Language . . . can never be a source of meaning and of life."[44] Such a view "is oriented toward, but also limited to, what can be brought to light about linguistic phenomena by empirical investigation."[45] Scientific views of language cannot be fully reconciled with phenomenology, which takes as its starting point "the relation between language and 'meaning-giving ek-sistence.'"[46] This distinction casts grave doubt on Chauvet's apology for the introduction of the linguistic sciences: "If Heidegger sees here a manifestation, dimly outlined, of the invitation by Being (always linked to the *Logos*) to the human being, linguistics and psychoanalysis attempt to show us the concrete process of this invitation."[47] Linguistics and psycho-

---

[40] Ibid.

[41] Ibid. Cf. the assertion of Jacques Derrida on the gift: "What I really do not know, and I confess I do not know, is whether what I am analyzing or trying to think is prior to my own culture, our own culture, that is, to the Judeo-Christian, Greek heritage of the gift . . ." ("On the Gift: A Discussion between Jacques Derrida and Jean-Luc Marion, Moderated by Richard Kearney," in *God, the Gift, and Postmodernism* [Bloomington: Indiana University, 1999], 73).

[42] Heidegger, *On the Way to Language*, Joan Stambaugh, trans. (New York: Harper & Row, 1982), 8.

[43] Heidegger, "Letter on Humanism," 252.

[44] Joseph J. Kockelmans, "Language, Meaning, and Ek-sistence," *On Heidegger and Language* (Evanston: Northwestern University, 1972), 7.

[45] Ibid., 5–6.

[46] Ibid.

[47] Chauvet, *Symbol and Sacrament*, 92.

analysis, however, make no attempt to show the invitation by Being to human beings; on the contrary, they are interested in all kinds of language acts (and subconscious movements) *between* human subjects, but only in these.

Illocutionary language acts provide an example of the gap between language as truth-revealing and language as human communication. When an illocutionary utterance is spoken in the right conditions and accepted, the relationship between speaker and addressee is altered. "I take this man [woman] to be my husband [wife]" is one of the classic examples.[48] Chauvet argues that every word has an illocutionary dimension and so requires a return-gift: a failure to respond "would be interpreted [by the speaker] as a personal insult, a wounding attitude ignoring the presence of the request, a symbolic murder."[49] Unfortunately, Chauvet overlooks the fact that the illocutionary dimension of language can itself be *used* to commit symbolic murder; not every linguistic exchange rises to "the invitation by Being." Chauvet suggests "I promise," "I baptize," "I confirm"; he does not make use of equally performative utterances of control ("I own you") or violence ("I'll kill you"), or dehumanization. All of these can be used to *negate* the identity of the addressee as a subject, to take away his or her voice. Repetitions of such illocutions are used in abusive relationships to enforce dominance, just as repetitions of positive performative utterances can build up positive relationships. Human language can be used to silence as well as to invite human beings, to dissolve and deny as well as to create relationships.

In the Sermon on the Mount, Matthew's Jesus cautions his disciples about precisely this kind of performative ambivalence of language: "You have heard that it was said . . . 'You shall not murder'; and 'whoever murders shall be liable to judgment.' But I say to you that if you are angry with a brother or sister, you will be liable to judgment; and if you insult a brother or sister, you will be liable to the council; and if you say, 'You fool,' you will be liable to the hell of fire" (Matt 5:21-22). The "quasi-languages" ("'supra-language' made up of gestures, mime, and all artistic endeavor; 'infra-language' of the archaic impulses of the unconscious"[50]) are subject to the same critique, so Jesus continues, "You have heard that it was said, 'You shall not commit adultery.' But

---

[48] See J. L. Austin, *How to Do Things With Words* (Cambridge, MA: Harvard University, 1975), e.g., 5.

[49] Chauvet, *Symbol and Sacrament*, 132.

[50] Ibid., 87, n. 8.

I say to you that everyone who looks at a woman with lust has already committed adultery with her in his heart" (Matt 5:27-28). The illocutionary dimension of language that Chauvet depends on is effective, but it is not at all clear that it is "outside the order of value."[51] In fact, in *How to Do Things With Words*, Austin's example "I bet you"[52] is efficacious within the order of economic value—which is, like symbolic exchange, a cultural construction.[53]

In the end, no cultural analysis of symbolic value is adequate to understanding grace. Chauvet says in his model,

> the communication of grace is to be understood, not according to the "metaphysical" scheme of cause and effect, but according to the symbolic scheme of communication through language, a communication supremely effective because it is through language that the subject comes forth in its relation to other subjects within a common "world" of meaning. It is precisely a *new relation of places between subjects*, a relationship of filial and brotherly and sisterly alliance, that the sacramental "expression" aims at instituting or restoring in faith.[54]

This is true of the sacraments, yet it is not adequate. The work of Miri Rubin on the eucharist in the Middle Ages, for example, shows how "a common 'world' of meaning," even among Christians, may yet be a world inimical to the universal love demonstrated by Christ, and "filial and brotherly and sisterly alliance" may be expressed by violence against others.[55] The eucharist is certainly symbolically effective, whether as a means for the subjection of Jews in the late medieval period or as a mediator of the unifying love Christ offers to his brothers and sisters; yet no theologian would wish to argue that both of these are equally a communication of grace. It is the efficacy of the sacraments *as a communication of grace* that interests the theologian and that is the object of such traditional phrases as *ex opere operato* or *in persona Christi*. The *symbolic* efficacy of ritual may effect both good and evil;

---

[51] Ibid., 100. Emphasis omitted.

[52] Austin, 5, example E.d. This example recurs throughout the text.

[53] In fact, economic value is precisely cultural and symbolic, which represents another problem for the distinction Chauvet is trying to draw between symbolic and economic exchange.

[54] Chauvet, *Symbol and Sacrament*, 140.

[55] Miri Rubin, Corpus Christi: *The Eucharist in Late Medieval Culture* (New York: Cambridge University Press, 1991).

sacramental efficacy, however, is an extension of the effective word of creation, in accordance with which God found his works to be good.[56]

Sacraments and grace are "outside the order of [human] value," not because they are language acts, but because they are part of salvation history, as I said in chapter 1. The language act model reinscribes the neoscholastic, Western hierarchy that privileges the word or form, the intelligible part of the sacramental ritual, above the embodied material and behavioral parts. Sacramental "meaning" then seems intellectual and obscure, accessible only to the knowledgeable elite. The model tends to suppress the exterior, material, and bodily parts of the rite in favor of a sacramental reading based solely on the text, like Chauvet's interpretation of EPII. This minimizes the performative nature of the rite and jeopardizes our appreciation of the ritual experience.

Another drawback of the language act model is its limitation with respect to prelinguistic, nonlinguistic, and extralinguistic dimensions of grace. This limitation becomes especially apparent with respect to infant baptism. For baptism of *infantes* is literally the baptism of those who are speechless. A linguistic model for the exchange that constitutes them as members of the community is particularly inappropriate, for they cannot receive any word "as such."[57] Nor are they capable of a quasi-linguistic return-gift, even if it is as simple as "a nod of the head, a look conveying our interest in what is being said."[58] The language act model thus casts doubt on the potentiality of nonspeakers to receive grace.[59] Yet the Christian tradition holds, in the practices of infant baptism and infant communion, that infants are in fact subjects of grace. The problem is not with this tradition: the problem is that the language act model represents the interlocutors' capacities as relatively equal, whereas infants have capacities that differ greatly from those

[56] Chauvet of course recognizes this distinction: it is acknowledged explicitly in *Symbol and Sacrament*, "A Reality Extra-linguistic Nevertheless," pp. 443ff.: "as with everything concerning God, from the first we declare grace to be *irreducible* to any explanations. . . . What we are proposing here is in no way a reduction of grace to the sociolinguistic mechanism of symbolic efficacy." The critique here is not meant to imply that Chauvet is reductionist toward the sacraments but simply to open a space for another model that explicitly examines the efficacy of sacraments as rituals.

[57] Ibid., 267.

[58] Ibid. Clearly, interest in *what is being said* is beyond prelinguistic persons by definition.

[59] Chauvet's reading of baptism is based on a sociolinguistic interpretive stance that cannot conceptualize the meaning of infant baptism *for the baptizand*: see ibid., 438–43. This point will be considered more fully in chapters 3 and 4.

of adults.[60] In fact, the linguistic model might camouflage the infinite difference in capacity for gift giving and gift reception between adult human beings and God.

The goal, then, of enlarging the methodological foundation to include ritual rather than linguistic efficacy is threefold: to account for the fact of grace experience in infants and other nonspeakers (even if it remains impossible to characterize), to differentiate sacramental efficacy from the ambiguous efficacy of language acts, and to open a broader view in order to respect the bodily and ritual nature of liturgical exchange. Although it would be possible to maintain the notion of "language" with the Heideggerian resonances it has in Chauvet's first part, such a move obscures the integral wholeness of the human person, whose use of body and imagination is not an "infra-language" but part of his or her dynamic self-development. Fortunately, the field of ritual studies provides models for seeing rituals as the field for human self-development.

Section 2.3
Efficacious Engagement

The drawbacks of the linguistic model stem from an oversimplified understanding of human (and thus Christian) identity as something relatively static, fixed by one's culture, and intellective-linguistic rather than integrative.[61] These factors quite naturally make infant initiation seem to be a benign or even malign abnormality,[62] given that infants are not only prelinguistic but also in a rapid state of development and still undergoing the process of cultural formation. Nonetheless, this oversimplified understanding is equally problematic with respect to adults (though the problems may be less evident): adults too have dynamic identities, are constantly undergoing personal change, and are shaped by but also defy their culture's assumptions and characteristics. Nonlinguistic practices play an important role in their identities as well and are highly integrated with their linguistic and symbolic fields.

---

[60] See ibid., 92–93.

[61] One might wonder whether the reduction to consciousness is the root of these problems, but the answer seems to be no. Other thinkers influenced by Heidegger (e.g., Levinas, Derrida, Marion) incorporate the concepts of symbol and of gift (though, especially in Derrida, in a very different form) without compromising the fluidity of human existence.

[62] See discussion of Aidan Kavanagh's famous critique of infant baptism in chapter 3.

Identity refers to the interface between continuity and change in a human being's experiences that allows him or her to incorporate new aspects of self.[63] Without continuity there is no identity, but identity is also the ability to improvise. Human development requires that some aspects of self be maintained; these enable the acceptance, revision, or change of other aspects. *Identity*, then, is intrinsically connected to *formation*. Identity develops through bodily and cognitive activity, through ritual and interpretation, through disciplines imposed by others and those one imposes on oneself.

In *Liturgy and the Social Sciences*, Nathan Mitchell suggests that contemporary liturgical studies may have more to learn from *emerging ritual*—improvisational practices arising from the search for self-understanding by a marginal group—than from the traditional "high church" theory that ritual recapitulates social consensus and reinforces the status quo. Emerging rituals exemplify the fruitfulness of an "identity" or "formation" model for understanding sacraments as a cultural reality.[64]

Contrary to popular belief, contemporary culture is not a "ritual wasteland": the diversity of contemporary culture causes ritual to proliferate because ritual participation becomes a more salient factor in determining group membership. Such participation may "generate social solidarity even in the absence of shared beliefs,"[65] making collective action possible. In the civil rights movement, "blacks and whites, Protestants and Catholics, Jews and gentiles, the devout and the doubting, joined in demonstrating . . . [showing that] ritual potency does not necessarily derive from a structured belief system to which all participants adhere."[66] Ritual participation creates social bonds that might not follow from genetic or propositional logic by identifying with a particular group and its way of life. If no shared system of meaning or symbolism is necessary for ritual to "work," then rituals must work, in some way, within, behind, or around our symbolic understanding of the world. Rituals do "encourage us to interpret reality in very specific ways,"[67] but this is more the *cause* than the *result* of a symbolic consensus among members of the created group.

[63] See Jean-Luc Marion, "*Mihi magna quaestio factus sum:* The Privilege of Unknowing," *Journal of Religion* 85, no. 1 (2005): 1–24.

[64] Nathan D. Mitchell, *Liturgy and the Social Sciences* (Collegeville, MN: Liturgical Press, 1999).

[65] Ibid., 39. Original italics omitted.

[66] Ibid., 41.

[67] Ibid., 39. Italics omitted.

Both emerging and traditional rituals are marked by an improvisational character. When people are marginalized, they may seek identity with fragile, invented rituals. They participate *in search of* a shared set of meanings; each seeks a new identity (a sense of family, hope for justice, freedom from debilitating addiction) and—reluctantly, cautiously, or recklessly—ritualizes toward this goal. Traditional religious rituals are also marked by improvisation. "Just as language is always being invented in the process of using it," Ronald Grimes observes, "so ritual is always in the process of being created as ritualists enact it."[68] Even if traditional rituals are "received (as part of a tradition) rather than invented,"[69] every new generation receives the pattern into their own bodies and so reinvents that pattern: to accept it is to change it. The inculturation of children is one social margin where traditional ritual is improvisational. Ritual systems evolve in part because they must adapt to each new generation. As a new generation "receives" cultural practice, they also transform it—and themselves.

The study of emerging ritual, then, suggests the possibility that (1) ritual and sacramental behavior is significant because of its potential for forming and transforming persons within their social settings and (2) infant reception of cultural practices is a particularly evocative example of such formation and transformation. These observations together lead to the potential for finding a model that is prelinguistic (and potentially a foundation for linguistic or symbolic formation) and embodied, which can approach the question of cultural formation from infancy. This model will keep in mind the character of grace as developing a desire to be self-giving in love and the ability to participate in that love. In other words, it will consider human persons in their attitudes and aptitudes as well as their symbolic and intellectual abilities.

What is it to engage in sacraments efficaciously? Christians participate in rituals, culturally and socially inscribed and inscribing, experiencing phenomena that *become meaningful through this participation,* not through importing outside meanings.[70] Since humans are embodied creatures, not beings in a body or with a body, sacraments can form identity in part by shaping the bodies of participants. Liturgical practice is linked to the formation of the self over time and the building

---

[68] Grimes, "Reinventing Ritual," *Soundings* 75 (1992): 24; cited in Mitchell, *Liturgy and the Social Sciences*, 47.

[69] Mitchell, *Liturgy and the Social Sciences*, 47.

[70] See ibid., 46–49.

of a "world" of meaning (becoming a "being-in-the-world" in a certain way). "Engagement" suggests an embodied and cognitive participation in the event, where both bodily and cognitive activity is based on the participant's ability, not judged by an exterior standard ("age of reason," "language act"). This allows sensitivity to human development, which depends on as well as facilitates cultural practice. "Efficacious" refers to the capacity of the rite to alter the status and identity of its participants, or to the participants' ability to alter their own identities through the rite. There is a link between this and theological concerns of "sacramental efficacy" (in both traditional categories of "validity" and "fruitfulness"), but this link will only be considered in chapter 5, since I believe that "the meanings of ritual unfold from within the ritual action itself [rather than being] imported from outside the ritual event."[71]

To see how a ritual process can develop embodied and inculturated identity, I will explore the contributions of Marcel Mauss, Michel Foucault, and Talal Asad. Maurice Merleau-Ponty's seminal work provides a foundation for thinking about embodied perception as world-forming. Finally, I will explain a method for understanding ritual "in its own right,"[72] which can "insulate" its practitioners from ordinary social constructs in order to transform "being-in-the-world."

Ritual Discipline and Identity Construction

Embodiment is the key to understanding ritual formation, but modern definitions of ritual are exclusively symbolic, divorcing ritual expression from the body's experience. In a 1997 essay, Asad argues that anthropology ignores the experience of the body and its emotions to focus on the culturally conditioned, symbolically constructed social effects of ritual practice.[73] Anthropologists have "regarded 'the body' (especially its innate impulses and feelings) as essentially non-cultural," despite significant evidence that the body, impulses and all, is culturally developed by the embodied person and his or her community.[74] The body is fully cultural but not passive: it is "the *self-developable*

---

[71] Ibid., 49. Italics omitted.

[72] Don Handelman and Galina Lindquist, eds. *Ritual in Its Own Right: Exploring the Dynamics of Transformation* (New York: Berghahn Books, 2005).

[73] Talal Asad, "Remarks on the Anthropology of the Body," *Religion and the Body: Comparative Perspectives on Devotional Practices*, Sarah Coakley, ed. (Cambridge: University of Cambridge Press, 1997), 44.

[74] Ibid., 44–45.

means for achieving a range of human objects—from styles of physical movement (for example, walking), through modes of emotional being (for example, composure), to kinds of spiritual experience."[75] Rituals are effective because the physical formability of the body enables the social and cultural development of the whole human person. Thus, *dividing* human activity into "physical" and "nonphysical," "utilitarian" and "symbolic," or ritual into "matter" and "form(ula)," is a distraction, because bodily activities can be used to develop certain desires and emotional capacities as well as physical skills.

The body becomes the first symbol of ek-sisting humanity because it is the original means of experiencing and changing the world. Through engaging with the world, the body mediates the human being's experience of being-in-the-world. The body, moreover, is amenable to formation, and when the body changes, the person's being-in-the-world is altered. The body's ability for self-development makes the body a symbol of the whole person and undermines the dichotomy between the "natural," "innate" body and "the (disembodied) mind [that] confronts 'the world' through the interface of 'symbols.'"[76] Discarding this dualism, Asad recognizes rituals are efficacious not only by *expressing* a particular kind of social structure but also in *forming* a particular kind of human living in the world.

Asad's work is based in part on Mauss's essay on the use of "body techniques"[77] to construct physical and social capabilities. Body techniques have two essential characteristics: they are culturally constructed actions, "assembled by and for social authority;"[78] thus they are *traditional*, although they are "felt by the author as *actions of a mechanical, physical or physico-chemical order*."[79] Body techniques are also *effective*: their practice transforms the practitioner in identifiable ways, adapting the body to practitioners' use.[80] For example, a culturally determined way of walking is an "education in composure . . . [that] allows a co-ordinated response of co-ordinated movements setting off in the direction of a chosen goal."[81] Body techniques make

[75] Ibid., 47–48.
[76] Ibid., 44.
[77] Marcel Mauss, "Body Techniques," trans. Ben Brewster, *Sociology and Psychology* (London: Routledge and Kegan Paul, 1979), 95–123.
[78] Ibid., 120.
[79] Ibid.
[80] Ibid., 121.
[81] Ibid., 121–22.

practitioners "*habilis*" (able). They have "a sense of the adaptation of all their well-co-ordinated movements to a goal, . . . are practised, . . . 'know what they are up to.'"[82]

Mauss's body techniques include initiation rites as well as more everyday practices such as particular modes of walking and swimming.[83] They are socially imposed in order to physically effect the transformation of the individual, because the body is a tool whose actions may shape the identity of the practitioner of these rites. Mauss hints that this transformation is effective not only on the physical and psychological level but even in the spiritual realm: "I believe precisely that at the bottom of all our mystical states there are body techniques which we have not studied, but which were studied fully in China and India, even in very remote periods. . . . I think that there are necessarily biological means of entering into 'communion with God.'"[84] The human body, as "self-developable" site of the self, is the key to attaining psychological, moral, and even spiritual capabilities. As Asad puts it, "The inability to 'enter into communion with God' becomes a function of untaught bodies."[85]

Foucault was also interested in disciplines as ways of attaining specific spiritual goals. He calls monastic disciplines "technologies of the self," which allow practitioners to change "their own bodies and souls, thoughts, conduct, and way of being," to reach "a certain state of happiness, purity, wisdom, perfection, or immortality."[86] Foucault saw monastic concern with sexuality and chastity, and especially the development of auricular confession, as a change from action as the site of transformation of self (the self-mastery of the Stoics) to thought and desire as that site (the self-renunciation of the monks).[87]

Asad shifts Foucault's focus, recognizing that Christian rhetoric about renunciation of the self cannot be taken in strict opposition with "self-mastery." Renunciation of Paul's "old self" and the desires connected with its disordered appetites was matched by pleas for another kind of self, one saved by God and desiring God. Creating this Christian identity was a ritual process, in which those celebrations that modern

---

[82] Ibid., 108.
[83] Ibid., 121.
[84] Ibid., 122.
[85] Asad, "Remarks on the Anthropology of the Body," 48.
[86] Michel Foucault, "Technologies of the Self," *Technologies of the Self: A Seminar with Michel Foucault* (Amherst: University of Massachusetts Press, 1988), 18.
[87] Ibid., 16–49.

people easily recognize as "ritual" played a dominant role. The Divine Office and the sacraments were practices "among others essential to the acquisition of Christian virtues."[88] These practices allowed a monk to become *habitus*, fitted to his vocation:

> If there are prescribed ways of performing liturgical services, . . . there exists a requirement to master the proper performance of these services. Ritual is therefore directed at the apt performance of what is prescribed, [which] involves not symbols to be interpreted but abilities to be acquired according to rules that are sanctioned by those in authority: it presupposes no obscure meanings, but rather the formation of physical and linguistic skills.[89]

By studying the monastic context, Asad identifies four relevant characteristics of ritual processes: (1) they are oriented toward a goal, the development of the virtuous Christian self; (2) they are prescribed ritual disciplines that come together in a particular system; (3) they prioritize physical and linguistic activities ("exercises") over symbolic interpretations; and (4) they presuppose authoritative structures that dictate the prescriptions and abilities required.

Asad's research shows that there is no necessary contradiction between symbolic and practical construction of attitudes. For example, Bernard of Clairvaux transformed sensual to spiritual desires with his adult postulants: he used "a skillful deployment of biblical language [to] resonate with, and reintegrate, the pleasurable memories and desires that had been fashioned in a previous secular life."[90] Bernard's authoritative rereading of his postulants' lives, done cooperatively with them, consisted in a symbolic reinterpretation of desire and sensuality. The "authorized reception" of this language, however, "was intrinsically connected to the regular performance of the liturgy."[91] Bernard's symbolic rereading of desire worked in part by resonating with the liturgies of Clairvaux. A ritual process, then, has an *authorizing function*, that of rendering a particular interpretation of the world compelling to the practitioners. This "world-orientation" includes symbolic relationships and physical behaviors, where the symbolic relationships

---

[88] Asad, *Genealogies of Religion: Discipline and Reasons of Power in Christianity and Islam* (Baltimore: Johns Hopkins University, 1993), 63, 155–58.

[89] Ibid., 62. Asad's work stands as a critique to the widespread belief that liturgical interpretation in the late Middle Ages was exclusively or excessively allegorical.

[90] Ibid., 142–43.

[91] Ibid., 143.

are authorized by the behaviors; that is, the symbolic world is ritually inscribed on the body.

An *authorizing structure*, then, is an action, symbolic system, or relationship that prioritizes ritual experiences facilitating consensus among a social group. The structures of authority and those of ritual reinforce one another: authorities are not (first) from books but from the ritual experiences of the members of the social group; at the same time, they authorize ritual elements by mandating disciplinary practices and offering symbolic or rationalist interpretations.

Rather than chastity, Asad focuses on humility as the central goal of the ritual process in the Rule of St. Benedict.[92] Different monastic traditions sought different ways of practicing voluntary submission: Asad argues that both the spectacular Divine Office of Cluny and the humbling manual labor of the Cistercians were designed as exercises in obedience.[93] While practices varied, the ritual process—goal, prescription, ritual disciplines, and authorizing structures supporting and supported by rituals—appear in each case.

The monks were not concerned with the social symbolism of their rituals but with the practical requirements ("physical and linguistic skills" oriented to "apt performance") and the ultimate object ("the acquisition of Christian virtues"). Monks did not seek virtue through heroic intentions but through practice, because virtues were considered skills. Like any other skills, they could be developed through bodily practice. Efficacious engagement in the ritual process alters the identity of participants by "practicing" their identity with a particular goal. The goal of the ritual process might be a physical or psychological ability (as for an athlete), a spiritual ability (as for a mystic), or both (as for a cantor).

I will use *techniques*, in a conscious echo of Foucault, to refer to practices done repetitively and attentively as part of a ritual process.[94] Asad's work suggests that such practices (in a particular cultural context) authorize and facilitate a particular kind of being-in-the-world;[95]

---

[92] Ibid., 125.

[93] Ibid., 147–53.

[94] Repetitive here might refer to variations on an internalized theme rather than strict iterations, and attentively means one's sensory, symbolic-linguistic, and spatio-physical abilities are brought to bear in and on the rite.

[95] The phrase, of course, comes from phenomenology; for an example of its use within an exploration of ritual processes, see the ritual studies work of Thomas Csordas, especially *The Sacred Self: A Cultural Phenomenology of Charismatic Healing* (Berkeley: University of California Press, 1997).

the world thus created is not only a symbolic world but also a world of action. Being-in-the-world will include behaviors and responses that are experienced as "natural" by those in the social group, although they are culturally dependent.

Efficacious engagement explores how participation in sacraments and the ritual processes integrated with sacramental practice allows practitioners to transform their identity. This model acknowledges the importance of the ritual goal, the system of practices, and authorizing structures in developing a sense of identity. While no person develops an identity outside of a social system of power, ritual processes may subvert the conventional power structures. The ritual process helps practitioners gain capabilities associated with their goals as well as changing desires. Practitioners participate to attain a new identity, one that is founded on a particular system of ritual and authority but that, in the end, the practitioner comes to recognize as his or her own (habit).

Merleau-Ponty: Perception and Behavior

The account of ritual process and ritual authority according to Talal Asad raises many interesting possibilities for examining sacraments as the exercise and acquisition of skills and aptitudes, but it also raises important problems for the current study. For example, the authority Asad examines in his study of Bernard is quite explicitly linguistic: it is a reorganization of the participants' worlds via linguistic imagery. The identity constructed by this imagery is embodied and enacted, but is it possible to see identity-construction at work in a prelinguistic or extralinguistic way? More generally, is it *really true* that the ritual process writes a new identity on the body, or is the body merely the "means of expression" of a new identity being processually written "into the mind"?[96] Maurice Merleau-Ponty's work on sensory perception shows that perception, which must precede symbolic cognitive ability, (1) is active, not passive, and embodied, not solely cognitive; (2) is an aptitude that can be acquired by ritual process; and (3) can be seen as "symbolic" and in continuity with linguistic behavior but is not in itself linguistic.

Merleau-Ponty's phenomenology was developed in part out of a concern that experimental psychology failed to produce a working model for human perception and behavior because it created condi-

---

[96] The parallels with historical questions of sacramental necessity are interesting but not, at this method level, immediately relevant.

tions that isolated the experimental subject (human or animal) from its natural environment. Psychological experimentation thus evoked only pathological responses, which it took to be characteristic of natural behavior.[97] Merleau-Ponty wished instead to understand psychological activities within their life context. He found that perception and learned behaviors—even in animals—presuppose a "meaning" intrinsic to the acts or a goal that directs the behaviors. Thus perception and learning are embodied realities that fully integrate cognitive, motor, and sensory actions.

For example, in *The Structure of Behavior*, Merleau-Ponty presents the example of an accomplished typist or organist who is able to improvise unknown pieces, even on unfamiliar instruments:

> A subject who "knows" how to type or to play the organ is capable of improvising, that is, of executing kinetic melodies corresponding to words which have never been seen or music which has never been played. One would be tempted to suppose that at least certain elements of the new musical phrase or of the new words correspond to rigid and already acquired sets [of physical motions]. But expert subjects are capable of improvising on instruments unknown to them and the exploration of the instruments, which is evidently a preliminary necessity, is too brief to permit a substitution of individual sets.[98]

In this case, perceptual activities (i.e., seeing words or music) and motor activities (performing the words or music) are clearly integrated into one cohesive aptitude. Moreover, this aptitude is broadly interpretive: the typist or organist does not see, then read, then re-create the words or music, but rather sees, understands, and performs simultaneously. The performance, not the symbolic meaning of the music, is the interpretation of the score.[99] The player has internalized a structure shared by perceptual cues and performative gestures that constitute one whole interpretive activity.[100]

Human behaviors can have a significance that is not cognitive but performative, even in cases where the notation is conventional. In other

[97] See, e.g., Merleau-Ponty, *Phenomenology of Perception* (New York: Routledge Classics, 2002), 8–11 (hereafter *Perception*); *The Structure of Behavior* (Boston: Beacon, 1963), 122ff (hereafter *Behavior*).
[98] Merleau-Ponty, *Behavior*, 121.
[99] This point has been made on several occasions by Nathan Mitchell; see, e.g., *Meeting Mystery* (Maryknoll, NY: Orbis, 2006), 45ff.
[100] Merleau-Ponty, *Behavior*, 121.

words, "meaning" has a motor component too, an embodied component that is evident when learning "aptitudes," which emphasize the ability to improvise. Not only complex behavioral capabilities, however, can be conceived of as aptitudes. Perception is an aptitude too, for it depends on the simultaneous coordination of the sensory abilities, motor skills, and world-orientation of the subject.[101] Perception is an aptitude in which both the human being and the world actively cooperate: the "world" offers itself to be perceived, and the subject participates by perceiving, because "to look at an object is to inhabit it" by intuiting it inside and out.[102]

The "form" that Merleau-Ponty attributes to motor and sensory behavior consists in an embodied "knowledge" (not solely cognitive and preconscious) of what, of all I could see, is relevant to *this* seeing. Without this knowledge, *no perception, activity, or learning can take place.* At the biological level, the body recognizes a "meaning" of the thing seen by knowing it as a "use-object."[103] Every instance of perception occurs as an improvisation on the basis of known structures.[104] Human and animal ability to do spatial visualization implies that every object is seen not in two dimensions but in three, together with an intuition of the whole object that dictates what forms it would take when rotated in a particular direction.[105] In general, Merleau-Ponty concludes, what is learned is not one behavior but "an adapted response to the situation by different means."[106]

Even fish demonstrate "an aptitude for choosing, a 'method of selection,'" which is learned in response to experimental trials.[107] The specifically human ability to learn "aptitudes" (that is, the creation of "meaning," performative, perceptual, or cognitive) comes from this simpler ability to adapt by discerning new kinds of value. Similarly, Merleau-Ponty's analysis provides a model for language acquisition: spoken words (and the meaningful structures they presuppose[108]) come

[101] See Merleau-Ponty, *Perception*, 18ff.

[102] Ibid., 79.

[103] Ibid. Here again the assumed dichotomy between symbolic and functional is broken by observation of human behaviors.

[104] Merleau-Ponty, *Behavior*, 88.

[105] Ibid., 89.

[106] Ibid., 96.

[107] Ibid., 97.

[108] "On the basis of a word as a physical phenomenon, as an ensemble of vibrations of the air, no physiological phenomenon capable of serving as a substrate for the signi-

to be relevant to a child's life-functioning and to be interpreted through his or her kinetic behaviors as he or she improvises a response to the intrinsic structures, conventional and cultural, of the words. Finally, Merleau-Ponty explains how the human subject and the world engage in world-construction: "consciousness projects itself into a physical world and has a body, as it projects itself into a cultural world and has its habits."[109] The aptitudes for perception and action, fully acquired, coalesce into habits.

In ritual processes, then, the development of perceptual skills and learning aptitudes is foundational both to habits of virtue and to symbolic understanding. Perceptual abilities as well as Asad's "physical and linguistic skills" can be developed by ritual processes. These abilities are acquired as embodied "aptitudes" that are "interpretive" in that they allow the practitioner to improvise performative, meaningful responses to the environment. This "ritualization" is crucial for the development of one's "being-in-the-world," because perceptual, learning, physical, and linguistic aptitudes allow one to be embodied within the world in a particular way.

Ritual Folding

To fully integrate phenomena and perception into ritual interpretation, we need to isolate ritual from its "ready-packaged" symbolic significance and focus on its body-forming meaning, its sensory phenomena, and its power to develop one's being-in-the-world. In ritual studies, it has been long known that rituals have the potential to reinforce a particular set of social and cultural norms; it has more recently been observed that they likewise have the potential to subvert these norms and reshape societal values, not through individual interpretation but through the rituals' own transformative use of cultural norms.[110]

In a recent volume edited by Don Handelman and Galina Lindquist, *Ritual in Its Own Right*, ritual theorists address this problem. The volume asks whether "particular [ritual] phenomena have degrees of autonomy from the worlds that create them; whether such qualities

---

fication of the word could be described in the brain; for we have seen that, in audition and also in speaking, a word as an ensemble of motor or afferent excitations presupposes a word as a melodic structure and this latter presupposes a sentence as a unity of signification" (ibid., 92).

[109] Merleau-Ponty, *Perception*, 158.

[110] See, e.g., Mitchell, *Liturgy and the Social Sciences*.

of autonomy are significant; and, if so, what such significance might be about."[111] The question stems from observations that ritual is a crucial aspect of certain kinds of personal transformation. Those undergoing initiation or recovering alcoholics depending on the rituals of Alcoholics Anonymous begin outside a given system of norms and proceed to a fuller integration of these norms; the ritual processes of initiation or of Alcoholics Anonymous help appropriate the new norms, relationships, and identity features.

Ritual autonomy from external cultural forces extends the work on ritual by Arnold Van Gennep and Victor Turner.[112] The idea of ritual process, introduced by Van Gennep and greatly expanded by Turner, posits that rituals transform people or systems by separating initiands from the social structures that bind them to specified roles, leaving them, for a ritual period, with an ambiguous social status (liminality). Finally, the ritual reintegrates the initiands into a new status, having altered their social standing. In order for ritual to be able to separate persons from their socially dictated roles, it must have some kind of cultural insulation from extra-ritual status assignments. Thus Handelman and the other authors of *Ritual in Its Own Right* consider the possible "degrees of momentary autonomy from social order" of ritual action.[113] These varying degrees of autonomy, as Handelman points out and supports with several examples, "seem to relate to what may be called the interior complexity of how phenomena are organized . . . [which is] related to what persons can do within [rituals], and how they act on persons."[114]

The capacity of ritual to generate social and personal change, then, cannot be explored if one limits the field to ritual that preserves the status quo: ritual as "a model of and model for cultural worlds . . . as representation . . . [or] as functional of and functional for social order

---

[111] Handelman, "Introduction: Why Ritual in Its Own Right? How So?," in *Ritual in Its Own Right*, 3.

[112] See, e.g., Van Gennep, *Rites of Passage* (New York: Routledge, 2004); Turner, *The Forest of Symbols: Aspects of Ndembu Ritual* (Ithaca: Cornell University Press, 1967). For an introduction to the concepts arising from their work on initiation rites, see Catherine Bell, *Ritual: Perspectives and Dimensions* (New York: Oxford, 1997), 94–108. A lucid account of the development of the ritual process concepts is also provided by Mathieu Deflem, "Ritual, Anti-Structure, and Religion: A Discussion of Victor Turner's Processual Symbolic Analysis," *Journal for the Scientific Study of Religion* 30, no. 1 (1991): 1–25.

[113] Handelman, "Introduction," 2.

[114] Ibid., 3.

. . . [or] as yet another arena for the playing out of social, economic, and political competition and conflict."[115] Instead, Handelman suggests a method

> whose prime locus of inquiry is initially within the rituals them-
> selves. . . . No assumptions need to be made immediately about
> how sociocultural order and ritual are related, neither about the
> meaning of signs and symbols that appear within a ritual, nor about
> the functional relationships between a ritual and social order.[116]

Even if this method reveals truth that is only true "to some extent," it offers a very important framework for understanding the transformational potential of ritual praxis. Therefore, to read Christian sacraments, I will "separate (to an extent, arbitrarily) the phenomenon from its sociocultural surround . . . [and then] reinsert the ritual into its surround, with the added knowledge of what has been learned about the ritual, taken in and of itself."[117]

Ritual is to some extent self-organized, "characterized by interior complexity, self-integrity, and irreducibility to agent and environment."[118] Some rituals are minimally interiorized and integral, but others are marked by greater degrees of self-organizational complexity. "Ritual folding" describes how a complex ritual is marked by its "curving towards closure and twisting towards openness . . . separable yet inseparable from its surround. . . . Ritual twists back into relations with the broader world within which it is embedded and from which it takes form."[119] In deeply folded rituals, the "greater interior complexity" leads to greater self-organization, greater "capacity of the ritual for temporary autonomy from its sociocultural surround," and greater "capacity of the ritual to interiorize the distinction between itself and its surround and so to act on the latter from within itself, through the dynamics of the ritual design."[120] More complex, deeply folded rituals have a greater degree of autonomy and a greater transformative potency.

Greater interior complexity does not refer to a ritual's "high church" formality but to the variety and depth of phenomenal self-reference

---

[115] Ibid., 2.
[116] Ibid., 3.
[117] Ibid., 3–4.
[118] Ibid., 10.
[119] Ibid., 13.
[120] Ibid., 12.

within a single ritual's sensory and kinetic requirements. Self-reference can create recursive meaning-giving structures in ritual practice, changing and perhaps even overturning (to adopt the geographical and curvaceous metaphor of Handelman) the symbolic and functional systems of its cultural surround. In Handelman's maximally folded example, Slovene pig-sticking, the temporal arrangement of the rite facilitates increasing insulation from the sociocultural surround, offering ritual "protection" from the dangers that would normally be associated with the practices of the rite. This allows culturally "marginal" features to become central and central features to be marginalized. In the end, "the exterior border [of the farmstead] destroys the interior border, changing both in the process, so that during the remainder of the fold's time/space, neither border exists. . . . The butchers re-entering the home are not the same ones who went out to kill the pig."[121] The rite transforms by "insulating" its practitioners from the norms of everyday life, and this insulation is created by "folding": phenomena within the rite reference each other in order to separate the rite from "ordinary" time and space. The rite becomes its own self-sufficient justification.[122]

Ritual folding may explain how Christian ritual systems such as that found in monasticism assist practitioners in developing toward their goals: Christian ritual progressively "folds away" aspects of the cultural surround in order to permit radical and transformative readings of reality and of practitioners' own bodies. To some extent, the order in which these realities are folded away is arbitrary, because the experience of ritual insulation will be different for each practitioner. There are two surrounds that maintain a voice (or perhaps a whisper) throughout the ritual analysis of chapter 4: the history of Christian initiatory practice and the cultural constructs surrounding infancy. These surrounds are maintained in order to allow the rite to speak, because they motivate the rite's interior momentum and allow its self-reference to be recognized: history has a voice in the interpretive method because some of the possible meanings of the ritual "in its own right" would have the ritual depart entirely from its concrete existence *as* Christian baptism. Although these readings might be very valuable, they will not contribute to our understanding of how baptism is a Christian sacrament (i.e., part of the sacramental economy of salvation).

---

[121] Ibid., 26.
[122] Cf. Mitchell, *Liturgy and the Social Sciences*, part 1; Asad, *Genealogies*, chap. 1.

The cultural constructs of infancy, on the other hand, maintain a voice in the analysis because the rite's complex dynamic of socio-cultural support and subversion can only be understood with these constructs as a background. The descriptive lens chosen for this study is the experience of the initiand, who is an infant; the infant's capabilities and development are therefore a necessary component of any embodied, phenomenal exploration of the ritual performance. In addition, the dynamics of the rite and of domestic life engage the infant's parents as "co-agents" of initiation; therefore these familial structures are "less folded away" (if such a comparison can be made) than other social structures. As the ritual analysis will show, such structures are maintained in the rite only to be subverted by the dynamic that allows marginal features to become central.

Section 2.4
Christian Ritual Process

If one considers "ritual processes" to be structures of ritual that facilitate self-development toward authorized goals through embodied experience, then the Christian sacraments can be seen as ritual process. This method prescinds from defining one Christian identity structure (as in Chauvet's work). Instead, the sacramental life is permeated by ritualized strategies for developing Christian identities. Christian identities are, first and foremost, Christian bodies—babies among them. The case study will examine the strategy for ritualizing Christian bodies in infant baptism according to the postconciliar Roman Catholic rite. The rite's phenomena and the ritual folding reveal how infant baptism redefines the body of the infant and the Body of Christ in the assembly simultaneously. This, in turn, marks Christian baptism as a distinctively trinitarian event.

Chapter Three

Initiating Infants

I n his influential *Shape of Baptism*, Aidan Kavanagh said that infant baptism was at best "a benign abnormality"—benign, that is, "so long as it is practiced with prudence as an unavoidable pastoral necessity."[1] He argued that adult baptism was implicitly normative in the patristic period and had been made explicitly normative for the Roman Catholic Church following Vatican II. His expression confirmed a general prejudice against the value of the practice of infant baptism and has been very influential both among theologians and lay Catholics. When I have discussed infant baptism in parishes, I am invariably asked whether, in view of the fact that infants "cannot get anything out of baptism," infant baptism should still be practiced in the church. Discourse on infant baptism, academic and popular, is still dominated by the question of "indiscriminate" baptism. Theological reflection on infant baptism is usually limited to the traditional, though trite, observation that infant baptism reveals that God's grace is offered freely to all, regardless of their deeds.

Mark Searle, on the other hand, argued for the distinctive theological emphasis of infant baptism and therefore of its legitimacy not only as praxis but also as a theological source, since "most sacramental questions come together in a particularly concentrated way in the issue of the sacramental initiation of infants. Here converge such problems as how to speak of God, the relationship between the order of grace and the order of history, the relationship between grace and freedom, the nature and role of the Church as mediating the mystery of salva-

[1] Aidan Kavanagh, *The Shape of Baptism* (New York: Pueblo, 1978), 109 (hereafter *Shape*).

tion, and the relationship between the language of faith and the basic experiences of human life."[2]

Liturgical theology must engage with the particularities of real celebration or risk being the theology of an individual rather than that of the church.[3] Infant baptism is a useful exemplar for the efficacious engagement model of sacramental participation for two reasons: on the one hand, infancy is the most dynamic period of human existence, which means that infant formation and identity is particularly rich and challenging; on the other hand, infants are incapable of symbolic and linguistic communication, and so whatever identity formation they receive from the rite of baptism is camouflaged by the symbolic model. Unlike other forms of lay participation, infant participation in the liturgy may be *less* adequately modeled by the symbolic view of sacrament than by the traditional causal view.

Kavanagh's belief that infant baptism is at best a benign abnormality springs from his conviction that it is necessary to focus on adult initiation as the norm so infant baptism does not become "a *malign* abnormality due to pastoral malfeasance, theological obsession, or the decline of faith among Christian parents into some degree of merely social conformity."[4] In other words, Kavanagh's preference for adult baptism accords with the modern understanding of religious identity as individualistic and voluntary. Children's religious formation and self-identity is considered to be entirely dependent on the commitment and self-identity of their parents. Since the religious commitment of "cradle Catholics" is popularly doubted, Kavanagh and others want to

[2] Mark Searle, "Infant Baptism Reconsidered," in *Living Water, Sealing Spirit*, ed. Maxwell Johnson (Collegeville, MN: Liturgical Press, 1995), 366.

[3] A case study is beneficial to any liturgical theology because "an *ordo* or pattern apart from its concrete doctrinal, cultural and textual expressions in actual liturgies *simply does not exist* in any independent or pure form. That is, an *ordo* or pattern is something deduced or abstracted from already existing liturgies and these already existing liturgies themselves concretize precisely the doctrinal, cultural, and textual expressions of the Church's faith for which the liturgy exists to serve and by which the faith and life of the worshiping community is nurtured and formed. In other words, there is no *ordo* apart from the ways in which this *ordo* of Gathering, Word, Meal, and Sending is actually expressed, performed, or 'done' in those liturgical assemblies called Church" (Maxwell E. Johnson, "Is Anything Normative in Contemporary Lutheran Worship?," in *The Serious Business of Worship: Essays in Honour of Bryan D. Spinks*, ed. Melanie C. Ross and Simon Jones [New York: T&T Clark, 2010]). I am indebted to Melanie Ross for calling my attention to this article.

[4] Ibid., 110.

turn to the proven commitment of converts who are making "an adult decision" for the faith. Adult identity, once this decision is made, is assumed to be static or at least irreversible; infants, meanwhile, are passive recipients of their parents' religious identity, and have no agency in their own religious development, let alone their parents' spiritual formation.

Is adult baptism normative for the Roman Catholic Church? The direct evidence Kavanagh claims for the normative status of adult baptism is contained in several conciliar and postconciliar documents of Vatican II, which are cited in *The Shape of Baptism* (pp. 122ff., nn. 4ff.). Clare Johnson has examined these citations in depth in her dissertation and concludes "that Kavanagh's long-influential assertion of the 'officially stated' theological normativity of adult initiation is based on an argument from silence in the documents of Vatican II."[5] Moreover, his "preference for the 'conversion model' of Christian initiation seems to have influenced his reading of these documents to some extent."[6] Certainly adult baptism has not been officially declared theologically normative.

What about the indirect evidence Kavanagh offers for the claim that infant baptism is abnormal? This evidence takes two forms. Kavanagh describes the Rite of Christian Initiation of Adults as the "last and most mature outcome of the postconciliar subcommission's work."[7] He argues,

> the document's purpose is less to give liturgical recipes than to shift the Church's initiatory polity from one conventional norm centering on infant baptism to *the more traditional norm* centering on adults. *Nowhere does the document say this in so many words.* If this is not the case, however, then the document not only makes no sense but is vain and fatuous. Its extensive and sensitive dispositions for gradually incorporating adult converts into communities of faith nowhere suggest that this process should be regarded as the rare exception. On the contrary, from deep within the Roman tradition it speaks of the process presumptively as normative.[8]

Thus Kavanagh's indirect evidence for the normality of adult baptism is an interpretation of the RCIA as the paragon of the postconciliar

[5] Clare Johnson, Ex Ore Infantium: *The Pre-rational Child as Subject of Sacramental Action* (PhD diss., University of Notre Dame, 2004), 282.
[6] Ibid., 281.
[7] Kavanagh, *Shape*, 105.
[8] Ibid., 106. Emphases added.

reforms and his view that the historical tradition of Christian initiation treats adult baptism as normative.

The argument that the RCIA presents adult initiation as normative is admittedly an argument from silence, and as such problematic. Its late date does not necessarily argue for its normative status; indeed, it was partly based on "collating reactions to the previously issued rites of baptism for children and confirmation,"[9] which might create a better-reformed rite, but one dependent on a previous norm. The judgment that the rite is "vain and fatuous" if adult baptism is not regarded as the sole norm can be sustained only if it is assumed that only one type of initiation, that for adults or that for children, can be regarded as really legitimate. Yet it is evident that the council regarded both adult and infant baptism as legitimate expressions of Christian initiation; adult baptism required more abundant reformation because, as Kavanagh notes, its practice had, in the wake of the Protestant and Catholic Reformations, been largely lost, so that adult initiation was in practice little more than the infant rite applied to a larger person.[10]

The argument that adult baptism has traditionally been regarded as theologically normative cannot be sustained either; initiatory practice has always been diverse, and the age of initiates has at times played a small role in this diversity. It would be as easy to construct an argument for infant communion from historical sources as it would an argument against infant baptism. This demonstrates the enormous variability of the church's traditional practice of infant initiation and suggests that any argument about infant initiation needs to be supported by more than a recounting of the historical practice of the church. In this chapter I will explain why infant baptism is a norm of equal weight as that of adult baptism in the postconciliar period. The efficacious engagement model makes it possible to see infants as true participants in infant baptism, giving a cultural and theological explanation of what infant baptism does. But the foundations of this model are the church's tradition of baptizing infants and the cultural acquisition skills of human infants.

The novelty of the postconciliar period is that the Roman Rite for the first time acknowledges two *different*, simultaneous, practical norms for initiation: one for adults and a different one for children under the age of reason. This is emphasized by the stipulation, in the Constitution on the

---

[9] Ibid., 105.
[10] Ibid., 104.

Sacred Liturgy, that the revision of the rite for baptizing infants should "tak[e] into account the fact that those to be baptized are infants."[11] Both rites are new, suggesting that the council felt that the single preconciliar norm resulted in a rite that was not appropriate to the needs of adults *or* infants. This dual normativity of initiation provides a rich new liturgical resource for theological reflection; nonetheless, theological reflection on the initiation of infants is deeply traditional.

Mark Searle has argued that there are several ways in which infant initiation provides an important *locus theologicus*.[12] Despite the fact that the current Roman practice is only partial initiation of infants (i.e., baptism and chrismation without confirmation and communion), these observations still hold of infant baptism. First of all, Searle argues, the characterization of adult baptism as "antique and paschal" and that of infants as "medieval and sociopersonal"[13] is inaccurate. The ancient catechumenates included children of all ages as well as adults. The novelty of the Middle Ages was not that infants were initiated but that they failed to be *fully* initiated, as Searle points out.[14] Furthermore, baptism in antiquity, whether celebrated on the Pasch or at another suitable time of year, was not merely paschal but also encompassed a wealth of other metaphors, including "adoption, divinization, sanctification, gift of the Spirit, indwelling, glory, power, wisdom, rebirth, restoration, mission, and so forth."[15] These metaphors tend to be crowded out by the heavily paschal and christocentric character of the RCIA but may be more visible in infant baptism, especially in the modern rite where references to original sin are more modest and reticent.

Maxwell Johnson, in his study *Images of Baptism*, acknowledges that "in our history we have often allowed some baptismal models (e.g., baptism as liberation from original sin or as death and resurrection) to function in . . . an exclusive manner."[16] The idea that a paschal model

---

[11] Austin Flannery, ed., *Vatican Council II: Volume 1, The Conciliar and Post Conciliar Documents* (Northport, NY: Costello Publishing Company, 1996), The Constitution on the Sacred Liturgy (*Sacrosanctum Concilium*), 67.

[12] Mark Searle, "Infant Baptism Reconsidered," in *Living Water, Sealing Spirit*, ed. Maxwell Johnson (Collegeville, MN: Liturgical Press, 1995), 365–409.

[13] Searle is responding here to Kavanagh, "Christian Initiation in Post-Conciliar Roman Catholicism: A Brief Report," in *Living Water, Sealing Spirit*, 3; cf. *Shape*, 196–97.

[14] Searle, "Infant Baptism Reconsidered," 370.

[15] Ibid., 385.

[16] See Maxwell Johnson, *Images of Baptism* (Chicago: Liturgy Training Publications, 2001), ix (hereafter *Images*).

for baptism is the normative or Western model, however, is actually a contemporary idea: "In spite of the fact that Romans 6 has become the dominant baptismal image in our own day and is often held up as *the* image preferred in the history of the Western liturgical traditions, . . . baptism as "new birth" or "adoption" along the lines of John 3:5 is likewise a dominant *Western* baptismal image and paradigm, and . . . Romans 6 itself is, quite surprisingly, relatively absent from the liturgical sources themselves."[17]

On the other hand, the images of birth, adoption, and new life (often connected to John 3) are quite common, even in the early period in the West, and these images tend to be more strongly associated with the Holy Spirit than the death-and-resurrection image. For example, Johnson quotes the Lateran baptistery inscription (432–40 CE):

> Here a people of godly race are born for heaven;
> the Spirit gives them life in the fertile waters.
> The Church-Mother, in these waves, bears her children
> like virginal fruit she has conceived by the Holy Spirit.[18]

Imagery of birth, womb, motherhood, and new life, Johnson concludes, "appears to be the preferred baptismal image" in Western liturgical texts, even if Western theologians like Ambrose of Milan appeal to Romans 6 for interpretive purposes.[19]

Easter baptism of adults in the West does not suppress this complex of imagery, as Johnson observes.[20] Nonetheless, these images are particularly appropriate to and naturally arise in the celebration of the baptism of infants, because the ritual participants themselves are potent symbols of new life, birth, infancy, and parenthood. Since infant baptism evokes these images particularly strongly, and these images are powerfully associated with the work of the Holy Spirit, which is neglected in Western sacramental theology overall, the study of infant baptism may prove helpful in uncovering the trinitarian structure of the rite of baptism. More important, a dual normativity of adult and infant baptism helps to preserve the inherent and essential multivalence of baptismal imagery, not only among scholars, but also among participants in the liturgy.

[17] Ibid., 36.
[18] Ibid., 39.
[19] Ibid., 48.
[20] See ibid., 52–54.

In the light of the extensive history of infant baptism in the Christian tradition, the unparalleled importance of this rite for Christian identity and church membership, and the relatively unproblematic status of that practice until the Reformation, Aidan Kavanagh's maxim that infant baptism is at best a "benign abnormality" is untenable.[21] Given the phenomenal diversity of initiatory practices in both East and West, it seems unnecessary to isolate this one common aspect of Christian initiation, its application to infants, as abnormal. Moreover, Christians who had been baptized as infants were universally admitted to communion until lay communication became exceptional, so the baptism of infants was not treated as abnormal in liturgical practice. Infant baptism, like adult baptism, was thought to be connected in some mysterious way to the condition of the human person (which was considered to be universal) and to the saving work of Christ (likewise universal). Even Augustine's question about infant baptism only led him to find an explanation in the common human condition and in the work of Christ, which was extended to all persons by virtue of the fact that "Christ baptizes" in the ritual of the church.[22] "Abnormality" is an evaluative criterion that is not substantiated by the Christian tradition.

Of course, most of the questions about infant baptism, including Kavanagh's, are raised by the question of whether baptism can really form any kind of identity in an infant. Therefore, I want to survey the baptismal tradition and its treatment of infants and of identity change before approaching the question of how to speak about infants' efficacious engagement in liturgy. Baptism of infants is a particularly difficult case, both because of its contemporary isolation from the other initiatory rites and because of the limited capabilities of the sacramental recipients. This work will explore identity formation in infant baptizands through ritual based on the proposed model of efficacious engagement.

Louis-Marie Chauvet used EPII as paradigmatic for sacramental exchange, but the eucharist is in many ways a special case among sacraments. It is the only sacrament, for example, in which the matter is permanently sacralized. Baptism, on the other hand, has in many ways been the paradigmatic sacrament for developing a theology of the sacraments in general.[23] It is the first sacrament to be connected to an

---

[21] Ibid., 267–75.
[22] Augustine, *Tractates on John*, 6.7.
[23] See chapter 6 for several examples of its paradigmatic function.

explicit soteriology in Christian literature (Rom 6) and theologies of the other sacraments, or of the sacraments in general, have often been developed around it.[24] Augustine's discussions on the minister, effects, and efficacy of baptism, inspired by the Donatist controversy, shaped the entire discipline of sacramental theology to the current day.[25] More important, using baptism as an exemplar avoids some of the problems of the exclusively linguistic-symbolic approach identified in chapter 2.

First, the language act model was linked to the narrative analysis of the eucharistic prayer. As mentioned, this isolates the cognitive (textual) "content" of the eucharistic rite as the crucial dynamic of sacrament. The eucharist is particularly vulnerable to a cognitive reduction because the current rite integrates body action in the rubrics at very few points, and most movement involves only the celebrant.[26] More important, the material elements (Thomistic "matter") of the eucharistic liturgy are differently valued than those of any other rite of the church. Their reservation and adoration call for special treatment, but additionally, they convey on the eucharistic prayer a special kind of importance that may not apply to other sacramental prayers. The baptismal rite, on the other hand, is more pervaded with ritual action and sensory phenomena: gesture, scent, procession, dressing and undressing. Baptism's "messiness" makes it more difficult to "extract" the linguistic content and consider the sacramental significance in it alone. The main prayer of baptism, the blessing of the baptismal water, does not seem to have the same comprehensive significance that the eucharistic prayer does;[27] on the other hand, the "formula" of baptism is not a prayer (and thus cannot share the narrative Chauvet attributes to the eucharistic prayer). The action of baptism also spans the whole rite, rather than being concentrated in the communion rite. Finally, whereas the eucharistic elements are the central feature of that sacrament, the

---

[24] For example, Tertullian compared baptism to the second plank for one shipwrecked (*On Repentance*).

[25] See, e.g., the structure of the treatise on the sacraments in the *Summa Theologiae*.

[26] This was not always the case even in the eucharistic liturgy. See, e.g., the description of the papal Mass around 700 CE: Theodor Klauser, *A Short History of the Western Liturgy* (New York: Oxford, 1979), 60–70. In addition, analysis of the whole Mass, rather than just the eucharistic prayer—especially in cases where the eucharistic liturgy is the site for celebration of another ritual, such as the dedication of a church, one of the preparatory rites for the RCIA, or the marriage vows—would also present a broader view.

[27] For instance, baptism can, in the imminent expectation of death, be performed without this prayer.

transience of blessing in the baptismal waters instead highlights the ritual action and the permanent effect of the sacrament resides in the initiand's body. Thus baptism might be a better choice to emphasize the ritual and embodied dynamic of the sacramental economy.

Another concern with the language act model was its tendency to restrict grace to linguistic channels, eliminating the possibility of extralinguistic mediations of grace. Clearly, infant baptism is an example of prelinguistic channels of grace; furthermore, the more obvious embodied qualities of baptismal celebration tend to focus attention on extralinguistic mediations of the economy. The combination of these facts leads to an analytical focus on the embodied experience of phenomena in the rite.

Third, the language act model represents interlocutors as relatively equal in their capacity for gift giving and gift reception, an assumption that can be justified in most human-human interactions but is dubious in cases involving infants on the one hand or the divine Persons on the other. This assumption can only be maintained by forgetting the tradition that the recipient of sacrament is radically altered—his or her very identity is changed—by the sacramental action. Because the eucharistic celebration is a repeatable sacrament of conversion, it is easy to forget this radical change in identity—the person who received communion last week, after all, is the same one going forward to receive it today—it seems.[28] Baptism, on the other hand, emphasizes this radical alteration. Since it is the entry to, not the summit of, sacramental life, it is clearly marked as a new beginning. Even more important, the practice of infant baptism is a potent reminder that the recipient of a sacrament has no gift of his or her own to offer; before the intervention of grace, the human person cannot offer himself or herself to God. Only by God's grace is this gift made possible.

Fourth, baptism lends itself to the exploration of sacramental efficacy that is qualitatively more than the cultural efficacy of the sacrament is able to explain. Chapter 2 cautioned against taking the ambivalent symbolic value of sacrament, which has historically effected evil as well as good in the world, for salvific grace. Baptism, of course, has a similarly checkered history (one considers, for example, forced baptism of Jews and Arabs). Still, the distinction between the ecclesial effect (character, which occurs *ex opere operato* and is the

---

[28] See Nathan D. Mitchell, *The Eucharist as a Sacrament of Initiation* (Chicago: Liturgy Training Publications, 1994).

res sacramenti of the ultimate effect) and the fruitful effect (grace, specifically the infusion of gifts and virtues under the influence of the Holy Spirit) served as a reminder, even in the scholastic treatises, of the mysterious gap between human and divine causality and objective and subjective efficacy. (Thus the scholastic treatises explored, for instance, the "revival" of baptism when the "obstacle" to its fruitfulness was removed—a counterintuitive assertion that was nonetheless necessary to do justice to the tradition against rebaptism. This peculiar framework revealed the inadequacy of human norms for causality in treating the sacramental work of God.[29])

Finally, baptism in the West more clearly preserves the trinitarian nature of the sacramental economy. While the eucharist, as consummate sacrament, evokes the Pasch as consummation of Christ's earthly ministry, baptism's imagery spans the whole of his work, from birth to resurrection.[30] Besides being more inclusive, this openness also means that baptism recollects those moments in Christ's life that represent the trinitarian essence of salvation history most strongly: the "overshadowing" of Mary at the incarnation, the theophany at the baptism, the sonship proclaimed at the transfiguration, the resurrection appearances and ascension.

Infant baptism, therefore, has some notable advantages for consideration of the sacraments "in general," that is, as ecclesial rituals that are part of the economy of salvation. These advantages span the sacramental dynamic from the work of God to the identity of the human person as a dynamic, interpersonal agent.

If human beings display dynamism, the same can be said of ritual practices. Here I will examine baptism's dynamics in three ways: over time, using history; in its cultural instantiation, using the postconciliar rite of infant baptism; and in its soteriological purpose, using a theological analysis of the rite. These can be seen as three interpretive keys to understanding what is happening in any particular rite of infant baptism. I count on the reader's experience to supply concrete ritual practices that can be contextualized with this discussion.

---

[29] The treatise on eucharistic presence in the *Summa Theologiae* is similarly counterintuitive, and for precisely the same reason (e.g., III, q. 76). But it is relatively easier to reduce the gaze on the eucharist to the elements, rather than the community action, and this, while retaining the odd causality, eliminates the component of human freedom. Baptism, by emphasizing new identity, highlights this component.

[30] See Maxwell Johnson, *Images*.

Section 3.1
Historical Practice of Initiation

Historically, practices of Christian initiation have been very diverse. Although water baptism has been central for most Christian groups from an early period, the details of practice and of recipients have changed. The value of tracking these changes is to put into perspective contemporary practice and attitudes toward contemporary recipients for baptism. Here, I pay particular attention to the initiation of infants and young children; to the importance of the identity change attributed to infant baptism; and to the period of greatest diversity, before and during the time of liturgical cross-fertilization (roughly taken to be the late third to late fifth centuries).

Comparative historical analysis is necessary as background to a ritual examination of the rite of infant baptism for several reasons. First, it provides perspective on the Christian tradition: just as EPII is not the one representative structure of all eucharistic rites, the postconciliar baptism of infants in the Roman Rite is not representative of the dynamics of all Christian initiation. The postconciliar rite examined here should be considered as a case study, though an extensive one. Second, it shows how ritual practice, cultural norms, and interpretations of initiation all mutually determine one another. No rite is practiced in a culture-free zone, and ritual process forms Christians within cultural, symbolic, and political spheres, often including interference with the goals of Christian initiation. Third, history grounds the analysis by keeping the cultural and historical origins of particular practices in view, precluding fanciful speculation while enabling the *speculatio* that explores the divine realm of grace through understanding the human realm of culture.

On a more practical level, historical analysis points to the most significant aspects, actions, and concepts of Christian initiation. Although elements common to several traditions are not necessarily most ancient, structures perceived as most important resist change.[31] Moreover, importation of elements (and thus commonality across rites) generally suggests that the structural elements imported are seen

---

[31] Paul Bradshaw, *Search for the Origins of Christian Worship* (New York: Oxford University, 2002), 11. This observation was the work of Anton Baumstark, who was of course only noting a tendency of liturgical history. Bradshaw's caveats in this section are important; for this work, preference has been for definite liturgical practices and their interpretation, rather than for prescriptive or specious liturgical works.

as strongly representative of Christian initiation.[32] The ritual analysis and the historical go hand in hand. For example, both suggest that the most important moments of the rite are the two anointings and the water bath. The perspective offered also gives a field for objection to particular points in the rite. For example, the historical significance of the proclamation of faith in the context of baptism makes the framing of the "renewal of baptismal vows" in the postconciliar rite suspect.[33]

The best example of the relevance of historical analysis as the background of ritual studies and liturgical theology, however, is the historical tradition of communicating baptized infants immediately as part of their initiation. This, alas, is no longer part of the initiation of infants in the West. Many arguments for the historical validity of infant communion have been made, but there is no accepted model for understanding how infants commune with Christ through the eucharist. By the perhaps paradoxical method of examining closely what is left of infant initiation in the West, efficacious engagement indirectly makes a case for the intelligibility of infant communion.

New Testament Period

In his study *The Rites of Christian Initiation*, Maxwell Johnson gives a comprehensive summary of the development of Christian initiation and the imagery used to interpret it.[34] Little is known about the specific structure of Christian initiation during the New Testament period. The most important structures seem to have been communal, indiscriminate meal sharing[35] and water baptism by submersion or immersion,[36] both of which probably have roots in the historical life of Jesus himself.[37] Footwashing and handlaying also have more elusive or perhaps eclectic connections to the earliest Christian initiations.[38] Finally, metaphorical imagery about Christian initiation in the New Testament (clothing, anointing, light) suggests ritualizations that may have been realized in the New Testament period itself, but in any case

---

[32] Of course, it could also be due to political power structures.

[33] See below and chapter 4.

[34] Maxwell Johnson, *The Rites of Christian Initiation: Their Evolution and Interpretation* (Collegeville, MN: Liturgical Press, 2007) (hereafter *Rites*).

[35] See Mitchell, *Eucharist as a Sacrament of Initiation*; Maxwell Johnson, *Rites*, 3–7.

[36] Maxwell Johnson, *Rites*, 23–28.

[37] Ibid., 5, 13.

[38] Ibid., 29–31.

were abundantly realized later in the Christian tradition.[39] There has been much argument over whether infants were initiated in the New Testament period. Because the purpose of contemporary liturgical practice is not to re-create any particular period of church history, I do not think it is necessary to rehearse and evaluate these claims here. Nothing is known with certainty about *how* infants were initiated in the earliest period or how their initiation was interpreted. On the other hand, it is quite clear that the texts associated with initiation see it as a dramatic identity change (e.g., John 3; Rom 6; Acts 9).

Pre-Nicene Period

In the second and third centuries, some of the distinctive elements of Eastern and Western rites are distinguishable in documents. Like the New Testament period, the pre-Nicene period is one of great diversity in both practice and interpretation. The Syrian tradition of initiation tends toward Jordan imagery, which is also associated in the East with Christ's birth and the manifestation of the Trinity as exemplified in Eastern celebrations of Epiphany. Therefore Epiphany was probably the preferred baptismal day in the Syrian churches.[40] The simultaneous celebration of Jesus' birth and baptism probably assisted the feminine gender of the word "Spirit" in Syriac in contributing to the image of the font as womb.[41]

Within the Syrian rite, however, the pneumatological emphasis of initiation does not fall on the water bath, as it does in most other Christian ritual traditions, but on the (prebath) anointing known as *rushma* ("sign"). This anointing was pneumatic and messianic, being identified with Christ's anointing with the Spirit at his own baptism in the Jordan: "it was the anointing that became, in Syria, the first and only visible gesture for the central event at Christ's baptism: his revelation as the Messiah-King through the descent of the Spirit."[42] The central image of fire is also here associated with the Holy Spirit, with anointing and with oil.[43] The later Syriac tradition gradually accommodated the majority emphasis on the water bath, without fully losing the significance of

---

[39] Ibid., 37–38.

[40] Ibid., 59–60.

[41] Ibid., 61.

[42] Gabriele Winkler, "The Original Meaning of the Prebaptismal Anointing and Its Implications," in *Living Water, Sealing Spirit*, 72. Cited in Maxwell Johnson, *Rites*, 59.

[43] Johnson, *Rites*, e.g., 57.

the *rushma*. In general, interpretations of anointings in the Christian tradition tend to change: because oil is associated with the Spirit, ritual anointings tend to accumulate pneumatic emphasis. Because oil is also associated with exorcism, however, which tends to exclude pneumatic interpretation, they also easily lose pneumatic emphasis.

The distinctive aspects of early Syrian practice—the emphasis on birth and the womb as symbols, the trinitarian (rather than solely christological) focus, and the paradigm as Christ's baptism rather than his crucifixion—lend themselves to seeing infant baptism as a central rather than abnormal Christian practice. This may be why the East, unlike the West, has never questioned full initiation of infants.

The dominant symbol of baptism outside Syria was the water bath. In Egypt Origen's homilies emphasized Christ's baptism in the Jordan, but it was seen through Israelite imagery: the exodus and conquering of the Holy Land.[44] Death and resurrection thus played a role, even within the context of Jordan imagery comparable to Syria: Origen integrates a reading of Romans 6 into the dominant paradigm of the Jordan event. He also witnesses to a creed (done in question-and-answer form) as part of initiation.[45] Finally, Origen testifies to the practice of infant baptism and speculates that it signifies some kind of impurity in infants that requires cleansing.[46] This becomes the germ of the theological argument for original sin eventually advanced by Augustine. Origen's testimony is a reminder that the same imagery for baptism can lend itself to dramatically different interpretations. In addition, it is clear that even in the very early period, the potential paradoxes of death and new life, creedal belief and recipients unable to personally profess faith were part of Christian baptism. Origen did not feel it necessary to find one side of these paradoxes abnormal; paradox was part of the proclamation of faith.

In the West, there is very little hard evidence of initiation at Rome before the medieval period; North Africa, on the other hand, is well attested and highly influential. In the West, the last major ritual act of a ritual complex was often the one that is considered efficacious. The rest were thought of as preparatory.

[44] Ibid., 71–73.
[45] Ibid., 73.
[46] Ibid., 74–75.

This tendency to focus on the last major action contributed to the gradual association of the Holy Spirit with the postbaptismal anointing in the West. Pneumatic emphasis is attracted to anointings and handlayings (based on scriptural motifs), and in the West one moment is often identified as the one in which the sacramental work gets done. Thus, in the West the water bath gradually became associated with cleansing (forgiveness of sins) and the postbaptismal anointing (originally what is now called "chrismation" but later confirmation) was identified as the moment in which the Holy Spirit was given. This later contributed to the Western dissolution of initiation.

Tertullian, in the early third century, witnessed to the beginning of this process when he said, "Not that *in* the waters we obtain the Holy Spirit; but in the water, under (the witness of) the angel, we are cleansed and prepared *for* the Holy Spirit." In Tertullian's rite, the Holy Spirit is given in a postbaptismal imposition of the hand following an anointing with chrism.[47] Here not only the prebaptismal anointing but even the water bath itself takes on a "preparatory" role, as tends to happen to any structural elements associated with cleansing or exorcism.

By Tertullian's time too, the distinctive Western emphasis on paschal baptism and its connection to Romans 6 is established.[48] The credal questions, like in the early Eastern initiations, were integrated with the submersions or immersions, which, in North Africa, were three in number. Tertullian also witnesses to, but critiques, infant baptism, implying that it is unnecessary and concerned that such children are likely to need to join the order of penitents.[49] Cyprian, on the other hand (as well as Augustine, later), considers infants to be the ideal sacramental subjects, since they cannot be hindered by personal sin from receiving grace.[50] Cyprian, in fact, considered the existential situation of babies particularly reminiscent of the status of catechumens repenting before baptism: "We think [baptism] is to be even more observed in respect of infants and newly-born persons, who on this very account deserve more from our help and from the divine mercy, that immediately, on

---

[47] Ibid., 86.

[48] Ibid., 87–88. But see also Johnson, *Images*, 36, which calls attention to the continuing diversity of interpretation in the West until the liturgical movement. Also, recall that parts of the East, especially Alexandria (Origen) and Jerusalem (Cyril), also use Christ's death and resurrection as paradigmatic imagery in baptismal contexts.

[49] Johnson, *Rites*, 89–90.

[50] Ibid., 91, 196.

the very beginning of their birth, *lamenting and weeping, they do nothing else but entreat.*"[51]

Infant communion, of course, was part of the initiatory practice that Cyprian is defending; infants were not only appropriate baptizands but perfect communicants. This argument comparing infant behaviors to catechumenal repentance is the close relative of ancient and modern understandings of Christ's sayings about children (Mark 9; 10; and parallels) that see in infants' dependence and helplessness an idealized picture of Christian behavior.[52]

The reconstructed document generally known as the *Apostolic Tradition* can no longer be assumed to be representative of any one community's worship at any particular period; it is not even certain that its various additions and redactions are all Eastern or all Western.[53] Nonetheless, it is interesting to note that it includes a reference to infant baptism as practiced simultaneously with adult baptism: "Baptize the little ones first. All those who can speak for themselves shall do so. As for those who cannot speak for themselves, their parents or someone from their family shall *speak for them*. Then baptize the men, and lastly the women . . ."[54] This seems to indicate that prelinguistic persons were baptized with minimal ritual adaptation, and that proxy confession was the norm. Bradshaw, Johnson, Phillips, and Attridge assign it to the earliest stratum of the document. The provenance of the document in question, however, remains so problematic that not much can be made of its testimony. Therefore its ritual specifications, besides this unique rubric, will be omitted entirely.

Post-Nicene Period

The post-Nicene period was largely one of increasing standardization and cross-fertilization in Christian liturgy. Three major alterations were occurring throughout the Christian churches. Following a brief synopsis of these, the discussion will concentrate on the post-Nicene West, where questions about infant baptism arose and the beginnings

---

[51] Ibid., 92.

[52] See Odd Magne Bakke, *When Children Became People: The Birth of Childhood in Early Christianity* (Philadelphia: Fortress Press, 2005), on the history of this common interpretation.

[53] Paul F. Bradshaw, Maxwell E. Johnson, L. Edward Phillips, Harold W. Attridge, *The Apostolic Tradition: A Commentary* (Minneapolis: Fortress Press, 2002).

[54] Ibid., 108; cited in Maxwell Johnson, *Rites*, 104. Emphasis added.

of the dissolution of (especially infant) initiation can be seen. This will lead naturally into the crystallization of Roman infant initiation during the medieval period.

First of all, the post-Nicene period was the age of the catechumenate, during which preparation for Christian initiation of adults was becoming longer, more formalized, and more intensive. This was largely because, after the peace of Constantine, the church sought "to ensure that its sacramental/baptismal life would have some kind of integrity when authentic conversion and properly motivated desire to enter the Christian community could no longer be assumed."[55]

Secondly, more ritual and doctrinal elements were exchanged between East and West. In the West, this meant that, in the wake of the councils resolving the trinitarian controversies, pneumatic language was increasingly attached to various parts of the initiation rites. Such language was attracted especially to anointings and handlayings because of obvious scriptural warrants. At the same time, elements that had been pneumatic in the Eastern rites, especially those preceding the bath, began to take on an exorcistic meaning influenced both by the West and by the desire to increase the emotional and spiritual preparation for the baptismal event.[56] In general a greater emphasis was placed on the dramatic and emotional character of the initiation rites, including a greater emphasis on the sin of those coming to baptism.[57]

Thirdly, theological interpretation of the event of baptism, in both East and West, was increasingly influenced by the death-and-resurrection imagery of Romans 6. While this image only came to dominate liturgical *texts* (at least Roman Catholic texts) as a consequence of the liturgical movement,[58] the post-Nicene period saw its increasing adoption as a major mystagogical theology of initiation.[59]

All these changes must have denormalized infant initiation. In the context of a long and intensive catechumenate, a ritual sequence "designed to heighten dramatically the experience and emotions of those being initiated,"[60] and a relative decrease of adoption and new life imagery, inattentive infants and chatty children must have seemed

---

[55] Maxwell Johnson, *Rites*, 119.

[56] Ibid., 115–57.

[57] Ibid., 141.

[58] Maxwell Johnson, *Images*, 1–5, 9–18.

[59] Potential reasons for this change, which seems to have originated in West Syria, are discussed in Maxwell Johnson, *Rites*, 137–44.

[60] Ibid., 119.

a cipher. It is hardly surprising that they tend to disappear from the theological landscape of initiation—though they did not disappear from its performance—reemerging only to pose a problem for Augustine. The roots of the difficulty in interpreting infant initiation were there from the outset (being one part of the paradox highlighted earlier) but it only became a theological issue when historical circumstances laid emphasis on the other aspect of initiatory interpretation.

Augustine seems to have been the first commentator on baptism to seriously consider whether the rites of initiation he knew, which were used for both adults and children, applied equally well to both. His theology of original sin went beyond those of his predecessors. It was motivated in part by a consideration that the church not only baptized infants but also exorcized them.[61] This seemed incongruous if infants were really innocent, so Augustine concluded that, like adults, they must need "to be liberated from sin, death, and the devil."[62] At the same time, Augustine saw *communicating* infants as "the model of the perfect subject for the sacraments. This is in part because the infant images the total helplessness of the human condition. The human creature must come to the Father with the same helpless abandon as the sucking infant does to his mother."[63]

The idea of infants as ideal sacramental subjects is thus retained in Augustine. His theology of original sin, however, provided an alternate justification for what was already a widespread church practice. This justification probably contributed to the erosion of the idea that infants were sacramental subjects by supplying an alternate clinical model for sacramental practice.[64] Perhaps as a consequence of developing ideas of subjectivity and expression, infant subjectivity and candidacy for initiation came to be questioned. This development was largely the *consequence of,* not the reason behind, the dissolution of initiation in the Roman Rite, which will be the final topic of this section. This dissolution was largely the result of a gradual conflation of several pneumatic postbaptismal ritual gestures and a Roman tradition that reserved one of them to the local bishop. The historical facts and their

[61] Ibid., 194–95.
[62] Ibid., 195.
[63] David Holeton, *Infant Communion: Then and Now* (Bramcote, Nottingham: Grove Books, 1981), 6; cited in Maxwell Johnson, *Rites*, 196. This metaphor of lactation in eucharistic context has enjoyed a long and illustrious history in the Christian tradition.
[64] See Searle, "Infant Baptism Reconsidered."

consequences are treated in Johnson's *Rites of Christian Initiation* and elsewhere; after a brief outline of the development of dissolution, the consequences will be the main concern here.

Dissolution of Infant Initiation

In the pre-Nicene period there is evidence of various postbaptismal ritual gestures in North Africa, including (from Tertullian) a single anointing, a pneumatic handlaying prayer, and (from Cyprian) the sign of the cross, followed, of course, by first eucharist.[65] Moreover, in this time period in the West the rite was schematically divided into pneumatic and non-pneumatic structures—or, more properly, elements that might previously have been associated with the Holy Spirit became associated instead with cleansing and forgiveness of sins.[66] In the post-Nicene period, this foundation combined with a Roman tradition that reserved a pneumatic postbaptismal anointing, having the form of the sign of the cross on the initiand's forehead, to the bishop alone. If no bishop were present, the presbyter would anoint the initiand with chrism atop the head, and the bishop would later sign the initiand with chrism in the consignation "reserved to the bishops when they give the Spirit, the Paraclete."[67] These two postbaptismal anointing structures were bound for eventual conflict.

This distinctively Roman pattern did not at first disrupt the overall structure of initiation. In Spain, for example, where the word "confirmation" first seems to have been applied to a postbaptismal rite performed by the bishop following the initiand's *complete* initiation, "it is not the newly baptized but the *sacramental ministry* of the local presbyter or deacon which is *confirmed* by the bishop's visit."[68] In the seventh and eighth centuries, witnessed by the Gelasian Sacramentary and *Ordo Romanus XI*, the ritual instructions for infant initiation still called for a full if brief set of catechetical rites (including the *traditio* of the gospels, the Nicene Creed in Greek and Latin, and the Our Father), paschal baptism, credal questions addressed to the candidates, an anointing with chrism, episcopal pneumatic imposition of hands followed by episcopal consignation with chrism ("confirmation"), white

---

[65] Maxwell Johnson, *Rites*, 85–87.
[66] Ibid., 87.
[67] Ibid., 162.
[68] Ibid., 183.

garments and coins given them by the bishop, first communion, and even a rudimentary mystagogy period during the Easter octave.[69]

The real progenitor of the dissolved Roman Rites of initiation, as well as of the postconciliar Roman Rite for infant baptism, was a ritual in the Gelasian Sacramentary intended for a "sick catechumen."[70] Johnson writes,

> In this particular rite, following a series of special prayers for the restoration to health, the catechumenal ceremonies of the *traditio* of the Creed and Lord's Prayer, together with all the rites associated with the seventh scrutiny on Holy Saturday morning above, formed merely an extended introduction to the rite of baptism itself. After an abbreviated blessing of the font and waters, baptism and the post-baptismal anointing were administered in the same way as we have seen already. But in *this* rite the postbaptismal anointing was followed immediately by the reception of first communion either at a special baptismal Mass or from the reserved Eucharist. The postbaptismal rites of handlaying and anointing associated with the bishop, there-fore, were added only *after* first communion had already been given![71]

This rite is substantially equivalent to the prevailing rites of infant initiation in the Roman West from the medieval period onward, including the postconciliar rite—except that the later rites make no provision for infant communion.

Thus, as Mark Searle observes in his article "Infant Baptism Reconsidered," "what had at first been the exceptional case eventually became commonplace as an increasing percentage of the candidates for baptism came in fact to be children in a period where infancy was itself so precarious a condition that to be a newborn was ipso facto to be in a life-threatening situation."[72] In other words, baptism of infants was justified not because infants had a superior capacity for grace (the traditional view) but because they were in imminent danger of death—physical death, and, as Augustine's views on original sin spread, spiritual death. This view of the development is supported by a twelfth-century French text that glorifies the post-Nicene adult model, celebrated on appropriate feasts, while it argues for *quamprimum* infant baptism. Restriction of baptism to specific feasts, it argues, "has adults in view.

---

[69] Ibid., 222–29.
[70] Ibid., 230.
[71] Ibid.
[72] Searle, 369.

In the early Church adults who were sick could say so, and then they were baptized. . . . But all this does not apply to little children, for who is more ill than an infant who cannot make it known that it is ill? The baptism of children should therefore not be put off, for they may die of the least ailment."[73] Augustine's view of the damnation of the unbaptized undoubtably plays a role here, but the argument explicitly ties infant baptism not to their eternal but to their mortal insecurity: infancy is an illness from which too few recover.

As *quamprimum* baptism became the norm, then, there was no time for the full set of catechumenal rites. The cultural formation of infants was camouflaged by the relative cultural homogeneity of "Christendom." Cultural artifacts and practices of Christianity became more and more integrated into the undifferentiated social sphere, so that Christian formation of infants became increasingly invisible and unnoticed. Finally, in the thirteenth century, with the gradual withdrawal of the laity from the chalice, infant communion (which was ordinarily restricted to the chalice) disappeared.[74] The dissolution of infant baptism, so long a matter of popular practice, became incorporated into canon law.[75]

So the emergence of confirmation as an episcopal reduplication of the North African or Roman pneumatic postbaptismal ritual gestures assisted the development of doubts as to the real status of infants as ritual subjects. That doubt in turn led to the discarding of the catechumenal rites altogether, to baptism of infants as a clinical precaution and the postponing of communion until the so-called "age of reason." The events of modernity—the emergence of pluralism as an identified phenomenon and, much later, the restoration of communion to laypersons in the liturgical movement—actually exacerbated the cultural and ritual isolation of Christian children. Before these, Christian children were ritually initiated into the social and cultural surround of Christendom. The ritual practice of laypersons did not normally include eucharistic reception, which meant that children were not "marked" by their exclusion from the table. Thus two of the most positive aspects of modern Christianity, intercultural dialogue and liturgical renewal, have paradoxically made children's cultural identity in the Christian community much more precarious.[76]

---

[73] Maxwell Johnson, *Images*, 214.
[74] Maxwell Johnson, *Rites*, 262–66.
[75] Ibid., 263–64.
[76] See Clare Johnson, Ex Ore Infantium, 257–96.

Section 3.2
Infants' Capabilities and Self-Development

The change in baptismal practices over time certainly calls into question the idea that one can identify one type of baptism, whether ancient or modern, adult or infant, paschal or Spirit-centered, as "normative." If the rite of infant baptism, however, is to initiate an infant into the cultural world of Christianity and the life of the Trinity, it must be addressed to the infant's identity and capabilities. In the face of widespread contemporary doubt about the infant's ability to undergo cultural initiation and receive grace (except in a quasi-magical, legalistic way that suggests that it is the state of the infant in God's sight, rather than the infant himself or herself, that is changed), I would like to consider an infant's developing abilities to be formed by ritual and experience.

Infants are fully cultural beings, with complex abilities to be formed and to undergo their own formation with agency. Their agency is at its finest when they actively cooperate with adult agents on experiences that are highly sensory, social, and well paced, with periodic reinforcement after the initial experience. Under the right circumstances, this describes infant baptism. The notion of cooperative agency, while difficult, is presumed not only by contemporary practices of infant baptism but also by the proxy confessions mentioned earlier. Even in adult baptism, however, there is a kind of cooperative agency assumed by Christian initiation.

Christians are "made, not born," as Tertullian famously said: they are made Christians by a process of initiation.[77] As a work of grace, becoming a Christian is beyond the ability of the initiand: it is the result of election by God and the community. At the same time, initiation requires the initiand's proclamation of faith and consent to the work of God and the church. In this sense, every initiand is an agent of his or her own initiation. The tension between the initiand's agency through personal faith and his or her consent to be initiated by the Christian community is essential to Christian initiation. Hence, a theology of cooperative agency is also required for any understanding of baptism.

In adult baptism, the necessary tension is maintained by balancing the community's election and "sponsoring" of a catechumen (in the postconciliar rite, this is ritualized by the rites of sending and of

---

[77] Tertullian, *Apologeticus pro Christianis*, 18.

election) with the catechumen's personal development, desire for initiation, and proclamation of faith. In infant baptism, however, the catechumen cannot proclaim faith and consent to be baptized. From the very early period, an adult spoke on behalf of the infant catechumen. In the patristic period, this seems to have caused little concern (though there were pastoral concerns about the baptism of infants, like Tertullian's). By the Reformation, however, concerns about this "proxy faith" of infant catechumens were deep and far-reaching, and these continue today.[78] A more robust understanding of how infants have agency and can cooperate in their own cultural formation should assuage this anxiety.

The modern concern about "speaking on behalf" of an infant springs from the specifically modern understanding of faith and, correspondingly, of the significance of the public proclamation of faith. The modern assumption is that faith is an ephemeral disposition perceptible only by the subject. Faith can only be affirmed by the person himself or herself, and he or she may deceive others. Moreover, faith is defined within a cognitively centered definition of the self (along the lines of Descartes). Since infants' cognitive ability does not allow them to affirm propositions, infant faith is not well defined.[79] Within this context, an adult's affirmation of faith "on behalf of" an infant catechumen, since the adult has no knowledge of the infant's inner state, is understandably interpreted as a pious falsehood or as only a promise of future development. Thus baptism of infants becomes problematic, and the Roman church's teaching that infants are baptized "into the faith of the Church" requires defense.

This meaning of faith was not the standard one at the time proxy professions for an infant (or an unconscious catechumen) developed; nor is it the standard against which the historical adage "into the faith of the church" should be judged. Augustine, for example, writes about a friend of his who became ill and was baptized while he was unconscious. The young man had been a caustic critic of orthodox Christianity, so Augustine considered his unwitting baptism insignificant and even absurd. When his friend was well enough, Augustine visited him and laughed at his baptism. Since the rite was something that "had been done *to his unconscious body*," Augustine assumed that it would not affect his opinions. Unexpectedly, his friend took the baptism gravely

---

[78] See, e.g.. Searle, "Infant Baptism Reconsidered," 396.
[79] Clare Johnson, Ex Ore Infantium, 263–66, 324–27.

and forbade Augustine to speak disparagingly about it.[80] This surprising experience no doubt influenced Augustine when he wrote, in *Merit and the Forgiveness of Sins*, about the baptism of infants. Augustine calls unbaptized infants "unbelievers," but infants who have been baptized are "believing."[81] Infant "faith," according to this, is accessible to outside analysis and decisively determined by ritual initiation. Clearly, Augustine does not see faith (at least in the context of Christian initiation) as an ephemeral cognitive state that can be known only to the subject.

There is a significant parallel between the change in the understanding of faith between the premodern and the modern periods and the simultaneous change occurring in the understanding of ritual. According to Asad, the medieval understanding of truth saw it as something that was marked on the body, an aspect of the self. This understanding of truth made attributing faith to infants (i.e., as a part of their socio-cultural body-makeup) perfectly comprehensible, and also correlated well with understanding ritual processes, in the context of religious communities, as "provid[ing] the discipline necessary for the construction of a certain kind of personality."[82]

In the Renaissance, on the other hand, truth became divorced from body-formation and ritual discipline. Before this, there was a specific kind of power, *virtus*, which required that truth be a part of one's own makeup. The existence of virtue (which was a capacity, a power) therefore implied that one's body was imbued with truth. For example, the early church called the martyrs "witnesses" because the ability to undergo martyrdom with courage was seen as a testimony to the *truth* of the martyr's convictions. *Virtus* indicated a particular kind of capacity for truth, not mere force of power or will, as *power* does today. In the Renaissance this understanding of *virtus* broke down, so that force of will could be brought to bear on deception as easily as on truthful communication. "By their fruits you shall know them" epistemologically gave place to *The Picture of Dorian Gray*.

When virtue proves strength rather than truth, one is assumed to have a public and a private self, where external attitudes may neither express nor inform internal beliefs.[83] The strategies governing behavior were altered in this new context, and the ideal of truth was

---

[80] Augustine, *Confessions*, 4.8. Emphasis added.
[81] Augustine, *Merit and the Forgiveness of Sins*, e.g., 28, 25.
[82] Ibid., 114.
[83] Ibid., 65–67.

"objective"—in conformity with the outside world (granting power over nature) instead of with one's own embodied life (demonstrating power over oneself). But the faith that is implied in baptismal proclamations of faith is not ephemeral and imperceptible, though it is personal. Instead, it is a complex, specific form of being-in-the-world that incorporates the physical with the cognitive and the spiritual, the cultural environment with the distinctive individual ways of assimilating experience. Thus it is more closely aligned with identity truths formed by ritual process than those constructed by cognitive affirmation. Baptism should immerse the initiand into a new way of being, not begin an intellectual conversion. The truth of the profession of faith transforms human capacities, rather than expressing the initiand's assent to an objective truth. The church's certainty guarantees the objectivity of the proclamation, but the ritual affirmation changes the initiand's subjective world and his or her way of being in that world. To call this "subjective" is to say it is more, not less, than an objective and legalistic change of status for the subject, as the ritual analysis of the next chapter will suggest. After all, the real obstacle to one's participation in the love of God is one's own self.

In the previous chapter the characterization of ritual processes as "technologies of the self" was discussed. That designation, of course, might cast doubt on the possibility of infant participants in such techniques. Infants, after all, have no conscious apprehension of socially designated goals for which they are striving. Even among adults, however, autonomy is easily overestimated. Foucault calls the disciplines "technologies of the self" in order to distinguish them from other ritual disciplines that are imposed without or even against the will of the subject of discipline, but Asad has shown that this distinction is a subtle one, and there are many ways in which ritual disciplines transgress the boundaries between intentionality and imposition. Monastic discipline can be seen in two parts: a goal that is both constructed by authority and desired by the individual, and a ritual process that is prescribed by authority and practiced by the ritual subject. The "technology of the self" might equally accurately be called "technology of the community," because it is from the community that the practitioner constructs and appropriates the goal and the ritual process used to attain that goal. If this is true, then nothing precludes examining infant baptism as a ritual discipline, a "technology of the community" that initiates the infant into particular goals, skills, capacities, and relationships essential to Christian life. Moreover, this initiation can and should take place on a preconscious level, like the infant's initiation to other cultural realities, rather than on an adult-appropriate cognitive level.

If infants, then, have the appropriate capacities to undergo and be formed by ritual processes, then the question of agency can be reframed more productively. Developmental psychology suggests that infants can be formed by ritual processes; in fact, it suggests the contours for effective ritual formation of infants. The Roman Rite of Baptism for Children (hereafter RBC) is intended for all children under the age of reason (i.e., from birth through six years of age).[84] Here I will focus on the developmental capacity of newborns (from birth to six months of age) to undergo formation, since they present the most difficult challenge to conventional understandings of faith and identity.

One undisputed fact is that infants of this age are not yet able to use "the symbolic function" to understand their world. Yet one must be cautious again: *symbolic* here does not mean an economic behavior as it does in Chauvet's work, but "the ability to use symbols, such as words, images, and gestures, *to represent* objects and events *mentally.*"[85] This ability develops gradually in tandem with language throughout young childhood.[86] There are more fundamental abilities, however, that do develop at this critical period, and these will be examined here. Moreover, the child at this age has a substantial *dynamism:* a propensity to rapid development and the progressive acquisition of skills. Many capacities cannot be clearly identified in young childhood; the child can use them in particular circumstances or assisted but not in other contexts or alone, for instance. This important facet of child psychology will also be treated in this section.

Since rituals are sensory events, we begin with infant sensory activity, which is surprisingly sophisticated and complex. To some extent, the work of Merleau-Ponty suggests this: human perception is organized for object recognition before any particular percept is recognized,[87] is "open to [learning] more complex structures" for behavioral organization,[88] and is "intentional" not in the sense of being consciously directed toward a mentally recognized goal but in the sense

[84] *Rite of Baptism for Children* (Collegeville, MN: Liturgical Press, 2002). Numbers indicate paragraphs, not pagination.

[85] E. Mavis Hetherington et al., *Child Psychology: A Contemporary Viewpoint* (Boston: McGraw Hill, 2006), 332. Emphasis added.

[86] Ibid., 332ff.

[87] E.g., Merleau-Ponty, *The Structure of Behavior* (Boston: Beacon, 1963), 88.

[88] Ibid., 109.

of being adapted to an end relevant to the person's functioning.[89] In a word, perception does not depend on memory, but memory depends on the ability of perception to identify relevant phenomena and suppress irrelevant ones.[90] It is thus less surprising to find that newborns are, in fact, highly attuned to their world, with sensory capacities that far exceed their motor capacities. "Researchers have discovered that babies' sensory and perceptual capabilities are quite well organized even at birth, allowing infants to begin adapting immediately to their new environments."[91]

The perceptual abilities of a newborn are "especially well equipped to respond to his social environment, including human voices, faces, and smells."[92] Infants can hear relatively well even before birth, can distinguish their own native language by their birth, and can make key distinctions between phonemes before one month of age.[93] Young infants not only prefer music to noise but can also demonstrate a preference for certain kinds of music over other kinds.[94] In fact, the very ability of infants to demonstrate preference (in studies, often by prolonged attention or by learning specific sucking rhythms in order to "request" particular kinds of stimulation[95]) suggests that infants actively engage to resolve sensations into phenomena and undertake agency with regard to those phenomena.

Although newborns' visual clarity and ability to recognize whole forms is limited, newborns are still able to recognize the contours of their mothers' faces within a few days after birth.[96] Similarly, infants demonstrate "shape constancy"—the ability to perceive an object's shape as constant despite changes in orientation and perspective—which is crucial to perceiving objects.[97] Newborns also have sophisticated senses of smell, taste, and touch. Research has shown that newborns prefer their mother's smell and the taste of her milk to other smells and tastes; moreover, infants become habituated to flavors they

[89] Ibid., 123–26.
[90] Merleau-Ponty, *Phenomenology of Perception* (New York: Routledge Classics, 2002), 24.
[91] Hetherington et al., *Child Psychology*, 137.
[92] Ibid.
[93] Ibid., 140, 284ff., 283.
[94] Ibid., 142.
[95] Ibid., 139-40.
[96] Ibid., 146–47.
[97] Ibid., 150.

experience in their mothers' milk, thus imbibing their native cultures.[98] Newborns are also sensitive to both positive and negative sensations of touch, including pain, and can use their sense of touch actively to explore objects in their hands at only two days of age.[99]

Besides being sensitive to these stimuli, newborns are also able to organize the information they are receiving with their senses into meaningful patterns, including localization of sounds,[100] discrimination of faces,[101] expectation of temporal patterns after a few repetitions,[102] and intermodal perception of objects. Intermodal perception is the ability to coordinate information from more than one sense in order to create meaningful (i.e., world-relevant) knowledge. For example, infants can identify textures by sight that they have been exposed to only orally and can identify video footage that matches audio tracks.[103] Infants are born knowing how to coordinate their senses to understand the world, and this ability improves rapidly during the first year of life.[104] Experience is necessary to the development of many specific kinds of perception and motor control, which suggests that ritual experience—understood broadly—is significant to newborns.[105]

The most important motor development during this period is learning goal-oriented methods for reaching and grasping objects. Even newborns have enough hand-eye coordination to "swipe" at interesting objects.[106] By six months of age, most infants can reach objects they see and grasp items of various sizes and shapes.[107] This, like the development of visual tracking, implies a simultaneous knowledge of how to coordinate sensory experience, how to control the appropriate muscles, and where one's body is in respect to the environment—in other words, the precognitive recognition of one's own body as an agent in the world. Even though the infant cannot recognize an image of his or her body as a symbolic representation of self,[108] he or she

[98] Ibid., 151–52.
[99] Ibid., 152–53.
[100] Ibid., 142.
[101] Ibid., 146.
[102] Ibid., 151.
[103] Ibid., 153–55.
[104] Ibid., 154.
[105] See, e.g., ibid., 145 (color), 149 (depth), 180–81 (locomotor), 182–83 (blindness).
[106] Ibid., 177.
[107] Ibid., 177–78.
[108] As in mirror experiments: see ibid., 259, 340ff., 675 (related to language ability); Chauvet, *Symbol and Sacrament*, 95–97.

inhabits it in a way that differentiates it from any other phenomena and exercises agency.

Besides the ability to perceive and alter the world through their sensorimotor skills, newborns have several crucial abilities for self-organization. One of these is state control. "States" refers to the level of alertness and engagement of young infants, from sleep through quiet alertness to fussy crying. These states are not "random" or "haphazard"; they "recur in a regular, periodic fashion as part of a larger cycle."[109] Even as newborns, "human beings are not passive, stirred into action only by outside stimulation. On the contrary, internal forces regulate much of our behavior and account for many changes in our activity levels."[110] State control allows the infant to adapt to the cultural environment: by two months of age, infants sleep much more at night and are awake more during the daytime than they are at two weeks of age.[111] The quiet alert stage, which is optimal for engagement with the world, shows a similar dependence on internal and external factors. One study of postural techniques on infant alertness showed that parents could soothe a crying baby or stimulate a sleeping baby to visually engage with the environment by bringing the baby upright on the parent's shoulder in 77.5 percent of cases.[112] Other postural techniques were effective in a smaller percentage of cases. Parents' postural technique *facilitates* engagement but does not guarantee it. One may see that there are "ritual processes" or "technologies of the community" at work even in infancy: the infant's state control is necessary to regulate when he or she can engage with the world and when he or she is too tired to do so; at the same time, the opportunities for engagement offered by the infant's "world" (both natural and cultural phenomena) gradually change the sleep-wake cycle to accord better with the infant's cultural community.

Further insight into the application of ritual processes to infancy can be found in Lev Vygotsky's sociocultural theory of cognitive development. Like Merleau-Ponty's understanding of perception, Vygotsky's model for human cognition accounts for how human capacities increase with time and practice. Human "cognitive development is, in good part, the result of children's interaction with more

[109] Hetherington et al., *Child Psychology*, 128.
[110] Ibid.
[111] Ibid., 129.
[112] Ibid., 133–34.

experienced members of their cultural community. . . . The child and her partners solve problems together, and through the assistance that her partners provide, the child has the opportunity to participate in intelligent actions beyond her current individual capabilities."[113] For Vygotsky, language is *one of several* "mediators, or psychological tools and signs" that permit more effective interaction with the world.[114] Mediators and their uses change over the child's lifetime, and different forms of mediation enable different skills and abilities. Mediators, and the skills depending on them, are culture-dependent. Language is only one facet of the complex "higher mental functions" that eventually enable the child to be an adult member of his or her social community.[115]

Vygotsky also suggests a dynamism to human development in "the zone of proximal development."[116] A child's abilities are not discrete: sometimes a child will be able to perform a task in a particular context, with a particular level of support, or under some circumstances, that he or she would be unable to do alone. Vygotsky not only recognizes these partial skill realms but also assigns much of the child's self-development to practicing skills under these limited conditions. The zone of proximal development differentiates "a child's 'actual developmental level as determined by independent problem solving' and his 'potential development as determined through problem solving under adult guidance or in collaboration with more capable peers.'"[117] The zone of proximal development acknowledges the indeterminacy associated with learning processes: skills, abilities, and characteristics are not acquired instantly. During the learning process, abilities may be exhibited under certain conditions and not exhibited under others, so a ritual process, with authorizing structures that facilitate the activity and prescribe it under particular conditions, may be necessary for the development of some skills. The zone of proximal development also marks out the imminent sphere of the child's development; the capacities in its range are those that the child is in the process of acquiring. It thus gestures toward the goal-oriented nature of ritual process. It also suggests a means for the acquisition of new skills and describes the process by which this is gradually accomplished: "more experienced

[113] Ibid., 350.
[114] Ibid.
[115] Ibid., 351.
[116] Ibid.
[117] Ibid.

learners are able to break down an activity into components to make it more understandable and accessible to the learner. More experienced partners also help the learner by modeling new strategies . . . and by encouraging and supporting the child's involvement."[118] There are several learning structures developed in response to this theory of cognitive development, including scaffolding, the community of learners, and guided participation,[119] all of which resemble aspects of the monastic disciplines described by Asad.

Infants certainly do not, as monks do, engage in ritual processes in conscious pursuit of particular self-goals, but the zone of proximal development—the development space where the child is currently learning new skills—is also the area where engagement is most rewarding. In other words, activities in the zone of proximal development are fun. Mihaly Csikszentmihalyi has done research into the psychology of enjoyment, and is particularly interested in what he calls "autotelic activities": those that are pursued "for their own sake," because they are enjoyable. These include games, sports, artistic endeavors, and certain types of work. These activities help practitioners focus their attention by narrowing the field of meaningful challenges, which is a kind of "scaffolding."[120] At the same time, they provide meaningful challenges to exercise individuals' skills. In fact, the most successful autotelic activities "present ever more difficult opportunities for action, so that the level of skills one can attain is in principle inexhaustible, and a person who takes advantage of the opportunities can feel that his control is increasing all the time."[121] Thus infants engaging in ritual processes that support their developing capacities in ways meaningful to the community (along the lines of the "technologies of the community" examined in the previous chapter) are likely to be fully engaged with those activities because they enjoy them. No extrinsic motivating force (such as understanding the goal) is necessary on their part.

[118] Ibid., 353.

[119] Ibid., 354.

[120] Mihaly Csikszentmihalyi, *Beyond Boredom and Anxiety* (San Francisco: Jossey-Bass, 2000), e.g., 192. Cf. experiment on planning and relevant context: Hetherington et al., *Child Psychology*, 383.

[121] Csikszentmihalyi, *Beyond Boredom*, 192.

Section 3.3
Infant Ritual Process

Infants, then, can be subjects of culturally determined ritual processes; in fact, these processes enable them to acquire later cultural skills such as language. Cognitive understanding of the "goal" of ritual is not necessary for fruitful engagement with it, and the skills developed through childhood rituals for acquisition of perception and behavioral adaptation are just as relevant for spiritual disciplines as they are for cognitive, emotional, and physical disciplines.

The history of baptism in both Western and Eastern Christianity reveals that such ritual processes are an indispensable part of the Christian tradition, by which people are initiated into Christian life. The age of the initiand plays an important but ultimately minor role in determining ritual practice and interpretation: infants generally were initiated in the same manner as adults until the contemporary reforms, so that other factors of liturgical variation (such as the status of Christians in the surrounding culture, cultural values, local practices, and language) played a greater role in dictating initiation practice. On the basis of phenomenology and ritual process, it is possible to assert that ritual techniques in which infants participate according to their abilities do have an effect (when properly supported) on their acquisition of identity structures; therefore, the Christian practice is comprehensible even on modern terms (with contemporary notions of subjectivity, etc.).

The limited capacities of infants are important when interpreting Asad as well; although Asad is following Mauss and Foucault in his construction of ritual disciplines, he changes the terminology referring to them in a subtle but significant way. Mauss describes his area of interest as "body techniques," which acknowledges the traditional character of the objects of study but (a) apparently limits it to traditions that have a strictly physiological character and (b) leaves notions of agency and intentionality unresolved.[122] Foucault, on the other hand, chooses the term "technologies of the self."[123] This choice explicitly acknowledges the continuity—organized by such techniques—between body and mind, soul, spirit, culture. On the other hand, this term answers the questions of agency and intentionality too precisely: the self is the

---

[122] Marcel Mauss, "Body Techniques," trans. Ben Brewster, *Sociology and Psychology* (London: Routledge and Kegan Paul, 1979), 95–123.

[123] Michel Foucault, "Technologies of the Self," *Technologies of the Self: A Seminar with Michel Foucault* (Amherst: University of Massachusetts Press, 1988), 16–49.

agent, provides the intention; yet at the same time the self is the object and goal of the technologies. Insofar as a technology is free of the imposition of outside power, just so much is it a technology "of the self."[124]

Asad uses the term "discipline," which preserves an inherent tension between self-agency and outside agency. A "disciplined child" can be one undergoing an imposed technique as well as one that, in part as a result of the technique, is at his or her own disposal. It refers to the child as the recipient of discipline but also as the practitioner on himself or herself. Similarly, Asad emphasizes that the monk of the Benedictine order chooses willing obedience as *his own goal*, and thus he attains the identity and character of a monk.[125] On the other hand, the cooperative imposition of authority in the Cistercian monasteries is the discipline that develops the commitment to the goal and its attainment. The abbot uses his authority to create in the younger monks and novices the possibility for willing obedience and give them a narrative that incorporates their experience in the monastic pattern. Thus, the processes by which the self is created have a cooperative agency: the individual undergoing transformation plays an essential role, but performance of that role relies on outside authority for its completion.[126]

Asad's examination of "discipline" makes it possible to examine practices that are simultaneously bodily, cognitive, spiritual. More, he suggests the possibility of examining coordinated agency between willing agents with drastically different roles. This, as is demonstrated by even the brief analysis of child psychology above, is essential to any proper understanding of children's developing social, cultural, ritual, and religious identity structures, but it is also essential—though more easily overlooked—in understanding adult ritual processes. In the following chapter, the case study will consider how the coordinated agencies occurring in the rite nevertheless leave room for the infant initiand to participate in baptism.

[124] Ibid., 18.
[125] Talal Asad, *Genealogies of Religion: Discipline and Reasons of Power in Christianity and Islam* (Baltimore: Johns Hopkins University, 1993), 125.
[126] Ibid., 125–69.

Chapter Four

Folds

U p to this point we have seen how baptism, especially of infants, is "folded up" within itself, made inaccessible to interpretation, by certain misunderstandings about sacraments in general, about human identity and culture, about baptism and infants. It is time to turn to baptism itself and begin the process of "unfolding" its richness for reflection. Here I will consider the folds of postconciliar infant baptism in the nonemergency case.

Contemporary understandings of baptism, being informed by the static image of Christian identity rejected in chapter 2, find it difficult to balance the agency of baptism between God, church, and initiand. A dynamic model for human participation in ritual, however, can see developing infant abilities for engagement as a real tool for participating in the baptismal liturgy. This model, therefore, can see infants as being fully active participants in their own initiation into the trinitarian life that is offered by baptism through the ministry of the church. Some postconciliar approaches have tried to evade the problem of infant agency and infant formation by an implicit interpretation of the rite as an elaborate catechism for the assembly or even as initiation of parents.[1] Annibale Bugnini, for example, in his history of the Second Vatican Council and the development of the postconciliar rite of baptism for children, says,

---

[1] Theologies of infant baptism often justify infant baptism on the grounds that it reveals theological truths and is therefore meaningful. These truths, however, are almost always to be cognitively appropriated by others besides the initiand him- or herself. While their revelation shows that the rite is meaningful for some participants, it does not show how it can be believed to be an effective initiation for children. Proponents have to fall back on undeveloped assertions about the ontological change that occurs in baptism.

Children are indeed the subjects of baptism but their *real condition* is taken into account, and therefore they are not questioned as if they were capable of responding. They are directly addressed only when such an address is *meaningful*: when the minister declares their acceptance into the community or performs rites directly on them. The rite is therefore performed *for* the children, but the celebrant addresses the Christian community and gets them involved, especially the parents and godparents.[2]

Although Bugnini explicitly calls infants the subjects of baptism, his language objectifies them and attributes the possibility of participation in the rite only to adults. One has only to envision the application of these directives for performance in the initiation of a chatty and curious child of six—or three, or two!—to realize that the ritual is no more appropriate to the "real condition" of all children below the age of reason than it is to that of adults. The result is a ritual that seems to waver between initiation of infants and initiation of parents—for it is the parents who "participate" and who are credited with a new identity and responsibility in the rite.

The problem is that the postconciliar initiation of infants and young children is not informed by a satisfying and coherent theory of infant ritual participation. Catholics have been unable to present a theologically coherent account of initiation for infants, so the elements of baptism related to identity formation have been partially displaced to the adult participants. This is actually facilitated by a partial understanding of the coordinated agency between parents and children, which relieves anxiety about parental authority and also camouflages the subtle but distinctive and essential role of the infant initiand in the rite. The resulting ambivalence about children's status as ritual agents and Christian persons extends beyond the liturgical practice of initiation, as Clare Johnson has shown in her work.[3]

Bringing the perspective of ritual play to the efficacious engagement model can provide a fruitful solution to this difficulty. The concept of play is crucial to examining infant participation in human ritual because the coordinated agency of infant-parent play facilitates effec-

---

[2] Annibale Bugnini, *The Reform of the Liturgy (1948–1975)*, trans. Matthew J. O'Connell (Collegeville, MN: Liturgical Press, 1990), 602. Emphasis mine. See analysis in Clare Johnson, Ex Ore Infantium: *The Pre-rational Child as Subject of Sacramental Action* (PhD diss., University of Notre Dame, 2004), 152.

[3] Clare Johnson, Ex Ore Infantium.

tive engagement for infant initiands; because play activities develop essential physical, linguistic, and cultural skills; and because the autotelic nature of play activities strengthens the coordination of the cooperating agents, including infant and parents as well as other actors. This chapter will consider in what way ritual play can allow infants to participate in the RBC as a ritual process and what the outcome of such participation may be.

Section 4.1
Disappropriation in the Postconciliar Rite of Infant Baptism

Chapter 3 explored how technologies of the self could more profitably be explored as "technologies of the community," that is, how authorizing structures organize ritual self-development. In the interest of seeking the formation of the infant in the postconciliar baptism of infants, then, one beginning is to look at the rite's treatment of authority. Applying this lens to the rite of infant baptism reveals a movement toward "disappropriation" of authority.[4] Despite infants' relatively undeveloped capacities for symbolic and linguistic communication, the momentum of the rite reveals that they are not passive recipients of an identity status offered by the agency of parents and church.

The identity of the child is the first question addressed by the rite at its opening. After the greeting, the celebrant addresses the parents: "What name do you give your child?"[5] A focus on the child's identity is appropriate to a ritual initiation. At the same time, the exchange recognizes the parents' authority as the source of the child's identity in the ecclesial context. The parents respond with the child's name. The celebrant continues by asking, "What do you ask of God's Church for N.?"[6] By using the child's name, this response accepts the name as a provisional answer to the question of the initiand's identity. The question moves the rite forward by requesting a basis for relationship between this person—whoever he or she may turn out to be—and the community that the celebrant represents. Like the problem of the

---

[4] On disappropriation, cf. Chauvet, *Symbol and Sacrament* (Collegeville, MN: Liturgical Press, 1995), e.g., 276, 279.

[5] *Rite of Baptism for Children* (Collegeville, MN: Liturgical Press, 2002), 76 (hereafter RBC). Numbers refer to paragraphs, not pagination. In the ritual analysis, the "Rite of baptism for one child" (72ff.) has been chosen for quotations for purely aesthetic reasons.

[6] Ibid.

child's identity, this relationship is referred to the parents' authority, and they request that their child be baptized.[7]

The celebrant responds to this request by explicitly identifying the parents' authority: "You are accepting the responsibility of training him (her) in the practice of the faith. It will be your duty to bring him (her) up to keep God's commandments as Christ taught us, by loving God and our neighbor. Do you clearly understand what you are undertaking?"[8] The parents respond in the affirmative, and the godparents, when questioned, agree to support them in their endeavor. Only at this point does the rite acknowledge the infant by welcoming him or her: "N., the Christian community welcomes you with great joy. In its name I claim you for Christ our Savior by the sign of the cross. I now trace the cross on your forehead, and invite your parents and godparents to do the same."[9]

This exchange has a contractual quality. The question about the child's identity is diverted and the question about the child's connection to the community is reduced to a reminder of the parents' connection and their duties with respect to that community. Only after receiving the parents' assurance of their efforts on the child's behalf will the community accept the child as part of itself (thereby giving the child a new identity, or beginning the process of the child's initiation into the community). The infant's initiation, from this part of the rite, seems to be something that can be offered at will by the church, which acts on the condition that the parents (promise to) put great effort into teaching, training, and raising the child as a Christian. Agency is restricted to the community, which can exercise its part freely and easily, and to the parents and godparents, who have a difficult task ahead for them.[10]

---

[7] In the postconciliar rite this request may take various forms according to the parents' desire, but the suggested response is "Baptism."

[8] *RBC*, 77. This unfortunate rendering of the Latin (a gentler translation would be "Do you *recognize* that you are undertaking the responsibility . . .") is perhaps intended to give parents a quick introduction to Derrida's *the* impossible.

[9] Ibid., 79.

[10] Chauvet's reading of psychoanalysis would incline to the idea that naming is decisive in the constitution of the sacramental subject (*Symbol and Sacrament*, 95–97). It is worth noting that his description of baptismal efficacy ("Symbolic efficacy . . . '[transforms] the perception these persons have of *themselves* . . .'") does not make sense in the context of infant initiation (439). Cf. also p. 443: "the baptized (supposed here to be adults) . . ."

This beginning seems to suggest a simple analysis, which would find meaning in infant initiation as a quasi-legal agreement regarding the child's future between parents and church, who together hold absolute authority over the child and whose ability to represent God is unquestioned. The baptismal rite would then be the ecclesial authorization and sacralization of parenthood: an initation of the parents into the duties, responsibilities, and tasks of Christian parenting. Speaking of it as "initiation" of the infant would be a perhaps justifiable equivocation on the basis of the fact that children will be immersed in their parents' parenting throughout childhood. This conclusion would find support in the proclamation of faith of the postconciliar rite, which is presented as a renewal of the parents' baptismal vows rather than as a profession of faith on behalf of the child.[11] The infant's new identity, then, would be bestowed on the condition that the parents raise their child as Christian parents, a condition reaffirmed by the parents' and godparents' participation in placing the sign of the cross on the child's body. But the rite deconstructs itself, for this condition—that of being Christian parents—is already imposed on them by their own baptismal vocation, which, whatever else may be said of the identity it creates, certainly imposes the necessity of performing all the regular tasks of human life as a Christian. Thus baptism would be a ritual of publicly acknowledging the parents' roles, but historically baptism has instead been recognized as affecting the child's status.[12]

Further analysis of the ritual confirms this complication. The second time the parents are exhorted about their responsibilities to the infant's Christian upbringing, the rite says, "If your faith makes you ready to accept this responsibility, renew now the vows of your own baptism."[13] The baptismal vows are linked to the new responsibility of raising the child as a Christian, but these vows do not create a new identity for the parents. The identity implied by the baptismal profession of faith has already been granted in the parents' own baptisms. The vows and the dialogue in the reception of the child are a public ritual repetition of a duty already implied by the parents' baptismal identity. Furthermore, this duty has already been acknowledged by them in the acts

---

[11] "If your faith makes you ready to accept this responsibility, renew now the vows of your own baptism" (*RBC*, 93). This departure from the tradition of speaking on behalf of the infant, without, as mentioned earlier, any true theology of childhood, is troubling.

[12] See chapter 3 above.

[13] *RBC*, 93.

of contacting the church regarding baptism, undergoing a formative process, being present at the rite, and formally requesting that the church baptize their child.[14]

In the reception of the child, then, the infant's identity appears to be a simple question: the issue is his or her membership in the community represented, and this is settled, apparently decisively, by the parents' relationship to that same community and their promise to raise their children in the faith. The promises that apparently secure this new identity for the child, however, are reproclamations of the parents' identity and responsibilities. Their agency in the reception of the child, then, does not truly change the identity status of any of the major participants. It remains, rather, a preliminary introduction to initiation. This introduction summarizes and publicly represents the cultural conditions (authority) that *justify* the infant's initiation. These cultural conditions, however, are progressively buried by the rite as the child's identity, rather than the preconditions for his or her initiation, becomes the focal point.

The liturgy of the word subverts the neat, juridical impression of agency. The readings themselves begin this subversion, drawing the gaze of the participants out of the apparently predictable realm of human authority, in which the destiny of a child can be packaged, handed over, and assured ahead of time, into the very unpredictable realm of grace.[15] In the reading from Mark 10, one of the possible readings for the rite, children are not only welcomed into Jesus' presence but also recognized as the privileged site where, contrary to the disciples' expectations, the kingdom of God is taking place.[16] Next, the intercessions attribute initiation to Jesus, whose death and resurrection give "the new life of baptism" and membership in the church. Furthermore, baptism, confirmation, holiness, and final salvation are all requested as gifts.[17] Suddenly, the agency of parents, godparents, and community is limited to a simple request for something beyond human power.

[14] Ibid., "Introduction," 5.

[15] See Nathan Mitchell, "Conversion and Reconciliation in the New Testament," in *The Rite of Penance: Commentaries vol. 3: Background and Directions* (Washington, DC: Liturgical Conference, 1978), 1–18.

[16] See the interpretation of the child sayings of Christ in Marianne Sawicki, "Chapter 2: Like Nursing Babies," in *Seeing the Lord: Resurrection and Early Christian Practices* (Minneapolis: Fortress Press, 1994), 27–50.

[17] RBC, 84.

Similarly, the prayer before the anointing attributes freedom from original sin and indwelling of the Holy Spirit to God's power alone.[18]

The formula of anointing clarifies this: "We anoint you with the oil of salvation *in the name of Christ our Savior*, may he strengthen you *with his power*, who lives and reigns for ever and ever."[19] In this culminating act of the liturgy of the word, juridical authority has given place to the power of Jesus Christ. The divine power comes with a physical contact with the child's body. Even though this touch is the work of the minister, the formula also calls attention to the inadequacy of any human power to accomplish the task. Paradoxically, then, the performance of this ecclesial ministry reveals the impossibility of it ever attaining its goal alone: the anointing is done "in the name of Christ" so that *his* power may meet the child's need.

This formula provides an opposing pole from the welcoming of the child. Both include a form of touch, an address, and provide a socio-cultural context and a new form of identity. The welcome, however, concludes the human act of naming by which the parents exercise their authority to determine the infant's culture. The context is a human ritual community that is bound by particular rules and expectations for one another—canons, in fact—and the new identity is effected by the application of a symbol to the infant, representing a reality (i.e., completed identity) that can only be completed in the future by full cognitive appropriation. This kind of identity, however, risks futility, for it seems meaningful only when one evades the question of infants that do not survive to full cognitive appropriation, either because they die prematurely or because they are developmentally disabled. The fact that modern Western commentators on the rite tend to avoid, although it was highly pertinent to earlier commentators, is the fate of children who do not survive.[20] In other words, the church baptizes infants for the sake of those who die, not only for those who live to adulthood. This is not to say that infant baptism is only valuable or necessary to those who die; in fact, I argue that an infant's engagement in the rite of baptism is an efficacious initiation into a new identity that directs his or her life. Nonetheless, any explanation of baptismal efficacy must grapple with the question of infant mortality; in particular, with the question of what benefit baptism can be to the precognitive dead. If

[18] Ibid., 84–86.
[19] Ibid., 87. Emphasis added.
[20] See section 3.1.

one believes that a baptized child only participates in his or her parents' faith by proxy until he or she develops the use of reason, the church's tradition that the baptized child who dies before the use of baptism is a believing Christian who has received the gift of faith is difficult to explain.[21] The simple explanation of the welcoming of the child is that infants are accepted as Christian because their Christian parents have promised to teach them to be Christian, and therefore that as soon as they develop the necessary cognitive skills, they will assent to the faith. But this explanation fails both because the tradition holds precognitive infants to be believing even if they never attain reason and because the rite itself is impossible to interpret as an initiation in such a case.

In addition, the explanation fails because the assumption that a parent's faith and teaching determines a child's future cognitive assent is clearly and demonstrably false, which is why this interpretation of baptism produces such acute anxiety with respect to "indiscriminate baptism." The question of whether the parents' faith is manifest enough and strong enough to reassure the church that this child will, in fact, cognitively assent to the faith at his or her maturity gives the pastoral minister, ordained or lay, the burden of being a gatekeeper of the sacrament. This is a lamentable and misguided burden that ignores the continued development of the parents' faith, the child's progressive autonomy and agency, and the work of the Holy Spirit in the lives of the people of God.

Again I turn to the rite for a corrective. The prebaptismal anointing is a ritualized *renunciation* of the idea that human persons are formed solely by the irresistible power of cultural formation—just as Jesus forced the disciples to renounce their ambitions for discipleship in Mark 10. This means renouncing the "contact lens" view of culture and recognizing developing children as subjects capable of discriminating between the cultural phenomena opened to them.[22] It also means rejecting any defense of infant baptism that argues that the parents' cultural influence is sufficient reason to admit infants into the company of the church—any "common sense" understanding of the church as a human institution must constantly be challenged by the realization that the infant is mysteriously appropriate, *ready* to receive sacramental grace, and that the church proclaims this grace for the infant because it recognizes his or her capacity for the life of God.

---

[21] See chapter 2 for the historical summary of this traditional belief.
[22] See critique of Chauvet in chapter 2.

To this end, the liturgy of the word reveals the body of the infant as a place where (the community can only hope and pray that) God is working outside of human (adult) understandings of potential. This partial renunciation of the power of human cultural authority opens up a space where, because the child is given a level of real agency, God can contradict human assumptions: the infant's body becomes the place where, beyond the imposition of the sign, the prayer is offered and God is invited.

The liturgy of the word subverts (but does not rule out) the human, cultural, and even legal understandings of authority in the reception of children. By discovering the futility of these authorities, however, it reveals another kind of authority and agency that is acting in the rite in tension with the authority of parents and church. This agency manipulates parents' and church's authorities for its own ends; they are the proxy speakers for the infant, but their only role is to "call out" for the acceptance of this child and to perform traditional actions "from time immemorial" on the body of the child, so that against all human reason, the water that touches the body may be believed to cleanse the heart.[23] This change follows naturally as soon as the community, having accepted the child as its own, begins to perform its natural function by praying for the child. In prayer the community must give its rightful authority over to the trinitarian God, for only in this way can it fulfill its calling and thus justify its authority.

The dialogue of the reception of the child implies that the authority of the church is parallel in some ways to the natural authority of a child's parents. Parents' authority over their children is goal-directed and self-moderating. The authority of parenthood is oriented toward the development of the child, a goal that is progressively realized. As it is realized, the authority of parenthood changes in degree and kind as it disappropriates each particular responsibility to the child's self-control. Similarly, in the rite of infant baptism, the church's authority over the infant's status as a Christian begins with discernment (before the rite[24]), proceeds to an (apparently) absolute affirmation in the reception of the child, but then retreats in favor of divine and human freedom in later parts of the rite. The authority of parenthood has an inherent tension, and this tension is preserved in the ritual authority of the rite of baptism. This tension is what allows the rite to become

---

[23] Augustine, *Tractates on the Gospel of John*, 80.3.
[24] *RBC*, "Introduction," 8.3.

a self-process, because the imposition of authority on the infant in the rite is oriented toward the creation of a new set of capacities and relationships with which the infant can fully participate. This will be demonstrated fully in the next section, but it is suggested by the disappropriation of the rite.

Section 4.2
The Authorities of Play

Chapter 2 considered ritual process, and chapter 3 explored its applicability to infant initiands. Authority emerged in both places but has come to the fore again here: in what way can the ritual relationships that are key to the performance of infant baptism be authoritative and yet incomplete?

One possibility emerges through the consideration of infant-parent interaction as play. Play, like ritual, has the potential to subvert authority structures by ludic behavior without eroding the activity's momentum. In addition, play has several characteristics in common with ritual that are relevant to self-process. The work of Mihaly Csikszentmihalyi reveals four aspects of play that are relevant to ludic and self-developmental ritual. First, play activities are *autotelic*: that is, engagement in the activity is itself rewarding; play is self-motivating. Second, play activities are linked to skill development and, as a result, to *self-orientation* in a world. Third, play activities, in order to support skill development and self-orientation, artificially *limit the relevant world* and its stimuli within a narrower range in order to provide more concrete challenges and feedback. Finally, within this narrow range, many play activities enable and support *cooperative agency*, in which two or more persons must work together in the limited field to continue the activity.[25]

This last point is crucial for infant play. Adult play activities like games *may* require group participation in which each person willingly follows a set of rules in order to ensure the emergence of the activity. Infant play activities, however, almost always require the participation of another person, generally an adult or much older child. Moreover, the cooperation of such play does not merely consist of self-limiting but

---

[25] See, e.g., Mihaly Csikszentmihalyi, *Beyond Boredom and Anxiety* (San Francisco: Jossey-Bass, 1980); *Flow: The Psychology of Optimal Experience* (New York: Harper & Row, 1991).

of active supplementation of the infant's nascent skills. This "cooperative agency" simultaneously (a) enables the child to use the capacities
he or she is developing, (b) encourages the further development of
these capacities through practice, and (c) rewards both infant and
older participant (hereafter called "parent" for simplicity). In infant
play cooperative agency is linked to efficacious engagement.

Some examples of infant participation in parent-child autotelic
activities will give the best introduction to the ritual study. These examples will also introduce a more nuanced concept of efficacious engagement in the context of infant play: the term "coordinated agency"
is adequate for labeling the coparticipation of more than one agent, the
real exercise of agency of each, and the goal-oriented nature of their
cooperation, but it does not acknowledge the real differences between
parent and infant agency in infant play or the special character of each.
To account for these things, the words "technique" and "engagement"
will be introduced here, although the terminology of infant participation will be elaborated later in the chapter.

Technique refers to the parents' role in orienting and introducing
the infant to the play activity. This term echoes Mauss and Foucault
because technique is *imposed on the infant's body* in order to create a
phenomenal, social, and cultural experience for the infant. *Engagement*,
on the other hand, refers to the *infant's use* of his or her skills (innate,
proximal, or mastered) in order to further the experiential effect,
practice developmental abilities, and learn about the world. Recall the
experiment mentioned in chapter 3, in which infants and their parents
each played a role in the infants' coming to the quiet alert state from
a sleeping or crying state.

Another example of technique and engagement in infant development is breastfeeding. A newborn, full-term infant who is introduced
to the breast soon after birth already has a relevant skill set: the infant
has practiced sucking in the womb, has an instinctive understanding
that bull's-eye patterns like those found on the nipple are likely places
to suck, has eyesight adequate to identifying these patterns, can root
and cry for food, and can suck and breathe at the same time without
detaching from the breast. These abilities, however, cannot attain their
goal without the cooperation of the mother, who must bring the infant's
mouth to the breast, assist the untrained muscles with achieving a good
latch, and support the head, since the newborn's neck muscles are too
weak to hold it in position. At the same time, unless the infant uses his
or her acquired abilities, the mother's intervention will be ineffective.

The mother's intervention to hold the infant's body in the proper position is technique; the infant's participation with the appropriate skill set is engagement. The two, clearly, depend on one another; technique is often spurred by the child's rooting, grunting, or crying; the infant's engagement requires the proper positioning. Technique and engagement together provide the rewards for infant and mother.[26] Clearly, the relevant field of activity is limited to the breast and the infant's mouth, and this limitation encourages the infant to make developmental advances in relevant skills. Over the ensuing few months, the infant becomes much better at sucking and breathing without aspirating any of the milk, at latching on independently, and at holding the mouth in the proper position. Eventually, he or she becomes four or five times as efficient as a newborn—able to drink twice the milk in half the time. At the same time, by breastfeeding the infant and mother are forming his or her identity.[27]

A second example, which is more clearly related to autotelism and thus to play, is the infant's gradual development of linguistic abilities. Like breastfeeding, the infant's development of relevant skills begins while still in the womb: studies have shown that newborn infants prefer their (mothers') native language over other languages and their parents' voices over other voices. Linguistic capacity seems partially dependent on inborn abilities; at the same time, the infant's exposure to a particular language and therefore his or her development in that language to the exclusion of other possible linguistic capacities is a result of technique. The infant begins to engage in linguistic activities as a form of play very early, first tracking utterances and connecting visual to sonic input. The newborn also experiments with vocalizations

---

[26] Research on the rewards for breastfeeding mothers is widespread and well established, even though breastfeeding is not always, or perhaps not primarily, an autotelic activity for mothers. For a recent compilation of studies on the benefits of breastfeeding for mothers and infants, including a summary and an annotated bibliography of primary studies, see "Breastfeeding and Maternal and Infant Health Outcomes in Developed Countries," Evidence Report/Technology Assessment 153, prepared for the Agency for Healthcare Research and Quality, available at the AHRQ's web site. Study accessed October 7, 2008, at http://www.ahrq.gov/clinic/tp/brfouttp.htm. Briefer, less official reports are readily available on the internet.

[27] For example, breastfeeding infants become acclimated to traces of the dominant cultural flavors (garlic, ginger, pepper, cinnamon) in their mothers' milk and thus are more likely to accept these flavors during and after weaning. Breastfeeding plays a role for culinary acculturation parallel to that of linguistic exposure for language development.

of different kinds as forms of communication with his or her caregivers. Later (around two to three months), the infant begins to develop the phonetic range specific to his or her native language, and this development leads gradually to the mastery of the phonetics, grammar, syntax, semantics, and cultural surround of his or her linguistic group.[28]

The interaction between technique and engagement in the case of language is more obvious (because the process is more gradual and well known) and yet more subtle (because technique is often offered unconsciously and engagement is taken for granted). This example is useful, however, in part because it shows that technique and engagement are more fundamental processes in the development of human identity than the cultural and linguistic lens that Chauvet identifies as the crucial medium for sacramental grace. If linguistic exchange were more fundamental to identity than effective engagement (i.e., if infants were unable to effectively engage in cultural processes), then infant baptism might indeed be, as Aidan Kavanagh labeled it, a "benign abnormality."[29] However, linguistic exchange is an ability that gradually develops as part of the identity processes of human persons.[30] Technique and engagement are required for the development of this ability, so they are more fundamental. They are, of course, not necessarily more important for adult identity than linguistic abilities—for example, linguistic and cultural orientation might largely overtake the functionality of technique and engagement in some or most adults. (Recall Vygotsky's zone of proximal development model and the different "mediators" available for intellectual development.[31])

Infant baptism, then, is important because the ludic and ritual elements of its formative processes are what lie behind, what (in part) determine the contours of Christian cultural orientation. In other words, infant baptism, like infant exposure to linguistic phenomena, provides a necessary experiential backdrop for the development of particular skills and cultural understandings: it effectively initiates a ritual process oriented to the formation of infants as Christian people, and this process is key to Christian being-in-the-world.

---

[28] See E. Mavis Hetherington et al., *Child Psychology: A Contemporary Viewpoint* (Boston: McGraw Hill, 2006), 140–43, 269, 281–86, and especially 174–76 (hereafter *Child Psychology*).

[29] See chapter 3.

[30] See *Child Psychology*, 269–70.

[31] Chapter 3.

First Bath

To demonstrate the applicability of effective engagement to infant baptism, it is useful to begin with a cultural analogue of infant baptism in the United States: the "first bath," which generally refers not to the first cleansing of the infant's body but rather to the infant's first partial submersion in a body (tub or sink) of water.

The "first bath" (distinguished from sponge baths, which are applied for the first few days) is a cultural milestone in the United States.[32] There are expected times, places, forms, artifacts, participants, and techniques to this event. There is also a near infinite amount of variability. Nonetheless, it is possible to sketch a "typical" first bath. For full-term infants, the first bath takes place around one week after birth, when the infant is between five and ten days old. There are two requirements: the infant must have lost the stump of his or her umbilical cord and must be able to regulate his or her own temperature (full-term babies can do the latter at birth). The first bath is at home, unless the infant is hospitalized. It can take place in a sink or bathtub. Participants usually include both parents and sometimes family visitors. It is not rigidly planned ahead of time and does not require an invitation. It is thus a "domestic" ritual. Photos are often taken to commemorate the bath. Techniques vary; generally either an infant tub is used to hold the infant in a partially reclined position or a parent holds him or her in this position. Sometimes the parent is seated in the bathtub and holds the infant in his or her lap. The child is partially submerged in warm water. The other parent or another participant wipes the infant with a damp washcloth that has a drop or two of baby soap on it, and then pours water over the child. The infant is then removed from the water and wrapped in a towel. Sometimes oil or lotion is used after the water bath, especially for infants who were born with skin conditions. Critically, the participants usually talk to the infant throughout the procedure, often asking him or her questions.

---

[32] Research for this example was done through searches of "baby first bath" on Google Images, YouTube, Blogger, and Flickr. The status of the first bath as cultural milestone, in my opinion, is best proved by "borderline" cases, such as blogs by parents whose children are hospitalized who make this event a grasping at "normalcy" for their children (or lament that the nursing staff "stole" it from their experience of parenting). Because these stories are so personal, and blog posts are written and read in an air (if not a fact) of ephemerality, I choose not to reveal those that influenced my reading here.

Despite important differences, there are significant parallels between this domestic ritual and the ecclesial rite of infant baptism. Most significant is the pouring of water over the child while he or she is held over or in a basin of water. This aspect of bathing is what makes a first bath "first"—not the symbolism of bathing (because the child has been cleaned by sponge bathing before this), but the experience of being wetted all over, chilled from coming out of the water, and then dried. The question asked of participants in the domestic ritual is whether the child enjoys the water bath or whether he or she cried (often, the answer is both). There is an emphasis on familiarizing the child with the experience of bathing, which will be a significant part of his or her life. The rite is not "unsuccessful" if the child does not enjoy the experience, because introducing the experience is the goal. Nevertheless, if the child does enjoy the bath, it is, in some sense, "more" successful: familiarity, comfort, and pleasure in this significant cultural norm have begun to be achieved.

The American first bath exemplifies a number of useful aspects of domestic parent-infant "play": (a) it is initiated by parents, who have a developmental and cultural goal for the activity; (b) it is a deeply corporeal activity adapted to the infant's abilities (for example, it includes tangible and olfactory experience as well as visual and verbal components, which rely on less well-developed sensory systems); (c) it evokes and is attentive to the infant's response; (d) it is ludic and improvisational; (e) celebration of the moment is combined with a looking toward a future, gradual development of the infant's cultural identity; and (f) it is not subjected to rigid judgments about its success or failure.

Can the rite of infant baptism be explored as a ritual "playground" for young infants? It is not an easy task, because the rite of baptism is not "designed" as "play." Yet there are significant parallels between the ritual play exemplified by the first bath and the rite of infant baptism. The role of parents' initiative in determining an infant's baptism has already been examined, and the other five elements (b–f) above are widely recognized as characteristic of many kinds of ritual activity.[33]

Thus it is possible to see the rite of infant baptism as a kind of playground. The ritual explicitly acknowledges the role of the parents' authority in directing the ritual process. The rite also explicitly acknowledges its goal-oriented nature in the conclusion, when the

[33] See, e.g., Catherine Bell, *Ritual* (New York: Oxford University, 1997), 138–70.

introduction to the Lord's Prayer projects the brokenness of infant initiation in the West by pointing to its fulfillment in confirmation and holy communion.[34] The Lord's Prayer (unlike the profession of faith) is "in the name of this child, in the Spirit of our common sonship." In other words, the momentum of the rite is *from* parents' authority and direction *to* the goal of Christian identity of the child, which is *both achieved and looked for* at the end of the rite, just as the nebulous cultural goals of the baby's first bath are both achieved and looked for at the end of that rite.

The rite is also highly sensory and corporeal, combining experiences of a visual, auditory, olfactory, tangible, kinesthetic, and social nature with opportunities for the child to respond. This aspect is particularly evident in the pacing of the rite. In the first moment when the child is both touched and addressed,[35] the parents and godparents, whom the infant knows well, play an important role in "echoing" the touch of the relatively unfamiliar celebrant. The unfamiliar social and tangible phenomenon is thus repeated to establish familiarity for the infant. Then there is a long period in which relatively little interaction is required of the infant, and the infant is allowed and perhaps encouraged to enter a more attentive state.

During this period, the infant is becoming accustomed to the ritual environment, with its accompanying cultural elements of word, space, song, assembly. Later, the infant's attention is again required in a more demanding way, by the application of oil and another period of direct address and eye contact by an unfamiliar person. Another quiet period intervenes, marked by activity near the font, where the infant is. The infant thus has the opportunity to focus on and assimilate phenomena associated with this activity.[36]

Then there is the high point of the rite. The infant is bathed, and the assembly watches expectantly to see whether he or she will gasp or cry. The infant is anointed again, this time on the head. The infant may be newly dressed in the white garment (this is specified by the rite, but

---

[34] *RBC*, 103; cf. on the reference in the intercessions: Clare Johnson, Ex Ore Infantium, 150. Johnson is troubled by the highlighting of the rites' disunity that is achieved by such proclamations, whereas I feel that a rite that has been broken by historical accident should shout out its brokenness as loudly and clearly as possible.

[35] See "Ritual Folding" below.

[36] Directing attention toward preferred objects is one of an infant's skills from birth: *Child Psychology*, 137–40.

not always actually done in practice).[37] A candle is lit and held near the infant, where he or she can see and smell it. Finally the celebrant may touch the infant's ears and mouth. Several direct addresses are involved here, and the whole assembly is looking at the child, which he or she may recognize.

There is usually a ludic feel to this ritual experience: in the context of infant baptism and the introduction of the relatively novel and unpredictable element of water and the child's reaction to water, the assembly is usually positively engaged. There is an interest in how the infant will respond—will he or she cry, gurgle, smile, fall asleep? At the same time, there is also an awareness that the ritual is future-oriented, expressed by certain formulae in the rite (see next section) as well as, on the more popular side, by the interest in keepsakes (baptismal gown, candle) and photographs.

Finally, there is no evaluation of whether an infant's baptism was "successful" or not: the rite is successful because by its performance it initiates the infant into the Christian ritual environment and thus creates for him or her an inculturated identity.[38]

Based on this paradigm of infant baptism as a ritual playground, the next few sections will examine some various aspects of the rite as they conduce to the development of a distinctive kind of identity for infants.

Ritual Folding

Ritual folding, as explained in chapter 2, is a ritual studies perspective that examines how rituals, first and foremost, exist "in their own right." That is, the ways rituals point to, intersect, and interact with their own parts logically precede their references to external cultural and social settings.[39] This is important because it is often the ritual folding

---

[37] Based on my experience in parishes in Illinois. When the baptismal garment is not put on during the rite, the infant is already dressed in his or her baptismal garment at the very beginning of the rite, and the infusion, done only on the head, does not require undressing. In some cases, an additional part of the garment, such as a stole or bonnet, is added at the moment for the dressing formula.

[38] This observation inevitably reminds one of the doctrine of *ex opere operato*, but in fact this is a human precursor or ritual aspect. *Ex opere operato*, strictly speaking, refers to the work of God that is inerrantly done in the ritual, whereas this kind of "success" is merely cultural. The two are linked, as the next chapter will show, but they are distinct.

[39] See Don Handelman, "Introduction: Why Ritual in Its Own Right? How So?," *Ritual in Its Own Right: Exploring the Dynamics of Transformation*, ed. Don Handelman and Galina Lindquist (New York: Berghahn Books, 2005), 1–32. Different terminology

of the rite, by juxtaposition of elements and nearness of association, that determines which of the rite's many polysemous symbolic associations will be raised in the ritual action. Depending on the ritual folding for example, a rite that evokes social stratification may support *or* subvert the cultural norms. Handelman's article persuasively suggests that deeply folded rites contain more power than less folded rites.[40]

Ritual folding is particularly important for infant baptism in two ways. First, children undergoing the RBC have a limited understanding of cultural contexts and symbols. Since ritual folding examines how ritual is shaped by its own intrinsic dynamic even apart from the cultural surround, it enables an analysis that is more pertinent to the experience of children, particularly infants. Second, ritual folding creates an implicit and progressive sense of the rite's "insulation" from exterior circumstances and roles. This is important in two ways. First, the progressive disappropriation of the rite of infant baptism is enabled by ritual "insulation" from the normal authorities and assumptions of ordinary life. This allows the infant's own capacities to be enabled, increased, and formed in new ways. Simultaneously, the ritual insulation produced by ritual folding provides the limitation of field necessary to produce the ludic atmosphere crucial to ritual play.

In the postconciliar rite of infant baptism, one example of ritual folding is particularly noticeable. This is the ritual element of a touch of the infant by the celebrant, or sometimes by the child's parents. The touches in the rite include the welcoming sign of the cross, the prebaptismal anointing, the water bath, the postbaptismal anointing, the clothing in the garment, and the ephphetha (if these latter two are performed). These points in the rite are significant in three ways: they provide culmination points of the periods of ritual action (see discussion of ritual pacing below), they are instances of ritually directed physical contact between the infant and the celebrant (and tangible phenomena are particularly important to the infant, as discussed above[41]), and they usually coincide with second-person direct

---

but similarly helpful concepts may be found in Bruce Kapferer's "Ritual Dynamics and Virtual Practice: Beyond Representation and Meaning" in the same volume. Both authors are of course drawing on and responding to the work of Fritz Staal, in, e.g., *Ritual and Mantras: Rules without Meaning* (Delhi: Motilal Banarsidass, 1996).

[40] Handelman, "Introduction."

[41] In fact, most of the phenomena that are readily accessible for assimilation by infants a few weeks old are concentrated at these ritual points.

addresses to the infant by the celebrant.[42] As such, these points are particularly important to the analysis of the ritual action that follows.

Section 4.3
Efficacious Engagement in Infant Baptism

Infant participation in initiation is about identity. In the modern period, we tend to think of Christian identity as something that is fundamentally cognitive: to be a Christian is to hold certain propositions to be true. I am suggesting, on the other hand, that Christian identity is about ways of being (and thinking and seeing), not ways of knowing. This is borne out by contemporary phenomenological and anthropological insights into human personhood on the one hand and by the approach of the patristic theologians to infant baptism on the other.[43]

Thinking about Christian identity and Christian initiation about the formation of ways of being is also quite faithful to the Thomistic tradition of sacramental theology, when one sees that Thomas was interested in the sacraments not as an intellectual advance on God but as a processual approach to God's own life, the life of grace. In his treatise on the sacraments, Thomas says that signs are "given to human beings, who reach the unknown through the known" and elaborates, "it is a property of the condition of human nature to be led through bodily and sensible things to spiritual and intelligible things."[44] The unknown are the spiritual and intelligible things to which the sacraments should lead, the capabilities of the life of grace: to do good and not evil, to walk with God, to love our neighbors as ourselves. These things are not fundamentally determined by our cognitive knowledge but by our orientation toward our world.

This correction of our modern misapprehensions about Christian identity should alter the way we think of liturgical participation. The goal of the liturgy is not "learn something new every day," but "be what you see, and receive what you are."[45] Christian identity should provide insight into the world and provide a structure for assimilating new insights from further experiences. In other words, identity is how one lives in the world and how one is able to learn new life skills. The

---

[42] Recall Bugnini's assertion that at these points in the rite such an address is "meaningful."
[43] See chapters 2 and 3.
[44] Thomas Aquinas, ST III, q. 60, a. 2; q. 61, a. 1. Translations mine.
[45] Augustine, *Sermon* 272, trans. William Harmless, *Augustine and the Catechumenate* (Collegeville, MN: Liturgical Press, 1995), 319.

anthropological method developed in chapter 2 suggests two facets to ritual identity development: authority and participation in the ritual process. I expand these two to four concepts to adapt this structure to the particular circumstances of infants to be baptized: authority, technique, phenomena, and engagement.

Authority

When I discussed self-development processes in chapter 2, I suggested that authority presents a goal and structures the ritual process that leads to the goal. Participants engage in the process and develop toward the goal. For infant baptism, parents and church serve as the authorities that present Christian identity as the goal and identify baptism as the beginning of the ritual process of acquiring Christian identity.

Talal Asad assumed that the goal of a ritual process (the monk's virtuous life) was the link between the authority figure and the participants' engagement. Since infants do not have a cognitive understanding of self-development, authority is constructed instead by established relationships and by the attraction of the phenomena involved in ritual celebration. For example, the celebrant is constructed as an authority figure parallel to the infant's parents by the ritual celebration. This construction relies on the authoritative relationship between parents and infant and on the celebrant's use of significant stimuli (oils, water) during the rite. Although we often think of authority in terms of unreasoning power rather than of relationality and stimulus, the play context emphasizes the cooperation between the agents to accomplish a common goal.

As the examples of parent-infant play suggest, when a parent plays with an infant, the parent chooses the context and environment, models play activities, and encourages the development of specific skills. This provides a ritual process animated by a goal: the infant's self-development, which, in different ways, is a goal shared between parent and infant. In the context of play, authority indicates the relationship between infant and parent, their drastically different capacities for the activity, and the cooperative functioning of those capacities to create enjoyment for both partners.

Technique

Technique is the practical application of authority in a particular situation. If parental authority is defined by the parent's ability to choose the environment for play, then technique is a parent's placing an infant on a colorful floor mat for "tummy time." In other words, technique is a parent's positioning of an infant's body so as to provide a particular range of experience or to give access to a certain kind of phenomena. "Positioning" here should be taken loosely: it can mean giving the infant a certain posture, placing him or her in a specific place, helping him or her perform tasks he or she cannot do alone, or, more metaphorically, introducing him or her into a social situation or setting. This metaphorical use does not overextend the meaning of the word precisely because a social situation or setting is offered to the infant through a set of phenomena that his or her parents, by technique taken more strictly, position him or her for. Having the metaphorical use at hand will simplify the analysis.

In play, the parent uses technique to initiate the activity by placing the infant in a position where he or she can play. For example, the mother may put her infant down on her lap and place her finger where the child can grasp it. Her authority includes her knowledge that this is how babies play in her culture, her relationship to the infant that reassures him or her through this change in position, and her physical ability to reposition the child's body and hers. The action that repositions the infant is an imposition of technique; it provides a link to the *phenomena* that the infant can interact with (e.g., her finger).

Phenomena

Unfortunately, young infants cannot explain their experience. However, they do engage their surroundings and respond to them. Although we do not know precisely how an infant understands his or her sensory experiences, we can often identify the experiences that he or she finds engaging. For example, if the infant who is playing with his mother grasps her finger, looks at her face, and moves his arms, we can identify the finger and face as phenomena that engage the child. The mother's authority has then effectively produced the child's engagement.

Engagement

When persons anticipate and experience enjoyment, they are able to participate more fully in activities that practice ways of being in the world. I call this participation *engagement* to emphasize the importance of enjoyment and the active use of skills. Specific skills are required for engagement in activity, which exercises these skills and encourages the development of other skills. A subject's emergent skills—those in the zone of proximal development—are especially dependent on engagement. The development of skills impacts one's identity by providing new avenues for engagement. In addition, by integrating skills through engagement the subject orients to her world and develops strategies for continued world exploration.

Engagement can be exemplified by the play of a two-month-old. The infant lies on her back in a dedicated play area (or blanket) and plays with her father, who begins the activity with exaggerated facial expressions and playful talk. Through previous experience, the infant knows that this environment and behavior initiates a certain kind of play. She responds (if in the mood) with smiles, giggles, hand waving, and kicking. Taking the hint, her father finds a favorite toy: bright-colored, noisemaking. He shakes it and the infant giggles more, intermittently sucking on her hand. The infant's attention drifts between her father's face, the toy, and a mirror hung in the play area where she can see her own face.[46]

The infant here is engaging with her sensory skills (tracking, recognition, association of tangible, auditory, and visual phenomena), her social skills (smiling, laughing, verbalizing, imitating), and her motor skills (waving and kicking, hand-mouth coordination, sucking). The activity is enjoyable for her and for her father. She is developing skills through practice. Her engagement rewards her with phenomena, which provide a means of world-orientation: she is learning about objects that sound when moved, about people and cooperative games, about her father and his personality, about her own body and its capabilities. These kinds of knowledge are important both in themselves (as world-forming) and as foundations for further world exploration (orientation toward future self-development).

Infant identity develops under parents' authority, because they shape the contexts within which capabilities are acquired. The most direct application of this authority comes in the form of technique, which is the parents' imposition of particular positions on the infant's body. The authority of the parents initiates a child's self-development through a formation of the body itself. The body is a malleable instrument, and through play certain postures, contexts, and stimuli become

---

[46] This example is developed from personal experience and examination of videos of infant play.

part of particular orientations in the world. By engagement, the infant is able to incorporate the phenomena offered through technique—particular settings, objects, and persons—into his sense of the world. Engagement also develops further skills and knowledge, which direct the acquisition of further orientations.

Efficacious engagement focuses on how human beings are involved in the world: orienting in it, responding to it, and altering it. World-formation, rather than self-understanding, is human identity. Even infants actively create their own identities by developing skills, relationships, knowledge, and heuristics applicable to all facets of life. The self-processes associated with this development are true initiations, bestowing a real identity on the infant and requiring the infant's active engagement.

Efficacious engagement also describes coordinated agency well. The agency of the child emerges naturally from his or her parents' authority, as authority leads to technique, which offers phenomena for the child's free engagement and enjoyment. Seeing the child as an agent in infant baptism clarifies its initiatory nature and also assuages unnecessary anxiety about the parents' power and responsibility.

Section 4.4
Ritual Analysis of Infant Baptism

The postconciliar rite of infant baptism provides, in its texts and rubrics, liturgical techniques to be used in infant initiation. In addition, the performance of the rite depends on mediating techniques, which are those used for infants' cultural initiation in a variety of contexts. Since the authority of the church over the infant depends on the parents' authority, the parenting techniques are the foundation for the liturgical techniques.

Mediating Technique: Continuity

To integrate a new cultural context into one's world-orientation, one must have techniques that mediate the strangeness of the new phenomena and link them to one's existing world-orientations. In the case of infant baptism, the parents mediate the infant's exposure to new phenomena using mediating techniques. Mediating techniques are techniques that are used outside the infant baptism context to help an infant engage in an activity. These techniques can be divided into four categories: (1) quieting or calming the infant, (2) making eye contact with and interacting with the infant, (3) directing the infant's attention to important actions and events, and (4) positioning the infant so he or she can engage interesting phenomena.

Mediating techniques create a nonthreatening situation in which the child can achieve engagement with the activity. The child is soothed so he or she does not become overwhelmed by the activity. Interaction with the parent provides reassurance and reward. The infant is introduced to the environment, and he or she is held in such a way as to encourage engagement. The child learns to move from familiar phenomena (the parent's touch, voice, and scent) to unfamiliar ones (the activity itself) and back.[47] This developing agency creates a self-process that can adapt and accumulate new identity elements from the child's new experiences.[48]

Accommodating the new experience offered in initiation depends on—without being reducible to—a previous identity structure. In the case of infant baptism, the identity structure that facilitates the infant's ability to become initiated into the Christian faith is the infant's relationship with and reliance on his or her parents.[49] Mediating techniques allow the infant's agency by facilitating engagement with a new environment. Parents and infants are capable of acting with coordinated agency at a level that cannot be attained with the same consistency and ease even by practiced and willing adults, so mediating techniques in infant baptism can be considered relatively effective.[50]

By the mediating techniques, the initiand enters the Christian environment as a playground in infant baptism and engages with its phenomena. The rite opens up the world of Christian phenomena so the infant *may* and *can* engage. Christian phenomena (not to be reduced, for children, to symbol, which is too cognitive and representational) are offered as a world for the children, in which children are free, encouraged, and enabled to practice becoming themselves.

[47] *Child Psychology*, 238–65.
[48] See Jean-Luc Marion, "*Mihi magna quaestio factus sum:* The Privilege of Unknowing," *Journal of Religion* 85, no. 1 (2005): 1–24.
[49] See *RBC*, "Introduction."
[50] See, e.g., *Child Psychology*, 278. The reasons for this superior capacity for coordinated agency between parents and infants are varied, speculative, and beyond the scope of this work. Possibilities include the limited capabilities of the infant, cultural transmission of techniques, coordination of goals, the developmental process, and, very probably, evolutionary pressures. This observation is not meant to exclude the possibility of failed coordination. Failure of coordination probably occurs very often.

Liturgical Technique: Folding

If the mediating techniques reveal the significance of the parent-child relationship within the ritual context of infant baptism, liturgical techniques show much more clearly the significance of the infant's body in mediating and accepting new identity roles. Ritual folding identifies the signing of the cross in the welcome, the prebaptismal anointing, the bathing, the postbaptismal anointing, the clothing, and the ephphetha as significant liturgical techniques in infant baptism.

One aspect of liturgical technique, clearly, applies phenomena to the skin: touch, water, oil. The phenomena move along the contours of the body, recreating its boundaries and changing its meaning. These "skin techniques" are a spectacular example of ritual folding: paired phenomena, nested within other paired phenomena and increasing in intensity, create the progressive insulation of the infant's engagement from the cultural surround. This insulation, as explained in chapter 2, allows ritual to be formative and potentially subversive.

The liturgical techniques on the outside of the nesting are the sign of the cross and the ephphetha. These are minimal skin techniques, involving only a slight touch of a hand, and the touch points outside the rite to social and symbolic relationships that are more meaningful to the adults than to the infant. The sign of the cross symbolizes the passion and the church, the ephphetha the infant's developing verbal skills. The ephphetha is optional, but because of the productive reduplication of ritual practice, its absence does not significantly impact the folding. (The structure depends on pacing and partial, building repetition, not on precise orderings.)

The liturgy of the word, with the readings and litany, follows the sign of the cross. It nests with the explanatory rites, which immediately precede the ephphetha. Both are symbolic calls for continued conversion, primarily relevant to participating adults because they are cognitively loaded. Within these folds, however, two anointings give more phenomenal engagement. The first anointing is on the body, the second on the head. Besides the tangible similarity of the oil on body and head, the scent folds the ritual.

The bath is the most deeply nested element and also has the most resonance with other parts of the rite. It reflects the two anointings in that each makes use of a fluid that highlights the presence of the child embodied by calling attention to the extensibility and limit of that body. This will be examined in more detail later. The bath also immediately precedes the postbaptismal anointing, and they are often both imposed on the head. The bath likewise has resonances with the clothing ritual (when this is done), in that each is part of a familiar domestic routine. The familiar elements of undressing, bathing, and dressing are "punctuated" by the less familiar anointing, which resonates with the prebaptismal anointing the infant has just experienced. The skin techniques will provide a major insight into the ritual's pacing, which will be examined in the next section.

Another aspect of the liturgical techniques is the attention to the infant's sensory abilities. Many of the touches are made on the infant's forehead, which means that the infant can engage them through his senses of smell and sight as well as touch. It also facilitates the infant's identification of the touches with the sounds of the celebration. Since the infant's sensory abilities of touch and smell are more developed than sight and motor skills, tactile sensations and scents play an extensive role in the ritual. The so-called "explanatory rites" include the second anointing, with its tangible and olfactory aspects; the process of dressing, which provides a tangible phenomenon over the whole body; the candle, which is primarily symbolic but may attract visual attention, especially through parents' mediating techniques; and the ephphetha with its touch of the ears and mouth, centers of hearing and taste.

Ritual folding calls attention to the infant's body, especially her skin, and to her sensory abilities as the infant's primary ways of being in the world. The rite addresses her existing abilities to orientate in a cultural world and asks her to engage with the phenomena that constitute being Christian using those skills. The ritual is meaningful to young infants in this way and offers an identity for even young infants to appropriate.

Liturgical Techniques: Skin and Boundary Exploration

The crucial moments of the ritual folding also have significant elements directed to the infant: sensory phenomena and personal address. These moments highlight the skin as phenomenal matrix where the person and the world meet.[51] In the first ritual touch, one parent is holding the infant, probably prone on one arm. The celebrant makes eye contact with the infant and calls him or her by name. After addressing him or her, the celebrant then makes the sign of the cross on

---

[51] See Ashley Montagu, *Touching* (New York: Harper Paperbacks, 1986).

the infant's forehead with the pad of the thumb. The infant has the opportunity to react to this unfamiliar presence and contact. He or she can make eye contact with the celebrant if he or she chooses. The touch also provides the opportunity for the infant to track the celebrant's movement and associate the tactile stimulus of the thumb with the visual and verbal stimuli of the celebrant's movement and address.

The parents and godparents then (usually rather awkwardly) shift about and each make the sign of the cross on the child's forehead in turn. This lengthens and repeats the opportunities for engagement offered by the touch. It also invites the infant into a resemblance, a resonance, between the unfamiliar adult and his or her parents and close friends or family. This resemblance is enacted for the infant's experience rather than presented for his or her cognitive appropriation. Such *enacted resemblances become part of the infant's authorizing structures*, which are thus expanded from the parents and their domestic domain into the other dimensions of human cultural life. For this process of expansion, it is crucial that the similarities and differences between the dimensions be enacted on the body, so the infant practices existing in each of these new cultural environments and begins to produce a self-orientation.

As such, the extensibility and limit of the infant's body is paralleled by the extensibility and limit of his or her cultural orientation. Like the skin, the infant's being-in-the-world is only revealed as such at the boundaries of his or her experience, where he or she is challenged to imitate or improvise an orientation and world structuring that is based in his or her experience so far but transcends his or her level of mastery. In this way, being-in-the-world is itself a skill that is capable of development, or, to put it another way, a self-process that incorporates other self-processes into itself.

The prebaptismal anointing deepens the constructive parallel between the infant's body and his or her cultural capability. A touch of the forehead gives way to a touch on the infant's chest; the dry thumb is replaced by the sensation of oil smeared on the skin; and the aromatic neutrality of the previous gesture is swept away by the scented oil of catechumens. The intensity of ritual gesture is certainly increasing, parallel to the ritual pacing acknowledged earlier; but this gesture is again followed by a period of dialogue and proclamation cognitively over the infant's head (blessing over the water, renunciation of sin, proclamation of faith, and question of intent). There is a difference, however—whereas the infant spent the liturgy of the word in the pews with the rest of the congregation (or, in the worst case, in the nursery[52]), he or she probably spends this period next to the font before the congregation.

With respect to extensibility, too, there is a new intensity to the prebaptismal anointing. The sign of the cross is a touch that remains confined within a space directly under the adult's control. The addition of oil as an element, however, both mediates and alters touch. The oil applied stays perceptible on the infant's skin, so that the phenomenon of the touch is extended in time. Moreover, the oil both spreads out on and soaks into the infant's skin. The boundaries of the contact are determined not only by the hand of the anointer but also by the contours of the infant's body. In other words, the infant as embodied person exerts some influence over the shape of this contact.

This observation about extensibility means that the enacted technique of the rite parallels the symbolic judgments that can be made about the sign of the cross and the anointing, as discussed above in the section on the rite's ambiguity about agency. The infant is never required by the rite to exercise fully conscious cognitive agency, but he or she does not remain passive in the ritual either; rather, his or her body capabilities exert their own distinctive power on the ritual, and the infant as an embodied person participates in the rite's enactment of identity. This participation is asymbolic but does depend on the infant's body and abilities for world-orientation.

This potentiality of participation in the rite is revealed yet more clearly in the next layer of ritual folding. So far in the ritual, the infant's head has been touched by the celebrant and his or her parents and godparents; his or her chest has been anointed with oil by the celebrant. The next ritual gesture, the water bath, deepens and expands the role of elemental mediation in these touches: water is a much less viscous fluid than oil (by two orders of magnitude at room temperature), and baptism, even when done minimally by pouring over the forehead, inevitably creates more splash, flow, and contouring than oil does. Water also conducts heat away from the body more effectively than oil, so that—even if warm water is used—temperature change is part of the phenomena of baptism. In other words, water is a substance more "out of control," more fluid, than oil is. This means that the infant's body plays yet a greater role in experiencing and directing the course of the ritual touch.

[52] RBC, "Introduction," 14. See also Clare Johnson, Ex Ore Infantium, 149.

In terms of world-orientation and engagement, the greater physical unpredictability of water is counterbalanced by the infant's more comprehensive experience of water's behavior in immersion and infusion. In other words, the water bath remains just outside the world-orientations or identity patterns that the infant can be expected to already have developed. It forces the infant to assimilate a new world pattern, but it does so in a way that is shaped and formed by a domestic rite already within the realm of the child's expectations, so that the activity falls into the infant's zone of proximal development.

There is a skill set that is crucial to human life that may be the object of development according to the "play" of the water bath: breathing. Infants' breathing skills are surprisingly complicated and often overlooked. An infant begins practicing breathing in the womb, and must establish an effective pattern immediately after birth. Moreover, the breathing pattern established in the nose must be able to coexist with the sucking patterns of the mouth and throat. Despite this considerable accomplishment, infants' breathing patterns continue to develop and mature for the first several months after birth. Eventually they discover how to alternate use of the mouth and the nasal passages to breathe, and these skills are obviously essential to the later development of speech.

Immersion or infusion of an infant (or an adult) causes an interruption of breath, which can be elaborated into a gasp or a cry. The response that is evoked by immersion or infusion, then, is one that is easily within the range of the infant's physical capabilities. Nonetheless, it provides room for development in that it provides association of the relatively familiar experience of being immersed or infused with the increasing pace of the unfamiliar ritual. This assimilation is a challenge to the infant's orientation in the world. Sometimes this challenge is such that the child begins to cry and must be soothed by the parents. Crying is an essential form of communication for the infant, by which he or she makes the parents aware of his or her need for help in assimilating this new environment. The crying infant is engaged in the world-orientation of the rite. His parents respond by soothing him, and this mediating technique is essential to the infant's successful negotiation of his or her new identity.

Immediately after the water bath, the infant is anointed again. The theme of the postbaptismal anointing is one of vocation, the prophetic, priestly, and kingly vocation of Christians, following in the pattern of Christ. For the infant, the main phenomenon offered for engagement is probably the scent. Notice the ritual folding: the anointing on the head evokes the sign of the cross on the forehead but intensifies it by the experience of the scented oil, which also resonates with the prebaptismal anointing. The return to another anointing also heightens the ritual significance of the water bath and provides the infant with another opportunity to assimilate the profound sensory phenomena of anointing. The infant's opportunities for engagement are very similar to those offered in the prebaptismal anointing, but the infant now has reason for more confidence and assurance in his or her engagement, and further practice at his or her capacity for integrating these phenomena into his or her world.

Up to this point, each of the ritual gestures has played a distinct role in the folding of the ritual, and thus in its suitability as "play" for the infant undergoing spiritual development. The final "explanatory rites," however (into which category, for both historical and ritual reasons, the postbaptismal anointing should *not* fall), are less important as instances of ritual folding. They are, in fact, "explanatory," symbolic, and, as such, directed more at the participating adults than at the infants. Nevertheless, they offer some phenomena that should be included in the analysis, and they will be examined, though briefly, here.

Dressing the infant in a garment following the baptism[53] has several significances. First, it is familiar to the infant, being part of the domestic bath ritual mentioned earlier; in fact, infants are dressed and undressed several times a day in their first few months. Yet the difficulty of the process without a flat surface, in the middle of a ritual in front of a crowd of people, gives the process of being dressed the same mix of familiarity and unfamiliarity that is crucial to the infant's assimilation of the water bath and the anointings. Second, the dressing is in some cases the most comprehensive ritual touch in terms of impacting the skin all over the body: when the baptism is performed by immersion, it is reduced to second place. In either case, its phenomenon of covering the whole skin is the final iteration of the ritual attention to extensibility and limit. As such, it provides an inversion of the extensibility discipline of the bath, for whereas the water conforms to the skin only to flow away and disperse, the garment conforms to the skin to remain

---

[53] Accompanied with the formula: "N, you have become a new creation, and have clothed yourself in Christ. See in this white garment the outward sign of your Christian dignity. With your family and friends to help you by word and example, bring that dignity unstained into the everlasting life of heaven" (*RBC*, 99).

and become, as it were, an extension of the skin and a new boundary between the child and the tangible phenomena of the environment. It thus has some resonance (in extent and inverted significance) with the water bath and likewise some resonance (in its permanence) with the qualities of anointing.

If the child's sensory capacities for touch and scent have been particularly exercised and occupied by the anointing and dressing, the candle and the ephphetha provide at least a gesture toward the senses of sight, touch, and taste, and the capacity for speech. These gestures, as said before, remain largely on the level of symbol and thus out of the realm of the infant's engagement; but the ephphetha does provide a ritual closing that seems to complete the folding of the rite by retreating to a bare touch of the child's head, in this case on the ears and mouth.

Section 4.5
Implications, Ritual and Theological

This look at the techniques of infant baptism seen from the vantage point of play, that is, as techniques that offer the infant opportunities for engagement, and that also further their development and expand their orientation to the world, leads to several conclusions about the ritual identity granted in the rite. First of all, as noted at the outset, it is an identity that does not depend upon the infant's explicit exercise of any autonomous and cognitive assent to the rite; rather, it is initiated by the parental and ecclesial authority in such a way that these authorities disappropriate themselves of power in order to encourage the development of the infant's own agency and to expect the intervention of God. Second, the manner of its bestowal is iterative, gradual, and not accomplished at any particular point of the rite. Rather, the rite itself enfolds and encapsulates ever greater significance of this identity, and the rite gives the infant the means to develop this identity fully. The new identity given is not a "thing," but a dynamic process that begins in the rite itself but is only fully accomplished in the infant's self-development through grace (ultimately, in eschatological salvation). Third, the identity is crucially involved in the child's familiarity and comfort—his or her ability to assimilate and improvise—with Christian phenomena within the context of Christian cult. These phenomena do not become significant once the child recognizes their symbolism much later in life (if at all); on the contrary, they provide the foundation for this symbolic understanding. Nor do they have significance only as catechetical helps to the parents, godparents, and other adults in the assembly. We can affirm that the rite bestows Christian identity both on those who will eventually develop into adults and on those who will die or are developmentally disabled, not by magic but by a deeply human change in one's way of being in the world.

The phenomena of Christian initiation gain their symbolic importance from the infant's experience of them in Christian initiation, which becomes the basis for their affective, cognitive, and symbolic significance throughout life. By being offered for the child's engagement, these phenomena become part of his or her world, part of his or her orientation, part of the identity process of being a Christian, and this allows the initiand to found new skills and capacities on these phenomena and to engage with these phenomena again as he or she develops new skills. Since the ritual process of Christian identity is unending, crucially, *a human person need not reach maturity to benefit from it.* In one sense, there is no "maturity" of Christian initiation in this life—rather, the ultimate phenomena of death provide the maturation of Christian initiation. Thus, *dead baptized infants are Christians*, as the tradition clearly proclaims. Moreover, *living Christians are infants*, still undergoing the processual formation of Christian ritual orientation.

These initial observations raise the interrelated questions of ritual studies and theology: What is ritual play? And what can be inferred about spiritual development from the ritual play of infant baptism? The analysis has identified a number of different elements: techniques and their impact on the infant's physical and social positioning, phenomena and their familiarity, and engagement and assimilation of unfamiliar elements. If these elements can be considered aspects of play, what is significant about infant play from a ritual and from a theological perspective?

To answer this question, recall some of the initial characterizations of infant ritual play: it is world-building, cooperative, and organized. These aspects are crucial to the understanding of play as ritual (from the social science perspective) and spiritual (from the theological perspective).

Infant Ritual Play Is World-Building

Infant activities, especially play activities, help infants develop and orient in the world. Ritual play is distinctive in that it provides an integrated play environment in which enriching stimuli are part of a meaningful network. While symbolic relationships guide most of adults' orientations within the field, infants' orientations tend to be guided more by sensory phenomena, associative memory, and adults' techniques. Despite this different mode, however, infants experience the ritual play environment as a distinct one with certain ties to their domestic experience (provided by similar sensory phenomena and techniques) but also with unique challenges (provided by ritual folding and the unique elements of the rite).

Theologically, this suggests that spiritual play draws on familiar play experiences to answer the specific challenges of spiritual development. The tone of translation, as it were, from the mundane to the spiritual is the task of the person at play. One resource for the task is the phenomenal field of ritual play, which allows the person a limited range within which to practice orientation to the tasks of the spiritual world. This opens up opportunities for spiritual activities within the other environments of his or her life.

Infant Ritual Play Is Cooperative

Infant play is cooperative in the specific way discussed earlier; that is, infant and parent (or other adult) agency complement one another in a way that is intended to supplement the infant's capabilities such that he or she can engage in the play activity. Significant within this context is the way that complementary agency is revealed as not only allowing engagement but even permitting the infant to enter into phenomena and relationships that, although not independent, are genuinely "his" or "hers." Thus an infant's new identity is acquired and a self-process is formed that requires, rather than is limited by, the infant's dependence.

Cooperative ritual agency, then, enables the infant to begin a self-process that would not be possible if the infant were left to his or her own devices and powers. Ritual play introduces cultural phenomena to the infant and demands that these phenomena become his or her own in a culturally acknowledged way. Even repeated gestures like the sign of the cross and the anointing, for example, by the ritual dynamic become part of the infant's skin and thus of the boundaries of his or her identity. The same ritual logic governs the repeated application of holy water to "reawaken" the boundaries of the Christian skin throughout life.

This cooperation, as observed above, is progressively accomplished through the dynamic of the rite. Theologically, the complicated interaction of parents', infants', and ecclesial agency indicate that the structures of Christian identity are not bounded by autonomous individuality, but neither are they compatible with complete and utter dependency. In fact, the spiritual play of Christian identity both acknowledges and creates interdependent competencies. This observation will be crucial to the next chapter.

Infant Ritual Play Is Organized

This is clear from the analysis, in which the ritual momentum is highly significant to the phenomenology of the event. Particularly significant in the case of infants are ritual pacing and skin techniques, which are easily overlooked by methods that focus on adult initiation and symbolic representation. Besides the ritual itself, additional—perhaps competing—organizational structure is provided by the infant's own abilities and preferences. From the ritual perspective, it is important not to overlook the infant as an agent of ritual performance—as a participant—even though his or her participation takes a very different form than that of an adult or older child undergoing initiation. One significant aspect of ritual play, then, is that the coordination of ritual specifications and techniques and infant engagement creates a specific kind of limited world with specialized and predictable demands. This type of stimulation is crucial to the development of new skills. The embodied experience of ritual pacing is one way in which prereflective apprehension of religious realities by liturgy can be more effective than cognitive comprehension.[54]

Theologically speaking, the result of ritual folding, in its limitation of field, is to iteratively create a projected reality in which the relationship of the infant with his or her parents becomes a foundation but gradually withdraws from the techniques and phenomena of the rite. Techniques, which at the outset are an expression of the parents' authority over their child, gradually become avenues that merely display the fluidity of initiation and mark the child's body as a place of excess.[55] In the Christian field, then, the child's embodied experience is opened to unexpected and uncontrollable phenomena. Moreover, the resonance of the fluid gestures (water, oil) with the nonfluid ones that follow (garment, ephphetha) ensure that although the rite closes, its significance to the body is retained.

---

[54] See, e.g., chapter 1, and especially Edward Kilmartin, *Christian Liturgy: Theology and Practice* (Franklin, WI: Sheed and Ward, 1988), 97.

[55] See chapter 6.

The limited field, then, ensures at least that spiritual play grants to the child a genuine kind of self-directedness. It does this by setting up a created world that is partially insulated from the infant's ordinary rhythms and granting to the infant's body, precisely as a body that is not yet fully under his or her (or anyone's) control, a degree of self-sufficiency. Spiritual play makes the child's limitations the means of grace.

These concepts of ritual and spiritual play—the limited field, the importance of cooperative agency within that field, and the impact of practices in the limited field to the overall orientation or orientations of the human person in the world—will be important in the following chapter, which examines the relevance of the ritual analysis to trinitarian theology. These concepts translate into three main questions that will be addressed in the following chapter: How is the Trinity constructed as belonging to the cultural group of the rite? How is identity bestowed within the rite? And how is the identity bestowed by the rite trinitarian?

Chapter Five

Threefold
The Trinitarian Dynamic of Infant Baptism

The ritual dynamic of postconciliar infant baptism is culturally effective because infant and adults cooperate together in the rite as a ritual process. This means the rite is effective at forming the infant's identity, providing the contours of the child's being-in-the-world, giving an opportunity for efficacious engagement in a meaningful world. As I said in chapter 2, however, cultural efficacy is not equal to theological efficacy: cultural identity formation is not the same as grace. A sacramental theology of infant baptism must start from the foundation of cultural efficacy and proceed with a theological hermeneutic.

I make this move cautiously but optimistically: although there is a chasm between the "Folds" of chapter 4 and the "Threefold" mirror of chapter 5, I believe there is also a bridge. This bridge has already been identified in chapter 1, where I observed that the sacraments are a part of the economy of salvation, and that liturgical participation in the church (which Robert Taft called *liturgie profonde*) is sacramental participation in the trinitarian mystery. I set this truth aside temporarily to focus on the anthropological efficacy of the sacraments (the order of nature: sacraments as acts of the cultural community of the church), but the continuity of the order of nature with the order of grace leads us back, finally, to the sacraments as a participation in the theological community of the Trinity through the church. When the infant's ritual experience of baptism is the focus of a trinitarian theology, it becomes clear that the Holy Spirit bridges the gap between Christian ritual processes as anthropogenic, historically conditioned cultural constructions and sacraments as acts of God in the world.

The chasm and the bridge were raised by a threefold question introduced at the end of the ritual study: (1) How does celebrating baptism allow the liturgical community to become the community that belongs to the Trinity? (2) how is the infant's identity recognized and bestowed as a trinitarian identity? and (3) how does the bestowal of the trinitarian identity in infant baptism reveal the trinitarian economy in action?

Section 5.1
The Community Belonging to the Trinity

The community celebrating the baptism of the child is the community of the Trinity because by participating in the ritual act of baptizing the assembly conforms itself to the body of Christ and the temple of the Holy Spirit. By "disappropriating" its rightful (but human and limited) authority over the infant, the church enacts its identity as Body of Christ.[1]

The rite begins (in the welcoming of the child) with human authority, affirming the natural structures of the child's life. The ecclesial structures are treated as extensions of parental authority: each has power that, rightly used, benefits the child, encouraging skills for the child's being-in-the-world. In this way the rite legitimates human authority, particularly the authority of parents over their children. The disappropriation that follows, however, shows that this authority is only legitimate where it is limited.

Of course the family's dynamic of authority (properly understood) has always been recognized in the Christian tradition as a vestige of trinitarian grace. Balthasar's depiction of the intratrinitarian dynamic, as discussed in chapter 1, explicitly attributes to the Logos the quality of obedience and a kind of receptivity.[2] In the sacramental ritual, however, the familial and ecclesial dynamics not only symbolize the Trinity but also enter into the trinitarian love.

The whole assembly is involved in disappropriation, which begins as soon as the community has accepted and begins to pray for the child. The anointing emphasizes the power of Jesus Christ and of the Holy Spirit, providing a climax. When the community prays for the child as one of its own, it must hand over the "natural" authority of parents over children, of elder over younger, into the hands of Christ.

[1] See section 4.1.
[2] See chapter 1; cf. Hans Urs von Balthasar, *Unless You Become Like This Child* (San Francisco: Ignatius, 1991).

This evokes the traditional image of baptism as adoption, not merely because God begins to care for the child, but also because the parents must "give up" the child for adoption. There is an element of pain here as well as much joy in the familial and ecclesial dimensions of the trinitarian economy.

Soteriology is participation in the Trinity, and participating in infant baptism saves the assembly as well as the infant, because it makes the Trinity present in the assembly. First, the assembly prays: in the Christian tradition invocation can only be made through the Holy Spirit (Rom 8:26-27; Eph 6:18; Phil 3:3). Clearly, the church's prayer for the child is accomplished in the Holy Spirit, but the disappropriating dynamic also reveals something about the church's identity in the Spirit by the way the assembly hands over the child.

Second, the assembly hands over the child to God through prayer, invoking Jesus Christ's name and authority. By giving up its authority over the child, the assembly takes up the role of Christ in the economic Trinity, because by his passion, death, and resurrection, Christ hands his power (back) over to the Father as a gift of love: "I do as the Father has commanded me, so that the world may know that I love the Father" (John 14:31). Christ participates in his own execution (John 10:18) but also in his begetting and in the Father's saving plan for human persons: "glorify your Son so that the Son may glorify you, since you have given him authority over all people, to give eternal life to all whom you have given him" (John 17:1-2).[3]

When the assembly gives over its own authority to the person of the Logos, it forms itself in the image of Christ, who is eternally handing over his authority to the Father (from whom he received it). The assembly becomes "the body of Christ" by having the same mind as Christ Jesus (Phil 2:5), being conformed to the image of the Son (Rom 8:29). This act of disappropriation realizes—makes real in a new place—the bonds of love between the Church and Christ and between Christ and God "in the Spirit." By disappropriation in love, the Spirit is made present in the assembly. The Spirit is the distance and the bridge between Son and Father and is likewise the principle by which Christians transcend historical ("natural") determination in order to affirm a future of love. Prayer always happens in the Spirit not because a preexistent presence of Spirit was required in the assembly in order

---

[3] See Balthasar, *The Last Act*, Theo-Drama, vol. V (San Francisco: Ignatius, 1998), 61–109 ("The World is From God") (hereafter TD5).

for prayer to be effective, but because the prayer itself reconfigures the assembly into the Body of Christ in the Spirit.

Another way of considering this is to take as a starting point the metaphor of the Spirit as space also mentioned in chapter 1. This is a ritually appropriate metaphor, since the anointing of the child at the end of the liturgy of the word asks that the child become a "temple of the Holy Spirit," which evokes the body as an architectural reality containing an empty (ritually defined) space. Within the world of this metaphor, the disappropriation discussed is a kind of self-emptying (*kenosis*) on the part of the assembly. Like the *kenosis* attributed to Christ in Philippians 2, the pouring out of power and authority here paradoxically establishes the identity of the one undergoing this *kenosis*, so that because the act links the actor (by the Holy Spirit) to the superabundant glory of the Father, the self-emptying has the end result of exaltation. (This exaltation, crucially, is given by the Father, not accomplished by the act of self-emptying: thus the prayers are requests for gift.) The Holy Spirit, then, is not something that enters in to fill the emptiness established by disappropriation; rather, the Holy Spirit is the emptiness and the act of disappropriation ("space," not "contents"). The assembly is not able to accomplish the act of prayer without the Holy Spirit's presence, but at the same time it is the act of prayer that opens up the Spirit's presence within the assembly, enabling self-emptying and thus the assembly's ability to anoint in the name and power of Christ.[4]

This expands Karl Rahner's trinitarian vision of grace: the transcendent aspect of salvation history, the Spirit's mission, does not just allow one to passively accept the historical dimension as past event, giving it ongoing relevance for oneself. Rather, the transcendent aspect renews the historical aspect by making it present again and again. This is not merely individual existential realization but historical, material, cultural, and communal renewal. The Spirit renews the Body of Christ in the church, not in the abstract, but through the rituals of the church's communal life. The church is Body of Christ because human life is bodily, cultural, and material. The transcendence of the trinitarian manifestation in the world actually renews the historicity of that manifestation, because the dynamic of acceptance and love creates a new historicity in the cultural, bodily, and institutional reality of the

---

[4] *Rite of Baptism for Children* (Collegeville, MN: Liturgical Press, 2002), 87 (hereafter *RBC*).

church assembled. Thus the liturgy becomes the privileged place of Christ's presence in the church (SC I.7) because the ritual enactment of liturgy creates a Spirit-filled field that alters the contours of the social body of the assembly into a Christ-shaped identity. The historical mission of Christ thus continues in the histories of the church and of each of its members (2 Cor 5:17-20). The Holy Spirit "overshadows" the church as it labors in the sacraments much as in the incarnation (Luke 1:35), so the "extension of the incarnation" is pneumatic just like Christ's own life.

This expands the work of Balthasar as well. The theo-drama is decisively realized in the created order by the incarnation of Christ (which, as "his hour," especially means his passion, death, and resurrection[5]). Nevertheless, theo-drama does not continue on its own momentum, or, more accurately, once the Trinity has invited in human actors, those human actors are essential to the continuation of the plot. It is the human enacting of Christ's obediential kenosis (for which liturgy is identity-forming "practice"—efficacious engagement) that allows the drama of human existence to retain its theological character. It is by the church's ethical life in the world that the world continues to be the manifestation of the absolute self-giving of Father and Son in the Spirit. This is not necessary for God, of course, but expresses God's will for the salvation of the world.

The disappropriation characteristic of the rite of infant baptism enacts the assembly's identity as Body of Christ. First of all, the structure of disappropriation, which Chauvet discovered by narrative analysis of a single eucharistic prayer, is neither a feature merely of that prayer nor of eucharistic worship. Rather, this sacrificial character (or as Chauvet wishes to call it, this "anti-sacrificial structure"[6]) is at least recognizable in the ritual dynamic of the postconciliar Roman Rite of infant baptism as well. Moreover, this sacrificial aspect reflects the sacrifice of Christ on the cross because the community acts in conformity with the incarnate Word, who eternally offers himself in love and obedience to his Father. This identification is a participation in the Holy Spirit, who alone identifies the church with Christ and enables it to make

---

[5] Balthasar, *The Action*, Theo-Drama, vol. IV (San Francisco: Ignatius, 1994), 238.

[6] Chauvet, *Symbol and Sacrament: Sacramental Reinterpretation of Christian Existence* (Collegeville, MN: Liturgical Press, 1995), 282–86; see chapter 2, note 19. Despite Chauvet's assertions, it is not clear that only Judeo-Christian rituals are kenotic, while other sacrificial traditions are manipulative.

an offering to the Father. Finally, the Spirit's sanctifying work is not constrained to a recognition now of Christ's saving work in the past but extends the historicity of that work by its sanctification of the assembly's acts.

The community is constituted as that of the Trinity not by individual membership in the Body of Christ but by collective action as the Body of Christ. This can be confirmed, again, through comparison with traditional treatment of sacramental efficacy. The Donatists asserted that the baptizer "cannot give what he does not have,"[7] and therefore those baptized by apostates did not receive the Spirit in their baptism. Augustine countered this argument with his observation that when anyone baptizes, "it is Christ who baptizes."[8] This gave rise to the axiom of Catholic sacramental theology that the sacraments are effective *ex opere operato*: when the rite occurs in the prescribed way, the church recognizes that God makes the sacrament effective.[9] In other words, the efficacy of sacrament depends on the performance of the rite itself, not on the personal holiness of the minister. The ritual performance makes God's power present because the rite makes the ritual assembly into the Body of Christ gathered in the Spirit.

Another important consequence of the specific momentum of disappropriation noted in the first part of the rite has implications for the infant's identity in the community context. If the momentum of the rite is a handing over of the infant's identity toward God, the infant himself or herself is the one being handed over. Again, there is a trinitarian significance to the ritual momentum: the child's body becomes the space where disappropriation is possible; thus the body is the place of the Spirit.[10] At the same time the child, by being handed over to God in order to complete God's plan for the salvation of humanity, becomes an extension of Christ's mission in the world. The body of the infant thus, like the community, becomes the body of Christ.

---

[7] This idea was adopted from Cyprian. Slogan adapted from William Harmless, "Baptism," *Augustine Through the Ages* (Grand Rapids: Eerdmans, 1999), 88.

[8] Augustine, *Tract. on John*, 6.7.

[9] *Ex opere operato* means "by the work having-been-worked" and refers to the fact that God gives grace in the sacraments. The scholastics used it in opposition to *ex opere operantis*, "by the work of the one working," which would designate a gift that came from the minister of the sacraments. The phrase *ex opere operato*, in its original context, was intended to preserve God's sovereignty as the author of grace.

[10] See *RBC*, 86.

If the original "justification" of the child's initiation into God's people seemed to be legal and contractual, this trinitarian embodiment of the initiand becomes an alternate justification. The disappropriation momentum reveals that the contractual reading of infant baptism fails, because the rite itself recognizes that the "conditions" for infant baptism—Christian parents committed to raising the child in the faith, the desire of the community to welcome the child into its midst, and their faith formation of the child—cannot secure to the child the end goal of baptism, that is, the life of God. At both climactic moments the celebrant underscores this inadequacy by calling attention to his or her proxy role.[11] The trinitarian analysis shows that the rite then continues in the mode of prophetic recognition—a recognition of the child as the location of trinitarian grace in the world.

The importance of recognition as an aspect of sacramental grace was treated by Nathan Mitchell in his "Conversion and Reconciliation in the New Testament: The Parable of the Cross."[12] In this essay, Mitchell argues that conversion in the New Testament, as gleaned from Paul's letters and from the parables of the Synoptic Gospels, is essentially a matter of letting go of the desire to be acknowledged (by self or others) as righteous. This conversion is provoked by a person's "*recognizing God at work in the world*, establishing a kingdom . . . which is surprising, unexpected, and even scandalous."[13] Seeing God at work redeeming the unredeemable liberates sinners from the futile effort of self-justification, thus allowing them to enter into the kingdom.[14]

The human attempt to earn salvation through righteousness is a manifestation of sin, so legalism is contrary to the gospel. Sacramental grace can never be a matter of a legal exchange between human beings and God but is rather a matter of the proclamation of God's salvific will already being put into effect.[15] This proclamation is not a static declaration of God's past and present work but provokes a crisis of recognition in the hearer, demonstrating that salvation is "both 'at hand' and 'yet to come.'"[16] In this way it can be considered prophetic,

---

[11] *RBC*, 79, 87; see chapter 4.

[12] Nathan Mitchell, "Conversion and Reconciliation in the New Testament: The Parable of the Cross," *Rite of Penance: Commentaries*, vol. 3 (Washington, DC: Liturgical Conference, 1978), 1–19.

[13] Ibid., 8.

[14] Ibid., 14–15.

[15] Ibid., 15, 17.

[16] Ibid., 8.

because in declaring the work of God it also evokes a recognition and response that becomes, for the hearer, justification and liberation.

The disappropriation momentum, especially exemplified by the anointing, the first ritual discovery of the fluidity of the infant's body,[17] can be seen as a prophetic recognition of this type. As noted in chapter 3, the disappropriation is an integral part of the very fact of prayer; in fact, the community's identity as place of the Spirit and Body of Christ necessitates that, having accepted the child, they must pray for it, and the prayer must be an act of disappropriation. On the other hand, this disappropriation would be self-deception if there were not a real possibility of identifying in the infant the trinitarian manifestation of grace already at work in the world. This is a prophetic recognition because in it the community recognizes the infant as a real locus of God's grace and simultaneously alters the infant's status in the community and potential for self-identifications. At the same time, this recognition alters the status of community as site of Spirit and Body of Christ, because it acknowledges in the infant a capacity for God's grace that is beyond the community's command. As such, the infant becomes for the community a prophetic proclamation of "the God whose predictable love appears in unpredictable places."[18]

The prophetic conversion reveals the community as "community of the Trinity" because the infant, an easily objectified *recipient* of the sacrament *administered* by the community gathered, suddenly becomes a microcosmic, privileged symbol of the community's ultimate calling (as Body of Christ and temple of Spirit). In baptism as in the eucharistic sacrifice, "The church is offered in what it offers."[19] In the case of infant baptism, as seen above, the infant becomes the place where disappropriation becomes a trinitarian dynamic intrinsic to the community's rite. The infant's body thus becomes a model for the (trinitarian) Body of Christ. Even the sign of the cross symbolically foreshadows what the ritual dynamic confirms: it not only inscribes the physical body but also inscribes the infant's shape on the social or ecclesial body of the church.

When Augustine observes that in the eucharistic sacrifice, the church "is offered in the offering [it] makes to God,"[20] he is reflecting

---

[17] See chapter 4.
[18] Mitchell, "Conversion and Reconciliation," 17.
[19] Augustine, *City of God*, X, 6.
[20] Ibid. (R. W. Dyson, trans.)

(through Romans 12:1ff.) on the nature of sacrifice. Bodily discipline of the members of the church is intrinsically connected to the liturgical practices, especially sacrifices and offerings, of that ecclesial body. Augustine concludes that the sacrifices prescribed by the Torah but repudiated in some of the prophetic writings are symbols of interior offerings of the self to God, which God desires because they are beneficial to his people, not on his own account.[21] In chapter 6, then, Augustine discusses "true sacrifice," that is, what is symbolized by these ritual sacrifices. The true sacrifice, in accord with Hosea 6:6, is mercy, but "even the mercy which we extend to men is not a sacrifice if it is not given for God's sake. For, though performed or offered by man, a sacrifice is a divine thing."[22] This is how the human body becomes an instrument of God's will: "a man who is consecrated in the name of God and pledged to God is himself a sacrifice insofar as he dies to the world so that he may live to God. . . . Our body also is a sacrifice when we chasten it by temperance, if we do so, as we ought, for God's sake, so that we may not yield our members as instruments of unrighteousness unto sin, but as instruments of righteousness unto God."[23] This, "the true sacrifice of ourselves," is Augustine's interpretation of Romans 12:1: "I beseech you therefore, brethren, by the mercy of God, that ye present your bodies a living sacrifice, holy, acceptable to God, which is your reasonable service."[24]

From the living sacrifice, Augustine proceeds to reflect on *logikēn latreian*, the "reasonable service" or "reasonable worship" of the ecclesial body. "The whole of the redeemed City," he begins, "that is, the congregation and fellowship of the saints—is offered to God as a universal sacrifice for us through the great High Priest Who, in His Passion, offered even Himself for us in the form of a servant, so that we might be the body of so great a Head."[25] The historical body of Christ, that is, became the means and instrument by which the Word could offer himself and his church to God: "For it was this form that He offered, and in it that He was offered, because it is according to it that He is our Mediator. In this form He is our Priest; in it, He is our sacrifice."[26]

---

[21] Ibid., X, 5.
[22] Ibid., X, 5, 6.
[23] Ibid.
[24] Ibid.
[25] Ibid.
[26] Ibid.

From the bodies of Christians Paul proceeds naturally to the ecclesial body: "For, as we have many members in one body, and all members have not the same office, so we, being many, are one body in Christ, and every one members of one another . . . "[27] This, the self-sacrifice of the one ecclesial body as instrument of God's will on earth, is the sacrament of the altar, "by which [the church] demonstrates that she herself is offered in the offering that she makes to God."[28] This theology of sacrifice facilitates seeing baptism, in which a child is "consecrated in the name of God and pledged to God"[29] so as to have his or her body become an instrument of God's will in the world, as a liturgical sacrifice. This sacrifice remakes the ecclesial body. The child is "given up" so that the church, by giving him or her up (for adoption—by handing over, by releasing, by letting go) may find itself in his or her body, because his or her body is conformed to Christ's body, which was given up, handed over, thrown away, discarded as unworthy (Acts 4:11).

In the signing with the cross, this link between the sacrificial character of the individual Christian's bodily conformity to Christ and the total conformity of the whole ecclesial body through its liturgical practice is enacted: the church is inscribed in what it inscribes. In writing the cross of Christ on the infant's physical body, the celebrant, parents, and godparents also rewrite it upon the ecclesial body, and thereby, by the shared sign, the infant's body is grafted into the Body of Christ, which the assembly, as if surprised, discovers itself to be in the act of signing.

This means that the infant also becomes a privileged site of trinitarian grace, so that he or she provokes the community to prophetically recognize his or her body as body of Christ, temple of the Spirit. The community finds its own identity—its rightful, desired identity—in the body of the child who seemed to be under its power. The child that seemed to be in the hands of the church is suddenly recognized as being under the hands of God, so that the church body is called to recognize itself as being "offered in the one it offers" into inexplicable grace. By accepting this challenge of recognition, the church binds itself to the trinitarian working of salvation history in all its mysterious and subversive peculiarity; as such, the church "belongs itself" to the trinitarian God by releasing its own workings of salvation in favor of

[27] Romans 12:4, as quoted ibid.
[28] Ibid.
[29] Ibid.

God's. Moreover, it is precisely by this offering, because the church "is offered in the one it offers," that the community is enabled to achieve its identity as Body of Christ. In other words, the dynamic of disappropriation is, at the communal level, a "technology of the community" with respect to the community itself, as well as to the child; it is a discipline or exercise, part of the ritual process of continual conversion into the Body of Christ through the indwelling of the Spirit; it forms the community's identity as much as the infant's (and each depends on the other).

This dynamic is also key to the eucharistic understanding of Augustine's reflection on the church's offering: the eucharistic community offers the sacrifice not only in the offering phrase of the eucharistic prayer but also as a dynamic central to the whole eucharistic action, exemplified in that offering phrase. This offering is a ritual discipline that forms part of a ritual process directed toward forming the community and the individuals within it as trinitarian; that is, it is oriented toward a goal that includes an experiential focus on God as the future of one's own history, an other-directedness, and finding one's own identity in absolute self-giving.[30] The offering of the eucharistic prayer is not, then, a merely ritual offering that represents (externally, though really) a future obligation to live in charity. Instead, it is a ritual discipline that lets the assembly, through its members' human activity in orienting themselves to the world, participate in the life of the Trinity. In Thomas Aquinas's language, it is the *res et sacramenti*, the body of Christ on the altar—as food which has been offered in prayer, not the words of the anaphora—that becomes the means by which the *sacramentum tantum* (the sign alone) can form the church into the *res tantum* (the Body of Christ).[31] The bread attains its meaning and its purpose when it comes to be offered as body of Christ on the altar, and only thus can it become the food that makes human beings one Body with the Word.

Section 5.2
The Trinitarian Identity Bestowed on the Child

The disappropriation of infant baptism, as a technology of the community, is a trinitarian dynamic. For this dynamic to be both honest and effective, the community must be able to justifiably recognize

---

[30] See chapter 1.
[31] Thomas Aquinas, ST IIIa, q. 80, a. 4, *respondeo* and *ad* 4.

in the child more than a deep dependence upon the community that is a reminder of our dependence upon grace. Rather, the child must have a trinitarian identity that corresponds in some way to the goal of the community's Christian ritual process. Only in this way can the community be "offered in what it offers" and therefore be enabled to become themselves Body of Christ, temple of the Spirit. At the same time, of course, baptism is a rite of initiation: as such, the identity "recognized" in the rite is also "bestowed."

Recognition and bestowal of Christian identity in the rite are closely related. As already noted above, the body of the infant appears in the rite as the body of Christ—as an essential part of the dynamic by which the assembly is enabled to recognize itself as the Body of Christ. Simultaneously, the body is also identified as the temple of the Holy Spirit, which emerges as an empty space, or a space filled with emptiness. Although it is the complete performance of the rite that creates this Christ/temple embodiment, it is possible to identify aspects of the ritual performance with each of these body images.

The phenomena offered by infant baptism are a foundation for Christian being-in-the-world: by offering these phenomena to the child, the rite affirms the child as a Christian subject, capable of creative self-orientation. The most significant phenomena of the baptismal rite are the wetting with water, the fragrant oils,[32] touch flowing over the body,[33] the touch on the forehead,[34] and other ritual touches.[35] Of these, three basic categories of experience emerge as particularly powerful: water, oil, and breath.[36] Moreover, these are easily recognized as three core symbols associated with the Holy Spirit in the Christian tradition. Together, as suggested in chapter 4, they define the contours of the infant's body and rewrite his or her bodily identity in a new form. The bathed and anointed body of the infant becomes identified with the bathed and anointed body of Jesus, speaking about how Christian embodiment is circumscribed by the Holy Spirit. The breathing body

[32] Although the two oils of baptism have distinct theological and historical meanings, in terms of the ritual event itself their most important phenomenal characteristics are echoes of one another.

[33] Water, in the bath, and the garment, when the infant is dressed.

[34] The postbaptismal anointing and the welcoming.

[35] The anointing on the breast and the ephphetha, if the latter is done.

[36] Note that all three of these emerge in the "core experiences" of the rite: the wetting and the postbaptismal anointing, which are also the historical and theological core of baptism in the West.

of the infant becomes identified with the breathing body of Christ in the Spirit.

The "skin techniques"—bathing and anointings—occur on the external boundaries of the infant's body and flow from the celebrant's hand, representing the community "in the name of" Christ, to and over the infant's skin. The bath is primary, marking one significant phenomenon: the fluid flows over the surface of the body, creating new boundaries with the world and a lasting sensation (temperature change). The alteration of status is not effected instantly, because the ritual folding implicates other parts of the rite, especially the anointings, in this dynamic. Rather, it challenges the community and instigates initiation, which will continue to develop in the infant's self-orientation. If the outside of the Christic body is limned by skin techniques, the interior workings and directedness are sketched by the body discipline of breathing. Thus the full body of the infant, inside and out, becomes inscribed by the Spirit in the ritual action.

If this was read according to the symbolic or linguistic model, one could affirm that the infant became identified with Christ (the baptized and anointed one) by the ritual action, but this identification could occur only on the level of cognitive access. Thus the rite would, for the assembly (at least, for attentive and symbolically literate members of the assembly), identify the child with Jesus, but for the child, the model would not account for any identity change. The child's identification with Christ would be a secondary construction, imparted to him or her by parents and church on the basis of their understanding of the symbolic rite. This "common sense" understanding of the sacrament, however, cannot easily be maintained, because it does not fit with the history of infant baptism. As Searle argues, infant baptism became the norm because of high rates of infant mortality;[37] in other words, infant baptism was more important for those who died than for those who survived.[38] Those who died in infancy, however, did not reach the symbolic capacity to identify themselves with Christ, so *for the initiand* the rite of baptism must have created a Christian identity.

---

[37] See discussion in chapter 3.

[38] This point should, however, be contrasted with the more positive theologies of infant baptism of, e.g., Cyprian of Carthage; if baptism in infancy was more urgent because of those who died, it was still immensely important to the formation of those who lived, as the ritual analysis of chapter 4 also suggests.

The ritual act, then, performs, not represents, a continuity between Jesus the Christ and the infant initiand. This requires a transsymbolic radical identification of the baptized one with Jesus, a transsymbolic power that operates not only in the realm of human understanding but also in the divine realm. Human symbolic behavior, metaphor or exchange, *cannot accomplish this*, but the Holy Spirit does. On the human ritual level, the assembly recognizes in the ritual washing a *likeness* to the baptism of the Anointed One, but only by faithfully relying on the work of God who effects a radical *identification* of the baptizand with the Anointed One.

The mission of the Holy Spirit thus emerges in this analysis as the one implicated in human experience, and also as that which acts like metaphor. The Spirit is the divine *poiēsis*,[39] by which the Father reaches into the world and alters the personhood of those he has chosen to be his own (John 17), so that they participate in Christ by means of their experience of the world. The boundaries of this significance are manifested in the rite at its borders: at the beginning in the sign of the cross and at the end in the explanatory rites. Now that the Spirit has been uncovered as the agent of identification, these two parts of the rite will be reconsidered.

In the welcoming, the infant is marked with the sign of the cross. If this part of the rite can be seen as adoptive, this gesture does not convey a particularly positive understanding of the adoptive act. Like the mark of Cain, the sign of the cross is simultaneously a reminder of violence and a pledge of redemption. The cross affirms that the body of the infant is and will be a suffering body (as are all human bodies), and it does not rush to find meaning in that suffering. Instead, it identifies that suffering, especially meaningless suffering (from colic to childhood leukemia), with the facticity of Jesus. The experience of pain is one boundary of the phenomenon of human personhood, a marking of limitation and lack that comes to be incomprehensibly identified with the fullness of Jesus. The rite thus faithfully maintains, by refusing to explain, that the infant is to be identified with Christ even in the experience of pain, which threatens the integration of his or her human personhood.

---

[39] *Poiēsis* can mean "making, fabrication, creation" as well as "poetic faculty, poesy, art of poetry" (H. G. Liddell and Robert Scott, *An Intermediate Greek-English Lexicon* [New York: Oxford University, 1975]).

At the other end of the rite the action focuses on the infant's sensorium, which is his or her way of interfacing with the world. If the experience of pain is the exterior world being inflicted on the human being, then the experience of the senses is the human being opening to the exterior world, ek-sisting into it.[40] This movement encompasses but is not restricted to pain, so trinitarian soteriology must not focus on the triune God's solidarity with suffering humanity at the expense of what we may call a trinitarian aesthetic of creation. The rite presumes that the whole interface between person and world—or, in the language adopted in chapter 2, the whole process of cultural world-construction—is consecrated by the act of baptism. Not only the baptizand's interpretations of the world but also the very fact of the world's interpretability and the processes by which it comes to be interpretable for the subject are conformed to the Christic pattern by the Holy Spirit. In other words, the whole of human identity, of being-in-the-world, is subject to (vulnerable to) the trinitarian dynamic.

In order for world interpretability to be infused with trinitarian meaning for prelinguistic human beings, there must be a correspondence between the body of the infant baptizand and the body of Christ that is significant *to the infant subject*—that is, prelinguistically.[41] Cultural phenomena, of course, not only function prelinguistically but create the basis for linguistic formation.[42] The data of revelation associate the phenomenal symbols of water, oil, breath with the Spirit and image the Spirit as beyond reason (John 3), the giver of words that are beyond human understanding (John 16:7-15). These suggest the possibility of the same role for the Spirit in the trinitarian manifestation through history: the Spirit's work is found in the prelinguistic and extralinguistic significance of the body as the impossible place for God's grace in the world. This is the basis for the traditional teaching that the sacraments bestow grace *ex opere operato*: the work of the Holy Spirit in the sacraments ties together the human cultural dimension of the sacramental action with the salvific activity of the Trinity. The incarnation and sacramental life together tell what Christianity is always forgetting: there is no conflict between *bodily* and *spiritual*. Without the mission of the Spirit, the Word could have no body: no text, no human incarnation, no church, no eucharist.

[40] See chapter 2 on ek-sistence.
[41] See section 4.6.
[42] See chapters 2 and 3.

Christian identity has historically, theologically, and culturally been tied to the process of naming ("christening") an infant baptizand. This association is suggested by the ritual dynamic of the rite of infant baptism, which begins with the name of the child.[43] After the parents respond with the infant's name, the trajectory of naming in the rite becomes quite complex, with the celebrant "claiming" the child in the name of "the Christian community";[44] the assembly invoking the names of the saints, which may include the name of the child and the church or its region;[45] the celebrant anointing the child "in the name of Christ our Savior";[46] and the assembly praying the Lord's Prayer "in the name of this child."[47] The central "naming," of course, is that of the trinitarian formula: "N., I baptize you in the name of the Father, and of the Son, and of the Holy Spirit."[48]

These naming incidents alter the child's name from an identity marker exclusively associated with his or her family status ("What name do you give your child?"[49]) to one that identifies him or her with the trinitarian love. The community gives this identity and implicates itself in this dynamic by the act of participating in the child's baptism. The community can only have the right to claim the child and give the gift by acting as Body of Christ by baptizing, disappropriating human power, and recognizing Christ in the world. The act of bestowing Christian identity on the infant is an act of faith: by baptizing, the assembly recognizes itself as gifted by the Holy Spirit in faith. The Christian identity of the assembly is offered by the work of the Holy Spirit, which is radically free (John 3). The trajectory of the name thus reveals the Christian identity bestowed on the infant and on the assembly.

First, the name is the specific name of the child himself or herself. In its particularity and incommunicability it thus shares qualities with

---

[43] *RBC*, 76; see section 4.1.

[44] Ibid., 79.

[45] Ibid., 85.

[46] Ibid., 87. The reference to "name" is not present in the Latin *editio typica*, although the identification with Christ is preserved, particularly by the ablative construction *in eodem*: "Múniat vos virtus Christi Salvatóris, in cuius signum vos óleo linímus salútis, in eódem Christo Dómino nostro . . ." (*Ordo Baptismi Parvulorum*, 50 [hereafter *OBP*]).

[47] *RBC*, 103.

[48] Ibid., 97. It is essential that this naming points back to the profession of faith, which elaborates the meaning of each naming of God (ibid., 95).

[49] Ibid., 76.

the child's body, already established as a powerful marker of his or her otherness and escape from the ultimate control of other people, even his or her parents'. It thus becomes a symbolic link to the phenomenological experience of touch, so that the ritual association of name and touch is effectual. This link allows the ritual to progress on the phenomenological level of the child's experience simultaneously with the symbolic-linguistic level of the assembly's social construction. Each part of the rite, then, signifies the transformation and progressive elaboration of the child's name by its link to a new kind of Christian naming.

The main aspect of name transformation in the welcoming of the child is the link of the child's name, with which the celebrant addresses him or her for the first time, to the name of "the Christian community," on behalf of whom the celebrant acts.[50] What ties the particular infant's identity to the group is a ritual action: the sign of the cross of Christ our Savior.[51] At this point, the infant's biological ties to his or her parents are deemphasized (ritually enacted by having the parents sign after the celebrant, rather than initiating the gesture) in favor of this new marking of his or her body as belonging to the body of those signed with the cross, the body of the crucified one.

The next appearance of the infant's name is (possibly) in the Litany of the Saints, where it may appear as the name of the child's patron saint. Once again, this acknowledges the particularity of this infant, the concreteness of his or her personal identity, while relativizing it with respect to the Christian community—no longer limited to the assembly but recognized as "all holy men and women."[52] The name that designates the child in his or her uniqueness is not unique—it belongs to the child alone only by being given in the context of this community in which it has previously belonged to another. Christian names are secondhand.

This provides the necessary backdrop to the anointing "in the name of Christ *our* Savior," since the identity between infant and community already established allows for Christ to (culturally) become Savior for the infant. The infant's body has been identified with the body of Christ (historical as well as ecclesial); now the infant's name is identified with Christ's name and with his power (*virtus*). Traditionally the

---

[50] The notion of "claiming" the infant "for Christ our Savior" is also absent in the *editio typica* (OBP, 41).

[51] In English, "the sign of his cross"; in Latin, *signo crucis . . . signo Christi Salvatóris . . .*

[52] RBC, 85.

prebaptismal anointing of infants was taken to imply the existence of original sin: the strengthening of the infant with Christ's virtue was exorcistic, intended to combat any demons that might be residing in the infant's soul.[53] But what is original sin, or equivalently, in what ways can the infant be newly identified with the (moral) strength of Christ in his or her infant state?[54]

Here postmodern philosopher and theologian Jean-Luc Marion's concept of original sin is useful. He argues that original sin must refer to a kind of guilt that eclipses individual wrong acts to be an origin for evil. Marion suggests that the original sin, then, is the desire for "justice." This desire is a natural and deeply human response to inexplicable pain: undeserved suffering prompts one to identify a wrongdoer. The "innocent," then, recognizing that his or her suffering is more than he or she has deserved, desires that the wrongdoer experience pain. The innocent believes that the wrongdoer "ought" to have suffering imposed on him or her in recompense for the existential wrong. The desire for justice then transforms the innocent into one who is guilty, wanting to impose pain on another sufferer. Thus the desire for justice, Marion argues, makes innocent people guilty of fault; no one is exonerated in the end, because none can suffer without seeking to be exonerated by leaving another responsible—none, that is, but Christ.[55]

Marion sees the sin recorded in Genesis 3 as most basically rendered in each participant's tendency to blame the next, and argues that the doctrine of original sin prevents Christians from repeating this pattern: "he who contests the doctrine of original sin, by arguing that he bears no responsibility for original sin, repeats, from the very fact of this argument, all the logic of evil (self-justification, refusal to take evil upon oneself so as to block its transmission, and so forth), and thus inscribes himself completely in that very sinfulness of which he claims to know nothing."[56] Marion thus transforms the doctrine of original sin

---

[53] Maxwell Johnson, *The Rites of Christian Initiation: Their Evolution and Interpretation* (Collegeville, MN: Liturgical Press, 2007), 194–98.

[54] See Clare Johnson, Ex Ore Infantium: *The Pre-rational Child as Subject of Sacramental Action* (PhD thesis, Notre Dame, 2004), 150–52, for a very different understanding of the prebaptismal anointing.

[55] Jean-Luc Marion, "Evil in Person," *Prolegomena to Charity* (New York: Fordham University Press, 2002), 1–30. For an exploration of the biblical terms that play a role in this argument, see J. P. M. Walsh, *The Mighty From Their Thrones* (Eugene, OR: Wipf and Stock, 2004).

[56] Marion, "Evil in Person," 10.

into a salvific teaching, arguing that the only true innocence consists of accepting an undeserved guilt.[57]

Although Marion does not explore the question of infant baptism in this essay, it seems that on this reading of original sin, the infant, by accepting in his or her body the mark of exorcism (the form of sinfulness, the label "original sin"), is conformed in the body to the body of Christ who suffered without laying claim to the innocence he merited, and thus broke the cycle of evil. The innocence of the infant, far from precluding his or her need for exorcism, makes his or her experience of exorcism (as an imputation of sin to an innocent) a perfect analogue of the one who was made sin for the sake of sinners (2 Cor 5:21). Thus the rite both recognizes and bestows the child's ultimate likeness to Christ in his salvific efficacy.

The baptismal formula, "N., I baptize you in the name of the Father, and of the Son, and of the Holy Spirit,"[58] has multiple resonances. Ritually, it is the site of the most fluid recognition of the child's identity; scripturally, too, it is washing "in water and the Holy Spirit" that alters the identity of a disciple of Christ. It is thus appropriate that this is also the most radical renaming of the child: the name of the child becomes the name of God, the Trinity. This points back to the profession of faith (RBC, 95), which specifies how the name of I AM comes to be known as a trinitarian name. This is, as suggested above, the most radical moment of prophetic recognition: the child is acknowledged as a manifestation of the mystery of God. Thus, this is likewise the moment at which the gift of the child's trinitarian identity is most fully expressed. What can be said about this identity?

The child's trinitarian identity is, first, the ground for participation in the trinitarian mystery of salvation. This means a filial love for God the Father modeled on that of the Son: that is, gratitude, obedience, and a kenotic commitment to the Father's will for the salvation of the world. It also means a radical freedom (perhaps Marion's "freedom to be free") for the capacity for these relationships: love for the Father, compassion with (a feeling along with, an ability to share the desires of) the Son,[59] commitment to the transformation of the world.

[57] Ibid., 10.
[58] *RBC*, 97.
[59] On "kind compassion," see Julian of Norwich, *Showings* (New York: Norton, 2005), 5 (chap. 2).

Curiously, this radical change is perhaps most fully manifest in the ritual dynamic at a moment that may be too pedestrian to attract any notice: the recitation of the Lord's Prayer. It is worth noting that this action points back to the trinitarian identity of the baptismal formula: *"In the name* of this child, *in the Spirit of our common sonship,* let us pray together in the words our Lord has given us."[60] At this moment the child's name comes to be parallel to the Spirit because it is the principle of the community's unity with one another and with God the Father. In other words, the whole trinitarian work of salvation is summed here and *attributed to the child.* Whereas before the community prayed for the child (as standing outside and facing him or her), now the community prays on the child's behalf (as able to speak in his or her voice); yet this very prayer reveals that it is because of this child that the community can (dare to) pray at all. The prayer shows how the child's new identity includes filial praise and petition of God the Father, emulation of Christ ("in the words our Lord has given us"), transformation of the world ("Thy kingdom come . . ."), freedom from sin, and the will to pass on that freedom to others ("Forgive us . . .").

To pray this prayer "in the name of this child" is, first, to assert in faith that the child is able to participate—indeed, is already participating—in these aspects of the trinitarian economy of salvation. The rite asserts this ability but does not defend it. Nor will this work attempt to do so; the child's ability to participate in Christ's saving ministry to the world is a mystery, except insofar as it is revealed—or revealed in its concealment—by the traditions of the church.[61]

Second, to pray is to assert that the child's trinitarian identity is the ground for the reformation of the trinitarian identity of the whole ecclesial community. The rite transforms the child's name by the invocation of the Trinity, and this change refers back to all the aspects of the child's name already emphasized by the practice of the rite: the child's relationship to his or her parents and their community, which is marked by the cross; the child's unique identity, which is nonetheless part of the universal church, living and dead; the freedom granted by participation in Christ's saving work and the indwelling of the Spirit. The baptismal formula invokes the trinitarian name as the

---

[60] *RBC,* 103.
[61] See Marianne Sawicki, *Seeing the Lord: Resurrection and Early Christian Practices* (Minneapolis: Fortress Press, 1994), chap. 2, on the importance of this mystery for the early church's preservation of Christ's sayings regarding children.

unique bond of all these. The act of washing in general both affirms and challenges cultural categorizations;[62] here, the baptismal action affirms the child's connection to the assembly while challenging the assumption that he or she is completely dependent on it. Renaming the infant with the trinitarian name creates a new authority structure: the infant's name is identified with the trinitarian name, which creates an equality between the infant and the other members of the assembly. The infant participates in the *virtus* of Christ who saves by embracing the identity of sinners, rather than the innocence he merits; he or she likewise becomes the site of the indwelling of the Spirit who is the freedom to participate in the trinitarian mysteries of love and creation. Thus baptism, as Thomas Aquinas says, delegates infants to the worship of God and the reception of the sacraments.[63]

It is the infant's ritual participation, the enactment on the infant's body, of these saving mysteries that allows the infant to become the body of Christ and temple of the Spirit. This in turn permits the assembly to recognize the infant prophetically as body of Christ, which is an exercise of the church's role within the trinitarian plan of salvation by recognizing Jesus' body (historical, risen, and sacramental) as the Messiah of God. The infant is the catalyst that renews the church community to act as Body of Christ, temple of the Spirit. The infant gives a gift to the community: the community bestows Christian identity on the infant, but the infant's initiation likewise bestows Christian identity on the community.[64] This fact, in turn, completes the infant's Christian identity: he or she is able to participate in the trinitarian economy by assisting in the constitution of the ecclesial Body of Christ.

Section 5.3
The Trinitarian Bestowal of the Infant's Identity

This project began with a concern about the traditional Western emphasis on the Word's place in the economy of salvation and a relative amnesia in the West about the role of the Spirit.[65] Sacramental theology, as is well known, has been no exception to this Western tendency;

---

[62] See Mary Douglas, *Purity and Danger* (New York: Routledge, 1984), 36–41.

[63] Thomas Aquinas, ST III, q. 63, a. 1.

[64] Cf. the initiand's renewal of the Christian assembly as expressed toward adults in the popular piety noted in Harmless, "Baptism," 86: "Those emerging from the font were thought to possess miraculous powers of healing and intercession."

[65] See chapter 1.

indeed, the medieval concern for validity (leading to an isolated emphasis on the minimal correct words and actions) apparently excludes the Spirit from both the text and interpretation of sacramental practice.

For example, Louis-Marie Chauvet critiques what he calls the "incarnational" focus of traditional sacramental theology and proposes instead a "paschal" focus that concentrates on the passion of Christ. This approach is intended to provide a platform for sacramentality that concentrates on the transformative power of narrative—specifically the narrative of Christ's suffering and victory over death—rather than on the "automatic" power of instrumental causality. In this way Chauvet intends to preserve the subjective and human aspects of sacramental efficacy even by his choice of christological vistas.[66]

Although this narrative Christology does help to reframe the sacramental account of the mystery of salvation, a pneumatically focused christological explanation would be even more helpful.[67] In the previous two sections the role of the Holy Spirit in the constitution of the community and of the baptizand as Christ's body were explored. In each case the Holy Spirit could be seen as a kind of sculpting, imperceptibly anointing the boundaries of the body (physical, ecclesial) in order to conform it to that of Jesus. The baptism of the infant suggests a similar role for the Spirit in the historical manifestation of the Word. The shape of Christ's body is not merely cruciform: the most powerful "body image" phenomena of baptism (washing, anointing, breathing) suggest three moments of Christ's life as formative for Christian identity—birth, baptism, and passion.

Both biological and cultural factors of birth are suggested by the phenomena of infant baptism. The first breath is the sign that a human being has traversed the first period of endangerment (in the womb) and the first great boundary to take over a significant new responsibility: providing oxygen to the body. The first bathing and first anointing are the sign of entry into the cultural world (an unwashed infant has been rejected by its family and is in danger of being depersonalized; cf. Ezek

---

[66] Chauvet, *Symbol and Sacrament*, 476–86. Chauvet's argument here depends on liturgiological evidence, which cannot be addressed here for reasons of brevity. See, e.g., Maxwell Johnson, *Images of Baptism* (Chicago: Liturgy Training Publications, 2001), for an alternate interpretation of the evidence with respect to initiation. As is clear from the structure of Chauvet's work, the choice of a paschal model is actually determined by the theological project.

[67] See, for example, Edward Kilmartin's trinitarian model in *Christian Liturgy I: Theology* (Franklin, WI: Sheed and Ward, 1988).

16). Christ's birth is the beginning of the voluntary-involuntary body discipline of breathing; the gifts of the magi suggest anointing, although no account of Jesus' bathing is recorded in the infancy narratives.[68] The baptism of Jesus is, of course, marked by washing. In the East it was also associated with anointing because of early Syrian accounts that had oil or fire in the baptismal water.[69] Jesus' baptism, like any baptism, interrupted the breath and its body discipline. Jesus' death, similarly, is marked by breath—a wordless cry. The "last breath" is, like the first, the mark of the boundaries of personhood. The passion is foretold by an anointing in all four gospels (Mark 14 and parallels; John 12) and closes with a flow of water from Christ's side (John 19). There are thus many parallels between the passion narratives and those recounting Christ's birth and baptism.

These moments in Christ's life, as suggested above, are also pneumatic moments. The Gospel According to Luke attributes Christ's incarnation to the "shadow" of the Holy Spirit (Luke 1:35). The infancy of Jesus is a paradox: how can the incarnate Word be unable to speak? Since the Spirit's manifestation always provides a witness to the relationship between Father and Son, the involvement of the Spirit in the incarnation (annunciation) and its symbols in human birth (first breath, first bathing) show how Jesus is Son of the Father even in his infancy.[70] Similarly, the passion shows Jesus as Son of the Father in his utter erasure: the wordless cry and Jesus' reproach of God for forsaking him are, in their different ways, still utterances of the Word Incarnate. The first breath and the last breath, then, are moments when the Word *fails to speak*, when not only human but divine language seems to fall short of expressing the reality of the divine love.

In the baptismal rite, the Holy Spirit circumscribes the body of the baptizand and of the community, creating bridges out of the boundaries between infants and adults, between the uninitiated and the initiates, between God and the human community. In the Trinity, too, the "filial

---

[68] The baptismal narratives were in a sense the "original" infancy narratives, giving the early faith's understanding of Jesus' origins as Messiah. Since these were already part of the origin story when the infancy narratives were added, no emphasis on washing during Christ's infancy was necessary. See Raymond Brown, *Introduction to the New Testament* (New York: Doubleday, 1997).

[69] See Maxwell Johnson, *Rites*, 57.

[70] Balthasar has provided an interesting theological account of the christological importance of Christ's infancy in *Unless You Become Like This Child*.

distance"[71] or the radical reciprocality between Father and Son[72] is accomplished through the Holy Spirit, who accomplishes the manifestation of the Father in his Word even when the Word is inarticulate. The inarticulate Word, then, is rendered communicative by the transformative action of the Spirit. When the Word enters human life, it does so by, in a sense, breaking it: the boundaries of humanity (the temporal ones of birth and death, the phenomenal ones of pain and transcendence) are not the same as they were before. Death is conquered, as the patristic exegetes argue, simply by becoming *God's death*.[73] This is possible because in the "separations"[74] effected by the history of salvation, as in the eternal filiation of the Son, the Spirit fills, or is, the intervening "space" and thus assumes distance into the divine life. The Spirit consecrates the experience of otherness. Because of the Spirit, then, the divine life is experienced in the traces of human existence;[75] or rather, the traces of human existence often result from the Spirit fragmenting human life with the divine entry.

In the economy, then, certain of the fragments resulting from Jesus Christ's entry into the world and its fracture during the passion and resurrection bear a special importance. These fully human celebrations, "made by human hands" from Christ's actions and the posthumous recognition of him as the incarnate Word and Savior, became specially privileged sites for the Spirit's continued breaking of the world and transformation of its distance into filiation—human filiation on the model of the filiation of the Son as a human being. Over time, certain celebrations were recognized as such privileged sites for transformation that they were considered to operate *ex opere operato*.

The cultural efficacy of ritual must not be confused with the *ex opere operato* efficacy of the Christian sacraments (i.e., with the working of grace). The rites operate *ex opere operato* only by the mission of the Holy Spirit. On the human side, however, cultural efficacy is required

---

[71] Marion, "Evil in Person," 24.

[72] Balthasar, *TD5*, 82ff.

[73] "The whole earth keeps silence because the King is asleep. The earth trembled and is still because God has fallen asleep in the flesh and he has raised up all who have slept ever since the world began. God has died in the flesh and hell trembles with fear" ("Ancient homily on Holy Saturday," translation in *Christian Prayer: The Liturgy of the Hours* [Totowa, NJ: Catholic Book Publishing Company, 1976, 1987]).

[74] Embodiment, death.

[75] Cf. Robyn Horner, *Rethinking God as Gift: Marion, Derrida, and the Limits of Phenomenology* (New York: Fordham University, 2001), 60–75.

in order to enter into the trinitarian manifestation in history. At the same time, this cultural efficacy is given a salvific significance by the intervention of the Holy Spirit, which is only known through faith. In the sacramental rites God acts "for us" but also "(through us) for the world," because sacramental grace given to one member is given to make the whole church Body, and the church is made Body so that the world can be reconciled with God. In the trinitarian sacramental economy, the Holy Spirit is then the one that breaks into cultural forms, phenomenal and significative, to take them into the reality of salvation. In other words, the sacraments rarely symbolize the Holy Spirit, but the Spirit acts in them to symbolize Christ.

The phrase *ex opere operato* has often been glossed as *ex opere operato Dei* or *Christi*,[76] but perhaps it should be *ex opere operato Spiritu*. According to God's will, the Holy Spirit takes the *opus operatum* (work of the church) up into the work of Christ the Redeemer. The work of the church then becomes the work of God by the gift of the Holy Spirit, which *re-creates* the sacramental identity between Christ and his ecclesial body.[77] The Spirit is then always a principle both of grace and of worship, the anabatic and katabatic dimensions of sacramentality. Nor is the Son inactive in this principle, for he actively cooperates in his dwelling in the body in the baptizand and his or her community. The power of the Holy Spirit, in short, allows the power of Christ to become manifest in the cultural construction of the community and its members, so that the cultural efficacy of the sacramental practice can be part of salvation history. The impetus to worship and the acceptance of grace are real human acts, but done "in the Holy Spirit": that is, within the space of filiation the Holy Spirit opens to human beings in the wake of Jesus Christ's mission.

The sacraments thus provide a particularly compelling example of the influence of the Holy Spirit in the world. This influence is always subtle and hard to distinguish from the workings of human nature, because the Holy Spirit's mission occurs in the depth of the human personality.[78] The Spirit's name designates an aspect of human personhood, so it is difficult to distinguish between the promptings of the human spirit and of the Spirit of God.[79] Similarly, it is difficult to dis-

---

[76] See Edward Schillebeeckx, *Christ the Sacrament of the Encounter With God* (Franklin, WI: Sheed and Ward, 1999), 71, 82–89.

[77] Ibid., 73.

[78] Cf. Rahner, *Trinity* (New York: Crossroad, 1999), 88–99.

[79] For example, both can be called "inspiration."

tinguish between human ritualizations and the effects of God's Spirit. Over time the need for a consensus recognition of the Spirit's work has led the church to acknowledge the saints in the one case and the sacraments in the other. This discernment is slow, partial, and made on a case-by-case basis. The Spirit is the principle of distance; its very procession is as a gap between the Origin and the Other.[80] In the human realm Spirit is characterized by discontinuity and paradox; phenomena that reveal its passing are marked by fluidity and unpredictability. No wonder its work is hidden so well that the Western theological tradition (excluding the mystical strands) practically forgot its existence.

There is more: the Spirit's mission succeeds precisely at the point that her influence is forgotten. In history, the presence of the Word in the world is fully realized at the point where the break between the divine and human realms becomes invisible, where God and humanity are truly reconciled in the person of Jesus Christ due to the "overshadowing" of Mary by the Holy Spirit. Similarly, the purpose of the passion and resurrection comes about when Jesus' humanity becomes invisible—going from unrecognizably present to recognized to unseen (see Luke 24; Acts 1)—because at that point Christ's relationship to the Father *comes to be shared in the visible ecclesial body.* Likewise, the salvation of an individual is complete only if his or her existence is truly pervaded by the love of God, so that the indwelling of the Spirit is a transparent phenomenon of which the subject is scarcely made aware. In all these cases the Holy Spirit is hidden because she does not add or take away phenomena but rather transforms them: the saint does not perceive himself or herself as holy, but his or her infinite distance from God is transformed by the Holy Spirit into holiness.[81]

All this raises the question of the Holy Spirit's special role in sacramentality. If the anamnesis ("remembering") is the proper revelation of the Son in the sacramental rites, the Spirit's role seems to be characterized, rather, as a forgetting. More precisely, the role of the Spirit is, in calling the memory of Christ forward and making it present in

[80] In the remainder of this work, I use *his, her,* and *its* interchangeably for the Spirit's work. Both the theological tradition and this work imply that the Spirit's revelation to humanity has been less marked by gendered human assumptions than the Father's and the Son's. None of the English pronouns is satisfactory, but I do not mean to imply either that the Spirit is gendered (male or female) or that he/she/it is less personal than Father and Son.

[81] Thus the saints always consider themselves as sinners but are usually considered holy by their contemporaries.

the bodies of the assembly, to erase the church's memory of the Spirit himself. They are called to live in the Spirit, not to watch his work. The Spirit has fully formed the bodies of the baptized into the Body of Christ when they can no longer remember an identity that is divorced from him (Gal 2:19-20).

In terms of the economy of salvation, how do we go from anamnesis to amnesia? One can see this as a reversal of the original human sin. The first sin of human beings is in an attempt to usurp the place of God as origin and end of all things; that is, human beings wished to be the Unoriginate Father to themselves and to all else. It was natural (*convenientia*, or "fitting") that such a perversion of the human role must be reversed by the Son, whose personhood is constituted by infinite reverence for and obedience to the Father, and that this reversal would take the form of self-emptying for the sake of the Father and his creation. This self-emptying reached its climax when the Son allowed himself to be handed over to sinners to endure their will. He thus acceded to the human demand to be Father; he handed himself over to human beings as if they were Father; he gave himself to the human race as to the Father. In so doing, he irrevocably gave to humanity the gift of the Holy Spirit, which is the gift and bond of love between Father and Son, thus taking the pattern of sin up into the trinitarian life. In future, then, the space of sin can be transformed by the ministry of the Spirit into filial love: repentance and reconciliation.

In infant baptism, then, this reversal is enacted on the infant's body. The contours of the infant's body are inscribed with the trinitarian gift of love, creating a dynamic of reversal in which the infant gives the community its identity as Body of Christ. In this process, the phenomena of Christianity are opened to allow the infant to begin creating a world with them in an embodied identity, forming the basis for his or her symbolic capacity. In so doing, the infant is enabled to act with confidence in conformity with the inarticulate Word, who was able to manifest the Father's love for the world precisely through the failure of language. The child's later development will be grounded in this identity, but infant baptism is not validated by the baptizand's potential for cognizant faith but by the action of the Holy Spirit.

Infant baptism is a theo-drama: a voluntary cooperation between the Trinity and human persons that essentially, dramatically, and irreversibly changes the course of history. The body of an infant is already a body formed by culture in a world where cultural formation often, if not always, implies power, oppression, suffering, and isolation. Infants are not only subject to pain but are already implicated in a cycle that inflicts pain and loss on others—a cycle in which gratuitous gift is rendered impossible. In this cycle, even the desire to do justice (as in Marion's analysis) leads to vengeance and thus to self-indictment. The only escape is to be freed from the desire to be Unoriginate Origin, Lawgiver, and Judge—but human causality cannot effect this freedom, no more than it can free people from the fact of culture. The very desire to be freed from culture, as Chauvet sees, becomes another instance of the desire to be one's own immortal lawgiver. In this ultimate paradox, the work of God (the Spirit) breaks into the world in the rite of baptism to write God's *oikonomia*: God grants humanity's desire to become, impossibly, the ones in charge, handing over his Son on the cross, the Spirit in the Church. This move, though, suspends the cycle of human economy, give-and-take, equal exchange, in favor of the break of God's *oikonomia*: when the Word dies on the cross, when the church invokes the name of Jesus, when the celebrant invokes the Spirit over the waters, control breaks out of its bounds, and the ones in control are revealed to be the bodies who are out of control. The crucifiers and the Crucified One, the assembly and the initiand reorganize the power structures: the one they killed kills death; the one they initiate initiates them into the work of God.

The work of God, then, is not only extended and reenacted by the sacrament but also renewed, because the Body of Christ can only be that body by continually reentering the break in the cycle of the world. Initiating infants, the church cannot be sure, by human wisdom, that it is doing the will of God—but by initiating the church takes its only possible chance, has its only hope of doing that will, of becoming the Body of Christ and inhabiting the space of the Spirit.

Chapter Six

The Spirit
Unfolding the Gift

C an liturgy be a source for theology? Catherine Mowry LaCugna's answer is a recognition that both liturgy and theology end in doxology, and so both coexist seamlessly in the work of any particular scholar and in the life of the whole church. She discounts from the outset, however, the possibility that any particular liturgical celebration could be the revelatory medium for new ways of seeing theological truths, limiting the sense of liturgy as source to "the fact *that* the Church worships and does so according to particular patterns."[1] LaCugna's insights are accurate and welcome, but it seems to me that there is more: the *oikonomia* does not take place in the abstract, but here; and humanity is not given the fact that the church worships according to particular patterns, but this, that, and those rites, and the responsibility to recognize in them the gifts of God.

I hope this study has made the case that a look at the nuts and bolts of the sacramental economy can be theologically fruitful, under certain conditions. First, the ritual approach of efficacious engagement should be complemented by a comprehensive historical understanding of the rite's development. This ensures that the ritual studies method is grounded in the tradition: for example, if the ritual analysis had indicated that the most important points of the rite were the sign of the cross and the ephphetha, I would be forced to conclude that I had made a mistake, interpreting the rite according to my own perceptions rather than in its proper cultural context. Since the ritual approach agrees with the tradition, however, in designating the washing and

---

[1] Catherine Mowry LaCugna, "Can Liturgy Ever Again Become a Source for Theology?" *Studia Liturgica* 19, no. 1 (1989): 1–2.

anointings the most important acts, the theological work can proceed with confidence.[2]

Second, the theological efficacy of the rite should not be attributed to or confused with the ritual efficacy that is the human result of human actions. To do this is to overlook the work of the Holy Spirit within the rite, which includes the risk of a sacramental Pelagianism. Infants do not enter into the trinitarian life because we say so, nor because they are innocent enough to merit it, nor because their parents are good Christians, nor because they have the potential to one day be full members of the church. We believe they enter the trinitarian life because God wants to save them, we act on that faith, and we believe that through our action both they and we are remade in the image of the triune God. At the same time, the theological efficacy must be traced to the ritual efficacy of the sacraments (*ex opere operato*), because it is in being immersed in—even disappearing into—human culture that the Holy Spirit accomplishes its mission.

The metaphor of "folding" the human experience of ritual is an enormously productive one for exploring the theological realm where the Holy Spirit is busy making Jesus Christ manifest in human culture. First of all, it is the Holy Spirit that folds human experience so that the experience of the finite can enclose the divine; second, it is the Holy Spirit that unfolds this experience so that human beings can glimpse the divine in their finite experience. I can do no more than gesture toward the implications of this folding metaphor in three areas: the symbolic tradition of sacramental efficacy in Thomas Aquinas's *Summa Theologiae* and in Karl Rahner's seminal article "The Theology of the Symbol,"[3] the question of the gift and of God's self-giving in trinitarian theology, and what a pneumatological rendering of eucharistic worship might look like.

Section 6.1
Symbol and Practice

In the *Sentences*, the basic medieval theology textbook, Peter Lombard quotes the common adage that the sacraments *efficiunt quod*

---

[2] The profession of faith is another very important element, which played a small role in the ritual analysis because of my focus on preliterate participants.

[3] Karl Rahner, "The Theology of the Symbol," in *More Recent Writings*, Theological Investigations, vol. IV (Baltimore: Helicon Press, 1966), 221–52.

figurant.[4] This provided the foundation for the sacramental signification
to be taken very seriously by Thomas Aquinas, but during the following
centuries the importance of this adage was often overlooked, so that
the link between the signification and causality of the sacraments was
forced or forgotten altogether. Karl Rahner reintroduced the connection with his commitment to a theological anthropology of spirituality.
His essay "Theology of the Symbol" reconfigured the concept of symbol, rather than that of cause, in such a way that symbolism, properly
understood, included a notion of causality. In this section Thomas's
and Rahner's work on sacramental signification and efficacy will be
compared to the pneumatological pole introduced in chapter 5.

Thomas Aquinas

Thomas Aquinas is bound by the tradition to connect the idea
of signification (Augustine's) with that of causality or grace in the
sacraments (also Augustine's). Interestingly, Thomas relies heavily on
baptism in constructing his model of the sacraments in general.[5] In
fact, baptism seems to be the paradigmatic sacrament: when Thomas
introduces the idea of sacramental causality, he chooses one quote to
provide the traditional understanding of sacraments *in genere*. "On the
contrary, Augustine says (Tract. lxxx in Joan.) that the baptismal water
'touches the body and cleanses the heart.' But the heart is not cleansed
save through grace. Therefore it causes grace: and for like reason so do
the other sacraments of the Church."[6] In his reply, too, Thomas takes
baptism as paradigmatic: "For it is evident that through the sacraments
of the New Law man is incorporated with Christ: thus the Apostle
says of Baptism (Gal. 3:27): 'As many of you as have been baptized
in Christ have put on Christ.' And man is made a member of Christ
through grace alone."[7]

Baptism, therefore, plays a crucial role in Thomas's project to
connect sacramental signification to sacramental causality. This is, of
course, related to his conviction that the efficacy of the sacraments
comes from their salvific purpose as "extensions" of the incarnation.

---

[4] That is, the sacraments "effect what they signify." The Latin can also be translated,
"effect because they signify," and this ambiguity has been central to its interpretation.
Peter Lombard, IV *Sent.* 4,1; quoted in Thomas Aquinas, ST III, q. 62, a. 1, ad. 1.

[5] See Thomas Aquinas, ST III, q. 60–65.

[6] ST III, q. 62, a. 1 *contra*.

[7] Ibid., *respondeo*.

Chauvet critiques traditional sacramental theology for its focus on causality, a reification of grace, the attribution of sacrament to Christ to the detriment of the Spirit's role,[8] and the focus on the hypostatic union rather than the paschal mystery.[9] When Thomas introduces his argument distinguishing different efficient causes, he refers back to the sign character of sacraments: "An instrumental cause, if manifest, can be called a sign of a hidden effect, for this reason, that it is not merely a cause but also in a measure an effect in so far as it is moved by the principal agent. And in this sense the sacraments of the New Law are both cause and signs. Hence, too, is it that, to use the common expression, 'they effect what they signify.'"[10] In other words, the sacraments are signs of salvation because they express God's will to save humanity. This clarifies Thomas's somewhat obscure general definition: "A sacrament properly so called is that which is the sign of some sacred thing pertaining to man; so that properly speaking a sacrament, as considered by us now, is defined as being the 'sign of a holy thing so far as it makes men holy.'"[11] This specificity is necessary because of Thomas's cosmic vision: every created thing is, in a sense, a sign of God (in part because God is cause of all created things), but not every created thing is a sacrament.

The signifying function of the sacraments refers to salvation history, especially to the passion of Christ. The three things signified by the sacraments are "the very cause of our sanctification, which is Christ's passion; the form of our sanctification, which is grace and the virtues; and the ultimate end of our sanctification, which is eternal life."[12] All these things are paschal-centered, because the passion of Christ was, according to Thomas, necessary for the salvation of humanity according to God's will. Not that God was compelled to enact the passion, but it was perfectly suited to the needs of human beings and therefore it was "fitting" that God save humanity thus.[13] On the other hand, human beings also needed to be connected to the passion of Christ so that its causality (merit, satisfaction, redemption) could be transferred to

---

[8] Louis-Marie Chauvet, *Symbol and Sacrament* (Collegeville, MN: Liturgical Press, 1995), e.g., 467.

[9] Ibid., 476.

[10] Thomas Aquinas, ST III, q. 62, a. 1, ad. 1.

[11] ST III, q. 60, a. 2.

[12] ST III, q. 60, a. 3.

[13] ST III, q. 46, a. 1. See 5.3.

them,[14] or, equivalently, so that its sign quality could function for their conversion.[15]

Thomas argues that the instrumental causality of a sacrament "belongs to it in respect of its proper form," but this causal power is not divorced from its sign function.[16] Thus baptism "produc[es] effects upon the soul in the power of God," but effects on the soul are recognized as cultural realities that operate in a properly human manner, including the symbolic realm, for "it is part of man's nature to acquire knowledge of the intelligible from the sensible."[17] Even Thomas's consideration of the validity of the sacraments, and thus of their "power" to convey ecclesial and spiritual effects, is based in cultural comprehension. The sacrament "touches the body through the sensible element, and the soul through faith in the words" and the words themselves are determined by the particularity of the language used in the rite and its use in ordinary life by native speakers.[18] Thus "the words produce an effect according to the sense which they convey."[19] The signification and causality of the sacraments have the same origin (God's will for the salvation of humanity) and outcome (union of the ecclesial body with Christ).

Unfortunately, Thomas does not explicitly attribute this union to the Holy Spirit in his sacramental treatise. On the other hand, his pneumatology does facilitate a rereading of the unity of sacramental signification and causality according to the Holy Spirit.[20] Christology and pneumatology are not mutually exclusive in the *Summa Theologiae*. In fact, they are mutually determinative. In the ecclesial realm, both operate in Christ's grace as head of the Church: "The head has a manifest pre-eminence over the other exterior members; but the heart has a certain hidden influence. And hence the Holy Ghost is likened to the heart, since He invisibly quickens and unifies the Church; but Christ is likened to the Head in His visible nature in which man is set over man."[21] Pneumatology is not absolutely absent even from Thomas's

---

[14] ST III, q. 48, a. 6, ad. 2.

[15] "Christ's Passion is the proper cause of the forgiveness of sins in three ways. First of all, by way of exciting our charity . . ." (ST III, q. 49, a. 1).

[16] ST III, q. 62, a. 1, ad. 2.

[17] ST III, q. 62, a. 1, ad. 2; III, q. 60, a. 4.

[18] ST III, q. 60, a. 6; III, q. 60, a. 7, ad. 2 and ad. 3.

[19] ST III, q. 60, a. 8.

[20] See, e.g., Chauvet's discussion in *Symbol and Sacrament*, 456–63.

[21] Thomas Aquinas, ST III, q. 8, a. 1, ad. 3.

explicit discussion of the christological principle in the church. Similarly, in the case of the sacraments, the christological principle implies a pneumatological pole, even though this is rarely articulated in the treatise on sacraments: "As in the person of Christ the humanity causes our salvation by grace, the Divine power being the principal agent, so likewise in the sacraments of the New Law, which are derived from Christ, grace is *instrumentally* caused by the sacraments, and *principally by the power of the Holy Ghost* working in the sacraments, according to Jn. 3:5: 'Unless a man be born again of water and the Holy Ghost he cannot enter into the kingdom of God.'"[22] The parallelism of this quote appropriates to the Holy Spirit the power of instigating the instrumental power of the sacramental rites. In other words, though Thomas lamentably did not explicitly draw out a pneumatology of the sacraments, the language of instrumental causality should not limit the efficacy of sacrament to the humanity of Christ. Rather, when the sacraments symbolize and effect grace, they do so according to the whole working of the Trinity; the gift of grace is always appropriated to the Holy Spirit. In particular, in baptism, the paradigmatic sacrament, the Holy Spirit is the principal agent of Christ's assumption of the rite as instrument.

Moreover, there is good reason in Thomas's theology why the gifts of the Holy Spirit seem to disappear, either into the humanity of Christ or into that of those who receive the sacraments, for the Holy Spirit is "Gift," and the Spirit given rests in the spirit of those who receive it: "Before a gift is given, it belongs only to the giver; but when it is given, it is his to whom it is given. Therefore, because 'Gift' does not import the actual giving, it cannot be called a gift of man, but the Gift of God giving. When, however, it has been given, then it is the spirit of man, or a gift bestowed on man."[23] For Thomas, too, the Holy Spirit's mission often remains "hidden" because that mission requires that it be camouflaged by the human person's own inner life. In fact, Thomas even comments explicitly on the spiritual quality of bodily exercise in the sacramental context: "Exercise taken in the use of the

---

[22] ST I–II, q. 112, a. 1, ad. 2. Emphasis added.
[23] ST I, q. 38, a. 2, ad. 3. This casts doubt on Chauvet's assertion (in *Symbol and Sacrament*, 462) that because "spiritual" can be used interchangeably with "intelligible" in the ST's treatise on sacraments, it does not refer to the Holy Spirit. I believe "intelligible" here should be taken in the sense of "significative," in continuity with the observations made about the Holy Spirit and signification above.

sacraments is not merely bodily, but to a certain extent spiritual, viz. in its signification and in its causality."[24] It is the unicity of signification and causality that, according to the *Summa*, allows the physical practice and the spiritual transformation of the sacraments to be linked.

This partial defense is not meant to suggest that Thomas's sacramental understanding of signification and causality is as pneumatologically driven as one might wish. In particular, the question of infant baptism was puzzling to him in the same way it is for modern proponents of a linguistic-symbolic model of sacrament. In his consideration of baptism, he asks in the objection why a sensible form such as the baptismal formula should be addressed to an infant, concluding, "the words which are uttered in the sacramental forms, are said not merely for the purpose of signification, but also for the purpose of efficiency, inasmuch as they derive efficacy from that Word, by Whom 'all things were made.'"[25] In other words, when pressed by the problem of infant baptism, Thomas retreats from pneumatology or signification as the means of efficacy into a "brute force" solution: the power of the creating Word. In the model I have proposed, on the other hand, the infant state brings the work of the Holy Spirit into a special relief.

Karl Rahner

In "The Theology of the Symbol," Karl Rahner transposes the question of efficacy and signification from the strictly sacramental realm to the broader category of ontology. According to his exploration in this work, symbolic function is characteristic of all being. Moreover, Rahner develops an ontology of the symbol from the "peak" of all potential reality: the Trinity. His argument treats the self-communication of the Trinity as the central point of symbolic behavior, from which all other kinds of symbolic function should be defined.[26]

The trinitarian foundation of symbolic ontology is implicit in the early part of the article, where the interplay of unity and multiplicity reveals it: "the 'one' develops, the plural stems from an original 'one,' in a relationship of origin and consequence; the original unity, which

---

[24] *Sed exercitatio per usum sacramentorum non est pure corporalis, sed quodammodo est spiritualis, scilicet per significationem et causalitatem* (Thomas Aquinas, ST III, q. 61, a. 1, ad. 1).

[25] ST III, q. 66, a. 5, ad. 3.

[26] Rahner, "Theology of the Symbol."

also forms the unity which unites the plural, maintains itself while resolving itself and 'dis-closing' itself into a plurality in order to find itself precisely there."[27] It becomes explicit later, when Rahner appeals to the trinitarian dynamic to explain the fundamental quality of symbol within Christian theology: "the Father is himself by the very fact that he opposes to himself the image which is of the same essence as himself, as the person who is other than himself; and so he possesses himself. But this means that the Logos is the 'symbol' of the Father, in the very sense which we have given the word: the inward symbol which remains distinct from what is symbolized, which is constituted by what is symbolized, where what is symbolized expresses itself and possesses itself."[28] Similarly, the incarnation becomes the extension of this principle "outward," as it were, beyond the Godhead and into the realm of human apprehension, so that, in Rahner's enduring principle, "the humanity [of Jesus] is the self-disclosure of the Logos itself, so that when God, expressing himself, exteriorizes himself, that very thing appears which we call the humanity of the Logos."[29] Thus the depth of symbolic self-communication reaches out from the Trinity as its source and center and "really arrives at" humanity in its concrete existence.[30]

On the other hand, Rahner intends his theology to provide a real symbolic ontology, such that "each being—in as much as it has and realizes being—is itself primarily 'symbolic.' It expresses itself and possesses itself by doing so. It gives itself away from itself into the 'other,' and there finds itself."[31] The ontological construction of reality, inasmuch as it is "symbolic reality," is permeated with the trinitarian dynamic. This is explicitly so with regard to the Word, of whom Rahner says, "the natural depth of the symbolic reality of all things—which is of itself restricted to the world or has a merely natural transcendence towards God—has now [in the incarnation] in ontological reality received an infinite extension by the fact that this reality has become also a determination of the Logos himself or of his milieu."[32] This must likewise be true of the Holy Spirit, by whom the Word became incarnate. If the Word as image of the Father is the foundation for

[27] Ibid., 227.
[28] Ibid., 236.
[29] Ibid., 239.
[30] Rahner, *The Trinity* (New York: Crossroad, 1999), 89.
[31] Rahner, "Theology of the Symbol," 229–30.
[32] Ibid., 239.

symbolic ontology, there must likewise be a pneumatic principle to account for the "being-there" accomplished by the symbolic function. It seems that the Western desire to establish the difference between the Persons by priority (i.e., the Son proceeds from the Father, so the Spirit must proceed from both Father and Son) motivated a selective forgetting of the Spirit's role as principle of the incarnation.[33] This led to a tendency to ignore the special mode of being of the Spirit and to miss her role in the sacramental life of the church.

As in Thomas Aquinas, who functions as a model, in Rahner's essay this pneumatological principle remains hidden, but there is a proto-pneumatology in his symbolic ontology. There is a resemblance in principle between the natural order of existence and the spiritual order, which is paralleled by use of the word "spirit" to name a realm of reality, an aspect of human personhood, and a Person of the Trinity.[34] One can connect this "natural depth" of symbolism, this "merely natural transcendence towards God," with the world-integrated aspect of the mission of the Holy Spirit. Is it because of the Holy Spirit's constitution of the world (Ps 104:30) that "all things possess, even in their quality of symbol, an unfathomable depth"?[35]

The Spirit emerges in greater relief in Rahner's discussion of the human body as symbol. "The body is the symbol of the soul, in as much as it is formed as the self-realization of the soul, though it is not adequately this, and the soul renders itself present and makes its 'appearance' in the body which is distinct from it."[36] This means that every act of the human person is to be attributed to the soul: "In every human expression, mimetic, phonetic etc. in nature, the whole [person] is somehow present and expressing himself [or herself], though the expressive form is confined to start with to one portion of the body."[37] Moreover, the body itself in its spatio-temporal existence bears the same relationship to the soul as these expressions do to the human person, so that "each part [of the body] bears . . . within itself the symbolic force and function of the whole."[38] The existence of the body is the soul's "taking form," and similarly, the existence of

---

[33] Augustine, The Trinity, e.g., bk. 5, chap. 14.
[34] See also Rahner, "On the Concept of Mystery in Catholic Theology," *More Recent Writings*, Theological Investigations, vol. IV (Baltimore: Helicon Press, 1966), 221–52.
[35] Rahner, "Theology of the Symbol," 239.
[36] Ibid., 247.
[37] Ibid., 248.
[38] Ibid., 249.

the embodied rituals of the church is God's grace "taking form": "As God's work of grace on man is accomplished (incarnates itself), it enters the spatio-temporal historicity of man as sacrament, and as it does so, it becomes active with regard to man, it constitutes itself. . . . the sacrament is precisely 'cause' of grace, in so far as it is its 'sign' and . . . the grace—seen as coming from God—is the cause of the sign, bringing it about and so alone making itself present."[39] Rahner follows Thomas in making the cultural existence of sacraments the effect (and thus, according to Aristotelian logic, a sign) of God's gracious will to save humanity. It is not hard, in this respect, to see the taking-of-form in the sacraments as the "embodiment"—that is, the act of coming to be in the world—of grace, or of the Holy Spirit. As the Holy Spirit is the principle of the incarnation and of sacramentality, perhaps he is also the principle of spatio-temporal existence of all things. If so, then the symbolic reality, the union of the essence of the thing with its "determinate quantity" or "species"—"which today we would call the given, concrete spatio-temporality, or spatio-temporal figure"—is the work of the Holy Spirit, binding the substance of the thing to its "given, concrete spatio-temporality."[40]

There are three fissures for this idea in Rahner's article, all related to the failures of symbolic function, or, perhaps more properly, derivative forms of it. First, Rahner hints at the human potential to degrade or empty the ontology of symbolism: "Every God-given reality, where it has not been degraded to a purely human tool and to merely utilitarian purposes, states much more than itself."[41] This is problematic, in that an ontology of symbolism implies that a created thing only exists insofar as it functions symbolically (and vice versa); surely the utilitarian use of created things does not cause them to cease existing. Moreover, sacramental rites and things often seem to symbolize precisely *in* their function as utilitarian acts (thus: washing, eating, "the collection" of donations). A second problem is Rahner's treatment of the derivative (ordinary) understanding of symbol, that is, "the concept of symbol where the symbol and the thing symbolized are only extrinsically ordained to one another."[42] Again, no doubt this is a very shallow definition of symbol,

---

[39] Ibid., 242. Rahner's argument here is clearly inspired by ST III, q. 62, a. 1, ad. 1.
[40] Rahner, "Theology of the Symbol," 233. This obviously carries potential implications for the theology of eucharistic presence.
[41] Ibid., 239.
[42] Ibid., 251.

but surely a full ontology of the symbol must account for this too? Yet if symbolic function is to be fully located in an "outpouring" of the thing itself into its spatio-temporal form, it is difficult to account for these "derivative" (or conventional) signs.[43] The final problem comes not in Rahner's article but emerges from the postmodern context of contemporary culture: what happens when symbols are surfaces that endlessly refer to one another, with no true "meaning" besides their own powers of association?[44]

All these questions are linked, and there is a possible answer in the light of the pneumatological interpretation here being proposed for Rahner's symbolic ontology. Rahner suggests that the parts of the body, while all informed by the soul, differ in "their power of expression, their degree of belonging to the soul, their openness to the soul."[45] If one attributes the embodiment of essence in existence (the in-formation of a reality or the cause of symbolic function strictly speaking, according to Rahner) to the Holy Spirit, which is suggested by the results of the case study in chapters 4 and 5, one can conclude that like the parts of the body, the existent beings in creation participate in the symbolic functioning of reality differently. Some things are the natural symbols of their own essence, as the human body is of human being; others are linked only by the arbitrary (free) connection of spirit. Some of these latter are due to the ingenuity of human spirit, which is indebted to the Holy Spirit but acts autonomously in the order of creation: these are cultural signs. Others are due directly to the trinitarian economy of salvation, and their signification and manifestation of a deeper reality are the work of the Holy Spirit. Most, though perhaps not all, of these latter also participate in the second category: they are human symbols that are informed by the Holy Spirit through the historical process of salvation so that they embody a real connection to that process. This is

---

[43] Rahner offers a partial solution when he argues, "Where a free decision is to be proclaimed by the symbol and to be made in it, the juridical composition and the free establishment is precisely what is demanded" (ibid., 240), but although, for example, the written word *Pax* may signify the freedom of human persons to create language and signs to represent that language, it must, at some level, also signify the reality meant by the word *Pax* in order to be an effective sign—and there is no way to account for that by the theology offered in this article. More broadly, this argument offers no way to account for conventional signs having different meanings.

[44] See Nathan Mitchell, *Meeting Mystery* (Maryknoll, NY: Orbis, 2006), 5–6.

[45] Rahner, "Theology of the Symbol," 249.

true not only of the sacraments but of other particular signs—especially the cross on which Jesus was crucified and the Sacred Scriptures.[46]

If this gestures toward a pneumatically determined ontology, it does no more than this. Many questions remain, of which the most important is, perhaps, what can be said of exceptionally powerful and effective symbolic forms that create cultural norms that are, apparently, directly opposed to the enactment of God's salvation in history? In other words, how can the human spirit depart so far, in its ability to subcreate, from the Spirit of God? This question seems unanswerable, except in hope, which might pray that, in light of the great subversion of these forces in the crucifixion of Jesus Christ, in the end, "all will be well."[47]

Section 6.2
Can the Trinitarian Gift Be Given?

The trinitarian analysis of chapter 5 inevitably delved into discussion of the Holy Spirit as "gift." This places the question of a pneumatology of sacraments squarely within the problem of gift and of the divine name in postmodern phenomenological discussion, particularly in the work of Jacques Derrida and his commentators. At root, the question of gratuitous gifts raises concerns about freedom, economic exchange, obligation, and—at the root of all—power. Though the question is not simply political, a political framing of the question helps to bring out the theological implications: does God give the Gift in order to bring human beings into his (quite deliberately gendered here) control? in order to oblige them to act as he wishes? If not (and surely God does not!), what are the implications of speaking in terms of obligation and exchange? What kind of gift can be given that does not bring the recipient into submission? These questions will certainly not be answered here: this section is merely meant to acknowledge the claims of this debate on the work done here and to point to some possibilities for further work in a sacramental phenomenological theology.

Perhaps it will be helpful to look one last time at the *Summa Theologiae*, for Thomas very directly considers the question of whether a divine Person can be said to be "given" as a "gift":

---

[46] On the cross, cf. Thomas Aquinas, ST III, q. 25, a. 4; on the Scriptures, ST I, q. 1, a. 8.
[47] Julian of Norwich, *The Showings of Julian of Norwich*, ed. Denise Baker (New York: W. W. Norton, 1995), 42–47 (chaps. 30–33).

The word "gift" imports an aptitude for being given. And what is given has *an aptitude or relation both to the giver and to that to which it is given.* For it would not be given by anyone, unless it was his to give; and it is given to someone to be his. Now a divine person is said to belong to another, either by origin, as the Son belongs to the Father; or as possessed by another. But we are said to possess *what we can freely use or enjoy as we please: and in this way a divine person cannot be possessed, except by a rational creature united to God.* Other creatures can be moved by a divine person, not, however, in such a way as to be able to enjoy the divine person, and to use the effect thereof. The rational creature does sometimes attain thereto; as when it is made partaker of the divine Word and of the Love proceeding, so as freely to know God truly and to love God rightly. Hence the rational creature alone can possess the divine person. Nevertheless in order that it may possess Him in this manner, its own power avails nothing: hence this must be given it from above; for that is said to be given to us which we have from another source. Thus a divine person can "be given," and can be a "gift."[48]

There are several important points here. First of all, although Thomas goes on, in the next article, to emphasize the importance of gratuity for the definition of gift,[49] in this first article he argues that a gift is such from its *potential* "givenness," not its actually being given.[50] Another important distinction is his concern with the relation of the gift to its receiver. He argues that the Holy Spirit can be possessed (i.e., can become a given Gift) by human beings only if they are united with God. In this case it is not so much that the human person "possesses" the Holy Spirit as that he or she is possessed by the Spirit and thus participates in God's (trinitarian) possession of God's self. These scholastic concerns are helpful for considering Derrida.

As John D. Caputo has argued at length, the musings of Jacques Derrida on the question of the gift should not be taken as hostile

---

[48] Thomas Aquinas, ST I, q. 38, a. 1. Emphases added.

[49] "[A] gift is properly an unreturnable giving, as Aristotle says . . . and it thus contains the idea of a gratuitous donation. Now, the reason of donation being gratuitous is love; since . . . we give something to anyone gratuitously forasmuch as we wish him well. So what we first give him is the love whereby we wish him well. Hence it is manifest that love has the nature of a first gift, through which all free gifts are given" (ST I, q. 38, a. 2).

[50] "Gift is not so called from being actually given, but from its aptitude to be given" (ST I, q. 38, a. 1, ad. 4). This seems to correspond more to Marion's "givenness" than to his gift.

to the possibility of gift, or of infinite gift, or even of God.[51] Rather, Derrida is committed to the encounter with the wholly Other (*tout autre*), or committed to the dream that this impossible encounter will come. Deconstruction is a preparation—a theologian might even say an ascetic discipline—for the advent of the impossible, because "if we have not adequately prepared ourselves in advance for the shock of alterity, the alter, instead of shocking us, will just pass us by without a ripple."[52] The crucial function of deconstruction, for Derrida, is to expose the impossibility of the Gift, to save it from becoming merely another "gift" in the human economy of exchange, so that if the Gift is given (or, rather, chosen), it will be the gratuitous (and thus impossible) gift that is truly desirable. "What I am interested in is the experience of the desire for the impossible. That is, the impossible as the condition for desire. Desire is not perhaps the best word. I mean this quest in which *we want to give*, even when we realize, when we agree, if we agree, that the gift, that giving, is impossible, that *it is a process of reappropriation and self-destruction*."[53]

Thus Derrida takes as a starting point the gratuitous character of gift, which is what makes it the impossible and, in turn, arouses desire. Pure gift would be, he argues, entirely outside any economy of exchange: "For there to be a gift, there must be no reciprocity, return, exchange, countergift, or debt. If the other *gives* me *back* or *owes* me or has to give me back what I give him or her, there will not have been a gift, whether this restitution is immediate or whether it is programmed by a complex calculation of a long-term deferral or differance."[54] Thus there is no common ground between gift (or Gift) and economy (or *oikonomia?*), because any particular gift, when recognized as gift, cannot escape economy. As Caputo puts it, "the gift is an event . . . something we deeply desire, just because it escapes the

[51] John D. Caputo, "The Apophatic," part I of *The Prayers and Tears of Jacques Derrida* (Bloomington: Indiana University, 1997), 1–68.

[52] Ibid., 22. Similarly Marion affirms a need for a kind of discipline: in order to describe the gift, "we have to commit ourselves by achieving the gift by ourselves, in such a way that we become able to describe it" ("On the Gift: A Discussion Between Jacques Derrida and Jean-Luc Marion," *God, the Gift, and Postmodernism*, ed. John D. Caputo and Michael J. Scanlon [Bloomington: Indiana University, 1999], 64 [hereafter "On the Gift"]).

[53] Derrida, "On the Gift," 72; cf. the concept of "saving" the name in "*Sauf le nom*," *On the Name* (Stanford: Stanford University, 1995), 35–85.

[54] Derrida, *Given Time I: Counterfeit Money* (Chicago: University of Chicago Press, 1994), 12.

closed circle of checks and balances, the calculus which accounts for everything. . . . The tighter the circle is drawn, the less there is of gift. For when a gift produces a debt of gratitude—and when does it not?—it puts the beneficiary in the debt of the benefactor, who thus, by giving, takes and so gains credit. Hence, there is no gift and what gifts there are, if there are any, turn to poison (*Gift*)."[55] Full gratuity would exclude the recipient from any obligation or possibility of return-gift; thus by emerging as a phenomenon (becoming visible) the gift erases itself.[56]

Despite manifest concerns about objectification of grace, Chauvet is willing to accept that the divine Gift cannot but enter into the economy of human exchange.[57] "Every gift received obligates. This is true of any present: as soon as the offered object—anything whose commercial or utilitarian value does not constitute its essence as a gift—is received as a present, it obligates the recipient to the return-gift of an expression of gratitude."[58] In other words, grace is economic, but it is an unusual economy (or "marvelous exchange") because "it functions *outside the order of value.*"[59] Chauvet wants to free (symbolic) grace from the problems of the gift not by eliminating it from the cycle of economic exchange (as Derrida thinks necessary) but by constructing it as interpersonal, concerned with subjectivity rather than "use" or "price." As feminist commentators have noticed, however, enshrining mediation favors the mediators; enshrining language empowers those who have controlled language.[60] Similarly, enshrining subjectivity seems to privilege those of high status: if the "liberality" of symbolic exchange "is really quite 'interested,'" the interest "has to do first with the desire to *be recognized as a subject,* not to lose face, not to fall from one's social rank, and consequently to compete for prestige."[61] Despite their association with subjectivity rather than cost, these considerations do not seem to be sufficiently divorced from self-motivation to apply to

[55] Caputo, *Prayers and Tears,* 160.

[56] See Robyn Horner, *Rethinking God as Gift: Marion, Derrida, and the Limits of Phenomenology* (New York: Fordham University, 2001), on the dialogue between Marion and Derrida on gift and "givenness."

[57] Most notably in Chauvet, *Symbol and Sacrament,* 99–109, 266ff.

[58] Ibid., 267. This discussion immediately precedes the characterization of the symbolic exchange of the sacraments as language critiqued in chapter 2.

[59] Ibid., 100.

[60] See, e.g., Susan Ross, *Extravagant Affections: A Feminist Sacramental Theology* (New York: Continuum, 1998), 144ff., 157, 167, for cogent feminist arguments against the universal validity of Chauvet's constructive theology.

[61] Chauvet, *Symbol and Sacrament,* 102.

the "marvelous exchange" of God's *oikonomia*. If God competes with humanity for prestige (symbolic power), Derrida is right: there is no gratuity to grace. Must one conclude that God, by giving gift, competes with humanity for power—establishes his power over us? Chauvet's construction does not appear to evade Derrida's critique; is his grace gratuitous?

Chauvet affirms that grace is *itself* gratuitous, but its entry into the human realm does implicate human beings in an obligatory return-gift—gratitude or charity between the brothers and sisters.[62] The entry of the "no-thing" beyond value, it seems, purifies human exchange, so that symbolic exchange, practiced as response to the always-initiating gratuitous giving of God, escapes the bounds of the circle because it (a) does not repay the giver but gives itself outwards toward the other, (b) represents a (divinely inspired) gift of self *for* the other, and (c) as gift owes itself to the originary gift of grace.[63] The criticisms offered against this construction of gift in chapter 2 still apply here; human gifts, even when (ostensibly) purified by contact with God's original gift, all too often fail to give. If there is a *sacramental* gift in the anthropological realm, it cannot be motivated by a competition for prestige.[64] Moreover, the charity that flows out of it must be its essential, defining characteristic, not an obligatory return-gift.

Jean-Luc Marion is differently motivated: less concerned with the question of gift as a phenomenon,[65] he is interested in how "givenness"—that is, the apparent passivity of intuition—is revealed by the range of experiences of gift.[66] He turns to Derrida's paradox in order to expose the way that gifts that escape the trap of the economy emerge as "given," or rather, emerge as paradigmatic experiences of "givenness," of how gift "gives itself."[67] Marion argues the essential characteristic of the givenness of a gift is not presence but *loss*:

> The gift, as soon as it has appeared in its presence, disappears as given, since the given according to givenness is precisely not installed in

---

[62] See discussion in chapter 2.

[63] Chauvet, *Symbol and Sacrament*, 108ff., 266ff.

[64] Derrida's work might suggest that Chauvet's problem here is his reliance on Heidegger, which inscribes him in the Western, privileged, Greek transcendentalist tradition: see Caputo, *Prayers and Tears*, 167. But cf. note, page 44.

[65] See "On the Gift," 56.

[66] Ibid., 70–71.

[67] Jean-Luc Marion, *Being Given: Toward a Phenomenology of Givenness* (Stanford: Stanford University, 2002), 74–83.

permanence—gift given as lost and never repaid on the part of the giver, given as never possessed and only conceded by the givee. But in thus disappearing as permanently present, the gift is not lost as given; it loses only the way of being—subsistence, exchange, economy—that contradicts its possibility of giving itself as such. In losing presence, the gift does not lose itself; it loses what is not suited to it, returning to itself. Or rather, it does indeed lose itself, but in the sense that it disentangles itself from itself.[68]

There are two striking resemblances to the results of the case study here. First is the identification of givenness with a kind of loss of the gift, an idea that corresponds well to the assembly's paradox of offering up or handing over the child (a renunciation of authority over that child) and simultaneously finding its own (true) self in the body of the infant. In the economy, this means that the body of Christ, handed over, gives over to humanity the impossibility that sin desired (the role of the Father), thereby allowing the Spirit to break into the distance of sin (replacing it with filial distance).[69] In this sense, Jesus did die "in place of" the other—not by releasing mortals from their own deaths but by allowing them to participate in his irreplaceability.[70] Redemption does not *take away* the death of human beings but *gives* them (a share in) God's death.[71] Second, and equally important, the presence of the gift means the disappearance of *givenness*, and vice versa: so Christ had to become absent for the Holy Spirit to come into presence (John 16:7). The Spirit, the givenness of God, broke into the world to make Christ the Gift visible, and his visibility had to withdraw in order for the Spirit to come into presence (invisibly, imperceptibly, in the self).

This does not mean, however, that Marion is doing trinitarian theology under cover of philosophy.[72] Rather, one of the exciting things about Marion's work from a theological point of view is precisely that it leaves space, one might wish to say, for the great, irreducible *hiddenness* of the Holy Spirit, in which the Holy Spirit seems to appear, or to

---

[68] Ibid., 79.

[69] Marion, "Evil in Person," *Prolegomena to Charity* (New York: Fordham University Press, 2002), 24.

[70] Derrida, *The Gift of Death* (Chicago: University of Chicago Press, 1996), 43.

[71] Cf. ibid., 41.

[72] Though many have accused him of this; see Horner, *Rethinking God as Gift* for an extended consideration of the various arguments (pp. 102ff.). Whether what Marion is doing can, strictly speaking, be called "phenomenology" is not my interest (see "On the Gift," 64–66).

be recognized by faith, precisely in disappearing into the human (and perhaps cosmic) realm. When defending his work as nontheological, he puts this very clearly:

> You can describe a phenomenon as given without asking any question about the giver. And in most of the cases, there is absolutely no giver at all. I am not interested in assigning a giver to a given phenomenon. I am interested in saying that our deepest and most genuine experience of the phenomenon does not deal with any object that we could master, produce, or constitute, no more than with any being. . . . When [phenomena] appear to us as given, of course, we have to receive them, but this does not imply that we should claim God as the cause of what we receive.[73]

Christians should not rush to assume that the givenness of phenomena amount to gifts from God, in part because of the need to distinguish cultural and theological efficacy but also because the Holy Spirit can only come to be present in phenomena (cosmic, perhaps, as well as cultural phenomena) inasmuch as identification with the Spirit is deferred, put off from knowledge to faith to hope.

With this background in mind, consider the ritual reading of infant baptism offered above. In what way are the phenomena of the rite of infant baptism, considered as phenomena, "given"? Do they rise to the character of "gift"? They are given in at least two ways: they are available to the senses of the infant baptizand (they are "there," *il y a*) and they are so in a way that precedes the infant's ability to desire their being there. At the same time, they are not present to the infant; they are characterized by withdrawal, because the infant's developmental state makes it impossible to maintain (an illusion of) mastery. One may say, on the one hand, that they are "offered" to the infant,[74] but it is difficult to say who offers: the parents defer their initiative in the process to the church (by bringing the child to church, ritually by the formal asking that the child be baptized[75]); the church, on the other hand, presses responsibility into the hands of the parents (is this the real purpose of the stress on the parents' responsibilities, in the face of the rite's blatant rejection of their capability to perform what they are required to promise?). Moreover, both undergo the rite on the assumption that the

---

[73] "On the Gift," 70.
[74] In chapter 3, the term chosen was, instead, "opened."
[75] "Introduction," *Rite of Baptism for Children* (Collegeville, MN: Liturgical Press, 2002), paragraph 5.

one who offers is, ultimately, God—and yet God, according to the rite, is really only "present" to and for the community in (or on the skin of) the body of the infant, who is (paradoxically) the receiver of the gift. Even the blessing of the water is transient, cannot be maintained in the face of time. In other words, the rite *may* maintain that the phenomena of its practice are "gifts," precisely by that unending deferral of giving. The rite "opens" the phenomena of the Christian world by refusing to "own" these phenomena but finding them in the body of the one who is not yet a part of that world.

This kind of givenness is even more appropriate to Marion's reduction to givenness than Derrida's paradoxical definition. Givenness, according to the reduction, consists in the receiver's free (never secure) recognition of the given *as gift*: "The gift character . . . comes from the suitability of what arises, or more exactly, from my admission of their suitability, from their recognition as given to me without me."[76] Thus the real gift consists not only in the gift itself but also in "the decision to identify who gives," which belongs to the receiver.[77] Moreover, Marion's reduction according to the gift itself reveals that in a symbolic enactment of gift, love, shared life, and the gift of self cannot be symbolized by the nearest and most perfect resembling entity (the body of the lover) because the objectification of that body invalidates the gift of self as gift. Rather, a conventional (and thus arbitrary) sign is chosen:

> The wedding ring . . . attests that the Other has given himself, through the bracketing of the giver, to me in giving me this object, and reciprocally; but the two gifts (the ring and the Other) never coincide. . . . By contrast, the ring attests *the gift that I became in receiving* (that of) the Other precisely because in reality it is *not* equal to it, but offers the symbolic index of this gift, without common measure with what is nevertheless shown in it.[78]

This excellent example demonstrates that the symbolic reduction of the gift occurs because the *gift does not (yet) exist*: the gift of self enacted in the marriage ceremony and in the life of commitment to the partner cannot be made available to the receiver because it is not present to the giver. The self offered in marriage never exists when it is given. It can, perhaps, come to exist only because it has already been given.

---

[76] Marion, *Being Given*, 100.
[77] Ibid., 101.
[78] Ibid., 105. First emphasis mine, second emphasis Marion's.

Derrida, Chauvet, and Marion thus agree that the only gift worth being given, so to speak, is the gift of self. But because self-giving uniquely and irreversibly changes (not to say risks) the one being given, the giver never possesses the self he or she offers. The gift comes to be acknowledged as gift by the receiver's *recognition*, yet that recognition can never quite exist in history but rather in the future: the self that the Other is (in the process of) making *will be gift* for me; the self that I am *trying to become* is hereby offered to you. Gift is, then, an interpretation of a process that always escapes certainty because it is never finalized.

Moreover, the giver of the gift of self actually receives the gift of self from the one to whom he or she offers it: this is because the giver cannot possess a self-as-gift unless he or she is recognized by the receiver as offering a self-gift.[79] The receiver is *not* obligated to a return-gift precisely because his or her acceptance of the gift *erases* the giver and leaves in place a new identity: one able to give the gift. In other words, the giver offers without being able to make good on his or her offer; he or she obliges oneself to deliver on a promise without being able to do so; it depends on the receiver to allow the gift to come into being—but if there is a coming-into-presence, the one who offered the gift no longer exists. The self who offered has been transformed into the self who was accepted. This transformation may be manipulative, coercive, or abusive; in fact, perhaps there is never a human relationship fully free of the economic cycle. The cycle is actually very fragile, and its very enactment tends to fracture it.

The giver thus offers a gift of self but cannot be the "cause" of the givenness of that gift; the receiver makes the givenness of self possible but likewise cannot claim mastery of the self he or she receives. The self, as in process, withdraws. Infants provide a good example of this. A newborn infant, neither knowingly nor willingly (yet not *unwillingly*), delivers himself or herself into the hands of his or her caregivers. He or she does not immediately have a sense of self to be offered; moreover, by the time the sense of self develops, the care that has gone into its formation is already being forgotten. Parents receive from the infant the capacity to offer themselves in service to the infant, and these services will never be remembered. The infant, as is much more commonly recognized, also receives his or her capacity to exist from his or her parents, and this too is never remembered.

---

[79] Cf. ibid., 100.

There are thus several levels of approximation of the recognition of gift. There is a zero level: an acknowledged "cash exchange" in which both participants agree that the exchange itself discharges all debts and transfers goods efficiently. This is, strictly speaking, an economic exchange. The first level of recognition of *gift*, then, is ingratitude or enmity: these recognize the gift insofar as it is given to them but refuse to be bound by any obligation to a return (perhaps because the gift does not meet the suitability criterion for givenness).[80] Marion recognizes that this, in a sense, frees the giver and the gift; but it also seems to fail in givenness *for* the receiver. The gift does not reenter the cycle of exchange so as to erase its givenness, but it erases itself as marked for the givee: it does not "arrive in the nick of time, at the right moment, save me just when I need it."[81] Many material gifts, though perhaps preserved from the cycle of exchange, are instead destined for the dustheap of waste.[82] The second level of approximation is gratitude and a conscious attempt to "make good" the gift by some level of reciprocation (perhaps by "paying it forward" to another recipient or to an anonymous receiver). In this case the gift emerges as *for* the receiver but remains partially indebted to the cycle of economic exchange. It is worth noting that both these levels of approximation are possible responses to a gift of self, and both invalidate the gift to at least some degree, as the self that is offered cannot fully emerge under conditions of ingratitude and hostility and the attempt to "make good" the gift cannot be sustained as a strategy for self-gift in the long term.

The final level of approximation, paradoxically, is superficially similar to the first: the receiver does not express gratitude for the gift or feel obligated to repay it. Instead, he or she is so caught up in becoming the gift—that is, participating in the Other who offers a gift of self—that he or she has forgotten the gift and all obligation. Another way of thinking of this is in terms of discovery: originally, the receiver does not know that he or she has any obligation to the (anonymous, unknown, reduced) giver, but only because he or she has not received any (worthy) gift.[83] This reduction is fragile, however, in that any especially suitable

---

[80] Marion analyzes these as a bracketing of the givee (here called receiver): ibid., 88–91.

[81] Ibid., 100.

[82] This remains true whether the gift is in itself unsuitable or is merely refused acknowledgment by the receiver.

[83] Recall Marion's slogan from *Being Given*: "what gives itself, shows itself."

gift (and those less suitable scarcely deserve to be designated gift) may provoke recognition, which threatens the givenness of the gift with a renewal of the cycle of exchange (suspended by ingratitude). The only retreat is a progression from anamnesis into amnesia: an amnesia that forgets the gift transferred by becoming the gift. But this amnesia is itself another phase of discovery: the discovery that obligation has, all along, been an illusion; obligations are entertained only to point toward joy—and joy is the participation in the thing, the discovery that the obligation was given only to discover in the law, spirit, and in the spirit, freedom.

There is one point at which this presentation of the gift becomes truly helpful, and that is with respect to theologies for women, children, and other historically marginalized groups. These peoples have historically been "obliged" to many things that actively harmed them and their brothers and sisters, in order to enrich the already powerful. In the light of the discovery of the gift, it is clear that the only obligations are those that lead to liberation—not to oppression—and the only purpose of obligation is to authorize and motivate the practices that allow one to discover joy in the obligation itself—life, abundantly. In this authentic mediations of the gospel can, in theory, be distinguished from inauthentic ones.

Infancy again offers an example: an infant has truly forgotten or, better, has failed to remember any obligation toward his or her parents. A parent's case is more complicated: he or she is knowingly obliged to offer a gift of self—and is thus incapacitated. He or she is trapped in a consciousness of obligation unless something can break the cycle, producing an amnesia with respect to obligation. In a word, one must be released by losing oneself in the gift, in joy. The infant in his or her naiveté does not offer himself or herself but rather offers a new self to his or her parents, who can thus offer a gift of self only by losing themselves in this gift. In a sense, the givenness emerges as something beyond both parent and infant, because it is the freedom to lose both obligation and reciprocity by participation in a reality that does not owe its existence to either of them. The givenness is an element of surprise, the failure of everything to add up neatly, the inexplicable surplus of meaning. No doubt families often fail to give the self-gift to which they are obliged. But if a parent *does*, for a moment, manage to give a gift of self—a gift of time, a moment of unconditional love—he or she will have received the self being given from the one who receives the gift. This gift that the parent receives does not obligate him or her to offer a self-gift: he or she owned this obligation before receiving the capacity, indeed before the child existed to be loved, because human beings *must* love—not only in justice to the other but also in order to exist, in order to flourish.

At this point it becomes possible to do justice to an observation that emerged in chapters 4 and 5, that baptism depends on and has resonances with the relationship between infants and their parents. One part of the disappropriation of the rite is intended to provoke the first level of approximation in parents: parents (and assembly) recognize that the secret of the trinitarian gift of baptism is that the baptizer has no gift to offer. Instead, the baptizand offers (unwittingly) a gift of self that enables the baptismal community to become the community of the Trinity. This gift is only visible in faith. The second level of approximation, however, suggests that the infant and the other participants become capable of being the gift they have offered (to one another and to the Trinity). This (fruitfulness) is the ultimate end of the sacrament, and cannot be affirmed even in faith, but only in hope.[84]

This turn to hope is necessary because the full release from the obligatory function of obligation, and into the full participation in the joy it sometimes camouflages, occurs only in death. For death is the one, verifiable, fully deferred gift, the one phenomenon that one fully becomes as one forgets the promise to have become it.[85] It is the gift one offers another—in fact all others[86]—but it is the same time the only gift that, received, contains an amnesia about its necessity. All other gifts that one attempts to give, or to receive, or to find oneself obliged to, reduce themselves at last to at least this one.[87]

Can death be given before the phenomenality of death obliges one to it? If so, death is a trinitarian gift (Rom 6). The obligation to self-gift that is associated with the baptismal vocation corresponds to Chauvet's ethical obligation. Is it possible that one is obliged to this gift on account of baptism, as if baptism opened a new ethical realm to which one was not (already) obliged by human existence? With regard to the general obligation of self-gift in charity to the human other, this obligation is, surely, already binding on all humankind. With regard to the specific obligations of the Christian cult, that is, worship, etc., the

[84] See Balthasar, *Dare We Hope "That All Men Be Saved"?* (San Francisco: Ignatius, 1988).
[85] Derrida, *Gift of Death*, e.g., 40.
[86] Marion, *Being Given*, 94–97.
[87] Balthasar, *The Last Act*, Theo-Drama V (San Francisco: Ignatius, 1998), 84.

case is more obscure—but if God exists for Christians to worship, they are obliged to worship not because they are Christians but because God is God. The purpose for the cultic obligations of baptism is to authorize the construction of a self who cannot see any reason not to praise God, who praises God for the joy of praise itself.

Baptism, then, *does not bestow the obligation to a return-gift*. It cannot, because any obligation that can exist—if any relationship can be so described[88]—between humanity and God exists independent of the baptismal rite. Baptism, then, offers a new identity (in the ritual process mode: i.e., a cultural world is projected around the baptizand and he or she is encouraged to effectively engage within it so as to "practice" its relevant skills) that allows human persons to fulfill the obligation that they have found imposed on themselves. This obligation, "discovered," is the true gift, in that it opens the eyes to the possibility of freedom and joy. Ritual allows the experience of egolessness that is crucial to the discovery of this givenness.[89]

If Spirit is the "givenness" of the trinitarian *oikonomia*, moreover,[90] it is not surprising that it is continually disappearing into the visible mission of the Son on the one hand and into the cultural life of humanity on the other. What is more, it cannot be lured back from either place: if no one moment of Christ's life can be decisively isolated as "the pneumatic pivot," no more can any one particular liturgical act be exclusively seen as pneumatic (as opposed to Christic, ecclesial, etc.). Finally, the only "space" that can be identified with the Spirit, is, paradoxically, the body, because the body is the only true visibility for a gift of self. Thus in infant baptism the church is radically confronted by the paradox that always threatens *human* confidence: when Christians wish to find the Body of Christ, they must go through the Spirit, and the Spirit can be identified with the church only through discipline and hope. In infant baptism, then, the church entrusts itself to the body of the infant, hoping against hope to find itself the Body of Christ (again) in the Spirit.

The phenomenology of givenness, and the recognition of gift in the trinitarian sacramental dynamic, then, allows a *rapprochement* of the trinitarian theology of Rahner and Balthasar. If "what gives itself

---

[88] God, of course, does not need human offering or sacrifice.

[89] On egolessness and the gift, see Marion, *Being Given*, 77.

[90] So Rahner was concerned that contemporary theologians did not identify trinitarian vestiges in creation (*Trinity*, 13–14).

shows itself,"[91] the trinitarian infinite gift, which embraces humanity in finitude and fallenness, is also the self-communication by which the Persons express themselves outside themselves. If this gift and expression never exhausts its own reality (and thus goes beyond the realm of phenomenology[92]), it never fails to enter into the world (even the cultural world). It does not so much transcend the world as stretch and break it.

Section 6.3
Liturgy in the Spirit

So far I have discussed, with great trepidation, the possibility that the Spirit is the basis for symbolic representation and for the givenness of the divine gift. There are two constants to the emergence of the Holy Spirit from these spheres: each is transformative of human identity and each recognizes the unitive principle of disparate phenomena. The Spirit also seems to be the origin of the fact of ritual folding. The fact of ritual folding, as originally discussed in chapter 2 and seen in chapter 4, "insulates" ritual participants from their ordinary assumptions so that they can undergo personal and communal transformation. The foldedness of a ritual creates a space, a temple for freedom. There a person can be transformed into the self-gift that, being human, he or she longs to be, and find in it joy. There he or she can undergo death without death on behalf of the other. There he or she can be freed from obligation and become the gift.

The Spirit is the one that folds human ritual, making the cracks that let God break in to remake the world. Perhaps better, the Spirit is the surface on which the rite is written, and her unpredictable bending and swaying can bring the words of the liturgy together in unexpected ways. Perhaps the Holy Spirit is like a parchment on which the theo-drama is drawn as a line, and when she folds history, events that are not linearly contiguous become contiguous in space, that is, in the Spirit. Perhaps the Spirit makes the passion present in the suffering, the confusion, the abandonment of the terminally ill patient who requests Viaticum. Her anamnesis of Christ is amnesia of herself, for she loses herself in the patient's experience of the passion.

[91] Marion, *Being Given*, e.g., 4.
[92] Ibid., 115.

The Spirit is fissure, fracture, and generating space in the world and in God. He unites what has been divided—most shockingly spirit and body—and by this highlights the differentiation of what has been made whole. The infinite distance between Son and Father, he becomes also the generative distance between Christ and the church, between the world and God. This distance is essential to recognize difference, but difference is only recognized by being bridged.

The Holy Spirit unites Son and Father in love by being the generative distance of the Son's procession from the Father. The Holy Spirit is the givenness of the Son, not only in his being given for the world, but even in his being given for himself. The Holy Spirit is the result of the generation of the Son, but the unity of Father and Son is not additive but results in the element of surprise: the Spirit, more than any expectation, is able to fracture every boundary and unite across any divide. In the incarnation, the Spirit is the unity of body and soul, the meetinghouse for the divine and the human. In the church, the Spirit is the givenness of the Gift of Christ, the givenness of the divine nature.

The Spirit renders Christ present in the eucharist. Breaking the boundaries by which we usually distinguish bodily from spiritual, the Spirit folds the universe so that the Body in heaven is present in the host as in a point, so that the gathered host can become the heavenly Body. The givenness of the gift is manifest when the ministers offer the Body and the Blood, when the Spirit makes Christ available to the church. Christ is not present in the eucharist in the same way a book is present in a bag, but in the way a black hole is present in black night: the Spirit of the eucharist pulls us forward, down the aisles, toward the altar on which we are offered, toward the Presence that draws us into itself. Nor does this satisfy the Spirit, for the divine thirst will not be sated until it has united us wholly with itself: the Spirit whispers to us in the psalms, pushes on us from our past, dwells in our bones, to ensure we answer the call. When we have swallowed the Body, we become Body, lose ourselves in finding ourselves in Christ.

Bibliography

Appleyard, J. A. "How Does a Sacrament 'Cause by Signifying'?" *Science et Esprit* 23 (1971): 167–200.

Asad, Talal. *Genealogies of Religion.* Baltimore: Johns Hopkins University, 1993.

———. "Remarks on the Anthropology of the Body." In *Religion and the Body: Comparative Perspectives on Devotional Practices,* edited by Sarah Coakley, 42–52. Cambridge: University of Cambridge Press, 1997.

Augustine of Hippo. *The City of God against the Pagans.* Translated by R. W. Dyson. New York: Cambridge University Press, 1998.

———. *Confessions and Enchiridion.* Translated by Albert C. Outler. Available in the *Christian Classics Ethereal Library,* http://www.ccel.org/ccel/augustine/confessions.i.html. Last accessed July 17, 2009.

———. *Merit and the Forgiveness of Sins.* Translated by Peter Holmes and Robert Ernest Wallis. Available on New Advent, http://www.newadvent.org/fathers/15011.htm. Last accessed June 9, 2009.

———. *Tractates on the Gospel of John.* The Fathers of the Church, vol. 90. Washington, DC: Catholic University of America, 1994.

Austin, J. L. *How to Do Things with Words.* Cambridge, MA: Harvard University Press, 2005.

Bakke, Odd Magne. *When Children Became People: The Birth of Childhood in Early Christianity.* Translated by Brian McNeil. Minneapolis: Fortress Press, 2005.

Balthasar, Hans Urs von. *The Action.* Theo-Drama, vol. IV. San Francisco: Ignatius, 1994.

———. *Dare We Hope "That All Men Be Saved"?* Translated by David Kipp and Lothar Krauth. San Francisco: Ignatius, 1988.

———. *Epilogue.* Translated by Edward T. Oakes. San Francisco: Ignatius, 2004.

———. *The Last Act.* Theo-Drama, vol. V. San Francisco: Ignatius, 1998.

———. *Seeing the Form.* Glory of the Lord, vol. I. San Francisco: Ignatius, 1982.

———. *Truth of God.* Theo-logic, vol. II. Translated by Adrian J. Walker. San Francisco: Ignatius, 2004.

———. *Unless You Become Like This Child.* Translated by Erasmo Leiva-Merikakis. San Francisco: Ignatius, 1991.

Barros, F. C., C. G. Victora, et al. "Use of Pacifiers is Associated with Decrease of Breastfeeding Duration." *Pediatrics* 95 (1995): 497–99.

Baumstark, Anton. *Comparative Liturgy.* London: Mowbray, 1958.

Bell, Catherine. *Ritual: Perspectives and Dimensions.* New York: Oxford University, 1997.

Bingemer, Maria Clara Lucchetti. "Postmodernity and Sacramentality: Two Challenges to Speaking about God." In *Sacramental Presence in a Postmodern Context,* edited by Lieven Boeve and Lambert Leijssen, 65–105. Sterling, VA: Leuven University Press, 2001.

Bracken, Joseph A. "Intersubjectivity and a Theology of Presence." In *A Sacramental Life: A Festschrift Honoring Bernard Cooke,* edited by Michael H. Barnes and William P. Roberts, 57–76. Milwaukee: Marquette University Press, 2003.

———. "Toward a New Philosophical Theology Based on Intersubjectivity." *Theological Studies* 59, no. 4 (1998): 703–19.

Bradshaw, Paul. "Christian Rites Related to Birth." In *Life Cycles in Jewish and Christian Worship,* edited by Paul F. Bradshaw and Lawrence A. Hoffman, 13–31. Notre Dame, IN: University of Notre Dame Press, 1996.

———. "The Homogenization of Christian Liturgy—Ancient and Modern: Presidential Address." *Studia Liturgica* 26, no. 1 (1996): 1–15.

———. "The Liturgical Use and Abuse of Patristics." In *Liturgy Reshaped,* edited by Kenneth Stevenson, 134–45. Garden City, NY: Anchor Press, 1982.

———. *The Search for the Origins of Christian Worship.* New York: Oxford University, 2002.

Bradshaw, Paul, Maxwell E. Johnson, L. Edward Philips, and Harold W. Attridge. *The Apostolic Tradition: A Commentary.* Minneapolis: Fortress Press, 2002.

Brown, Raymond E. *The Community of the Beloved Disciple.* New York: Paulist, 1979.

———. *An Introduction to the New Testament.* New York: Doubleday, 1997.

Buckley, James J., and David S. Yeago. *Knowing the Triune God.* Grand Rapids: Eerdmans, 2001.

Bugnini, Annibale. *The Reform of the Liturgy (1948–1975).* Collegeville, MN: Liturgical Press, 1990.

Cabie, Robert. "The Organization of the Ritual of Initiation until the Spread of Infant Baptism (Mid-Second to Sixth Century)." In *Sacraments,* The Church at Prayer, vol. 3, edited by A. G. Martimort, 17–63. Collegeville, MN: Liturgical Press, 1988.

Canals, J. M. "Liturgia y Metodologia." In *La Celebración en la Iglesia,* edited by Dionisio Borobio García, 33–47. Salamanca: Ediciones Sigueme, 1985.

Caputo, John D. *The Prayers and Tears of Jacques Derrida.* Bloomington: Indiana University Press, 1997.

Caputo, John D., and Michael J. Scanlon. *God, the Gift, and Postmodernism.* Bloomington: Indiana University, 1999. Chapman, David M. "Infant Baptism and Sacramental Grace." *Epworth Review* 25 (1998): 83–88.

Chauvet, Louis-Marie. "The Broken Bread as Theological Figure of Eucharistic Presence." In *Sacramental Presence in a Postmodern Context,* edited by Lieven Boeve and Lambert Leijssen, 236–62. Sterling, VA: Leuven University Press, 2001.

——. "Le Sacrifice Comme Echange Symbolique." In *Le Sacrifice dans les Religions,* edited by Marcel Neusch, 274–304. Paris: Beauchesne, 1994.

——. *The Sacraments: The Word of God at the Mercy of the Body.* Collegeville, MN: Liturgical Press, 2001.

——. *Symbol and Sacrament.* Collegeville, MN: Liturgical Press, 1995.

Chauvet, Louis-Marie, and Francois Kabasele Lumbala. *Liturgy and the Body.* Maryknoll: Orbis, 1995.

Congar, Yves. *I Believe in the Holy Spirit.* New York: Herder and Herder, 1997.

Congregation for the Doctrine of the Faith. "Guidelines for Admission to the Eucharist between the Chaldean Church and the Assyrian Church of the East." July 20, 2001.

Covino, Paul. "The Postconciliar Infant Baptism Debate in the American Catholic Church." *Worship* 56, no. 3 (1982): 240–60.

Crichton, J. D. "A Theology of Worship." In *The Study of Liturgy,* edited by Cheslyn Jones et al., 3–30. New York: Oxford University Press, 1992.

Csikszentmihalyi, Mihaly. *Beyond Boredom and Anxiety.* San Francisco: Jossey-Bass, 2000.

——, and Isabella Csikszentmihalyi, eds. *Optimal Experience.* Cambridge, UK: Cambridge University Press, 1992.

Csordas, Thomas. *The Sacred Self: A Cultural Phenomenology of Religious Healing.* Berkeley: University of California Press, 1997.

Daly, Robert J. *The Origins of the Christian Doctrine of Sacrifice.* Philadelphia: Fortress Press, 1978.

Deflem, Mathieu. "Ritual, Anti-Structure, and Religion: A Discussion of Victor Turner's Processual Symbolic Analysis." *Journal for the Scientific Study of Religion* 30, no. 1 (1991): 1–25.

Derrida, Jacques. *A Derrida Reader.* Edited by Peggy Kamuf. New York: Columbia University Press, 1991.

——. *The Gift of Death.* Chicago: University of Chicago Press, 1996.

——. *Given Time I: Counterfeit Money.* Translated by Peggy Kamuf. Chicago: University of Chicago Press, 1994.

——. *Of Grammatology.* Baltimore: Johns Hopkins University, 1997.

——. *On the Name.* Edited by Thomas Dutoit. Stanford: Stanford University, 1995.

——. *Writing and Difference.* Chicago: University of Chicago Press, 1992.

Division of Christian Education of the National Council of the Churches of Christ in the United States of America. *New Revised Standard Version Bible.* 1989.

Douglas, Mary. *Purity and Danger: An Analysis of the Concepts of Pollution and Taboo.* New York: Routledge, 2003.

Downey, Michael. "Trinitarian Spirituality: Participation in Communion of Persons." *Eglise et Theologie* 24, no. 1 (1993): 109–23.

———. *Altogether Gift.* Maryknoll, NY: Orbis, 2000.

Dupre, Louis K. "From Silence to Speech: Negative Theology and Trinitarian Spirituality." *Communio* 11 (1984): 28–34.

Fagerberg, David. *Theologia Prima: What Is Liturgical Theology?* Mundelein, IL: Hillenbrand Books, 2004.

Ferguson, Everett. "Baptism According to Origen." *Evangelical Quarterly* 78, no. 2 (2006): 117–35.

———. "Inscriptions and the Origin of Infant Baptism." *Journal of Theological Studies* 30 (1979): 37–46.

Foucault, Michel. "Technologies of the Self." In *Technologies of the Self: A Seminar with Michel Foucault,* edited by Luther H. Martin, Huck Gutman, and Patrick H. Hutton, 16–49. Amherst: University of Massachusetts Press, 1988.

Frank, Georgia. "'Taste and See': The Eucharist and the Eyes of Faith in the Fourth Century." *Church History* 70 (2004): 630–37.

Fry, Timothy, ed. *RB 1980: The Rule of St. Benedict in English.* Collegeville, MN: Liturgical Press, 1981.

Gelineau, Joseph. "La Prière Eucharistique Comme Acte de Langage de L'assemblé." In *Liturgy and Muse,* edited by Anton Vernooij, 37–47. Dudley, MA: Peeters, 2002.

Grabert, Colman. "The Rite of Penance/Reconciliation: Christian Existence in a Reconciled Humanity." In *Background and Directions,* The Rite of Penance: Commentaries, vol. 3, edited by Nathan D. Mitchell, 104–22. Washington, DC: Liturgical Conference, 1978.

Green, Garrett. *Imagining God.* San Francisco: Harper & Row, 1989.

Greene-McCreight, Kathryn. "When I Say God, I Mean Father, Son and Holy Spirit: On the Ecumenical Baptismal Formula." *Pro Ecclesia* 6 (1997): 289–308.

Greimas, Algirdas. *Structural Semantics.* Lincoln: University of Nebraska Press, 1984.

Grimes, Ronald. "Emerging Ritual." In *Reading, Writing, and Ritualizing: Rituals in Fictive, Liturgical, and Public Places,* 23–38. Washington, DC: Pastoral Press, 1993.

———. "Reinventing Ritual." *Soundings* 75 (1992): 21–41.

Hall, Jerome. *We Have the Mind of Christ.* Collegeville, MN: Liturgical Press, 2001.

Handelman, Don. "Introduction: Why Ritual in Its Own Right? How So?" In *Ritual in Its Own Right: Exploring the Dynamics of Transformation*, edited by Don Handelman and Galina Lindquist, 1–32. New York: Berghahn Books, 2005.

Handelman, Don, and Galina Lindquist, eds. *Ritual in Its Own Right: Exploring the Dynamics of Transformation*. New York: Berghahn Books, 2005.

Harmless, William. "Baptism." In *Augustine Through the Ages*, edited by Allan D. Fitzgerald, 84–91. Grand Rapids, MI: Eerdmans, 1999.

Heidegger, Martin. "The Age of the World Picture." In *Off the Beaten Track*, translated by Julian Young and Kenneth Haynes, 52–72. Cambridge, UK: Cambridge University Press, 2002.

————. "Letter on Humanism." In *Basic Writings*, edited by David Farrell Krell, 213–66. New York: Harper & Row, 1977.

————. "Nietzsche's Word: 'God Is Dead.'" In *Off the Beaten Track*, translated by Julian Young and Kenneth Haynes, 157–99. Cambridge, UK: Cambridge University Press, 2002.

————. *On the Way to Language*. Translated by Joan Stambaugh. New York: Harper & Row, 1982.

————. "The Origin of the Work of Art." In *Off the Beaten Track*, translated by Julian Young and Kenneth Haynes, 1–51. Cambridge, UK: Cambridge University Press, 2002.

————. ". . . Poetically Man Dwells . . ." In *Poetry, Language, Thought*, translated by Albert Hofstadter, 209–27. New York: Harper, 2001.

————. "The Thing." In *Poetry, Language, Thought*, translated by Albert Hofstadter, 161–84. New York: Harper, 2001.

————. "What is Metaphysics?" In *Basic Writings*, edited by David Farrell Krell, 89–111. New York: Harper & Row, 1977.

Hemming, Laurence Paul. "After Heidegger: Transubstantiation." In *Sacramental Presence in a Postmodern Context*, edited by Lieven Boeve and Lambert Leijssen, 299–309. Sterling, VA: Leuven University Press, 2001.

Hetherington, E. Mavis, et al. *Child Psychology: A Contemporary Viewpoint*. Boston: McGraw Hill, 2006.

Horner, Robyn. *Jean-Luc Marion: A Theo-logical Introduction*. Burlington, VT: Ashgate, 2005.

————. *Rethinking God as Gift: Marion, Derrida, and the Limits of Phenomenology*. New York: Fordham University, 2001.

Hugh of Saint-Victor. *On the Sacraments of the Christian Faith (De sacramentis)*. Cambridge, MA: Mediaeval Academy of America, 1951.

Hughes, Graham, and Daniel Hardy. *Worship as Meaning*. New York: Cambridge University Press, 2003.

Johnson, Clare. Ex Ore Infantium: *The Pre-rational Child as Subject of Sacramental Action*. PhD thesis, Notre Dame, 2004.

Johnson, Maxwell. *Images of Baptism.* Forum Essays, vol. 6. Chicago: Liturgy Training Publications, 2001.

————. "Is Anything Normative in Contemporary Lutheran Worship?" In *The Serious Business of Worship: Essays in Honour of Bryan D. Spinks,* edited by Melanie C. Ross and Simon Jones. New York: T&T Clark, 2010.

————, ed. *Living Water, Sealing Spirit: Readings on Christian Initiation.* Collegeville, MN: Liturgical Press, 1995.

————. *The Rites of Christian Initiation: Their Evolution and Interpretation.* Collegeville, MN: Liturgical Press, 2007.

Joncas, Jan Michael. *Preaching the Rites of Christian Initiation.* Forum Essays, vol. 4. Chicago: Liturgy Training Publications, 1994.

Julian of Norwich. *The Showings of Julian of Norwich,* edited by Denise Baker. Norton Critical Edition. New York: W. W. Norton & Company, 1995.

Kapferer, Bruce. "Ritual Dynamics and Virtual Practice: Beyond Representation and Meaning." In *Ritual in Its Own Right: Exploring the Dynamics of Transformation,* edited by Don Handelman and Galina Lindquist, 35–54. New York: Berghahn Books, 2005.

Kavanagh, Aidan. "Christian Initiation in Post-Conciliar Roman Catholicism: A Brief Report." In *Living Water, Sealing Spirit,* edited by Maxwell Johnson, 1–10. Collegeville, MN: Liturgical Press, 1995.

————. *On Liturgical Theology.* Collegeville, MN: Liturgical Press, 1992.

————. *The Shape of Baptism.* New York: Pueblo, 1978.

————. "Unfinished and Unbegun Revisited: The Rite of Christian Initiation of Adults." In *Living Water, Sealing Spirit,* edited by Maxwell Johnson, 259–73. Collegeville, MN: Liturgical Press, 1995.

Kelleher, Margaret Mary. "Liturgical Theology: A Task and a Method." *Worship* 62, no. 1 (1988): 2–25.

————. "Hermeneutics in the Study of Liturgical Performance." *Worship* 67, no. 4 (1993): 292–318.

Kilmartin, Edward. "The Active Role of Christ and the Spirit in the Divine Liturgy." *Diakonia* 17, no. 2 (1982): 95–108.

————. *Christian Liturgy: Theology and Practice.* Franklin, WI: Sheed and Ward, 1988.

————. *The Eucharist in the West.* Collegeville, MN: Liturgical Press, 1998.

Kingsbury, Jack Dean. "Baptism." *Interpretation* 47 (1993): 229–98.

Klauser, Theodor. *A Short History of the Western Liturgy.* New York: Oxford, 1979.

Kockelmans, Joseph. "Language, Meaning, and Ek-sistence." In *On Heidegger and Language,* edited by Joseph J. Kockelmans, 3–32. Evanston: Northwestern University, 1972.

————. "Ontological Difference, Hermeneutics, and Language." In *On Heidegger and Language,* edited by Joseph J. Kockelmans, 195–234. Evanston: Northwestern University, 1972.

LaCugna, Catherine Mowry. "The Baptismal Formula, Feminist Objections, and Trinitarian Theology." *Journal of Ecumenical Studies* 26 (1989): 235–50.
————. "Can Liturgy Ever Again Become a Source for Theology?" *Studia Liturgica* 19, no. 1 (1989): 1–13.
————. *God for Us: The Trinity and Christian Life.* San Francisco: HarperSan-Francisco, 1993.
Loades, Ann. "Trinitarian Theology, Baptism and Person." *Theology* 97 (1994): 82–120.
Lohmann, Johannes. "M. Heidegger's 'Ontological Difference' and Language." In *On Heidegger and Language*, edited by Joseph J. Kockelmans, 303–63. Evanston: Northwestern University, 1972.
Madigan, Shawn. *Liturgical Spirituality and the Rite of Christian Initiation of Adults.* Forum Essays, vol. 5. Chicago: Liturgy Training Publications, 1997.
Marion, Jean-Luc. *Being Given: Toward a Phenomenology of Givenness.* Translated by Jeffrey L. Kosky. Stanford: Stanford University, 2002.
————. *In Excess.* New York: Fordham University Press, 2004.
————. "*Mihi magna quaestio factus sum:* The Privilege of Unknowing," *Journal of Religion* 85, no. 1 (2005): 1–24.
————. *Prolegomena to Charity.* Translated by Stephen E. Lewis. New York: Fordham University Press, 2002.
Mastrogiannopoulos, Elias D. *Nostalgia for Orthodoxy.* Athens: Zoe, 1959.
Mauss, Marcel. "Body Techniques." In *Sociology and Psychology*, translated by Ben Brewster, 95–123. London: Routledge and Kegan Paul, 1979.
McCall, Richard D. "Imagining the Other: Toward an Aesthetic Theology." *Religion and the Arts* 8, no. 4 (2004): 479–85.
————. *Do This: Liturgy as Performance.* Notre Dame, IN: University of Notre Dame, 2007.
McDonnell, Kilian. *The Baptism of Jesus in the Jordan: The Trinitarian and Cosmic Order of Salvation.* Collegeville, MN: Liturgical Press, 1996.
McKenna, John H. "Eucharist and Sacrifice: An Overview." *Worship* 76, no. 5 (2002): 386–402.
McManus, Frederick R. "Back to the Future: The Early Christian Roots of Liturgical Renewal." *Worship* 72 (1998): 386–403.
Merleau-Ponty, Maurice. *Phenomenology of Perception.* Translated by Colin Smith. New York: Routledge, 2002.
————. *The Structure of Behavior.* Translated by Alden L. Fisher. Boston: Beacon Press, 1963.
Milhau, Marc. "Hilaire de Poitiers, De Trinitate, 2,1: Formule Baptismale et Foi Trinitaire." *Studia Patristica* 38 (2001): 435–48.
Miller, Vincent J. "An Abyss at the Heart of Mediation: Louis-Marie Chauvet's Fundamental Theology of Sacramentality." *Horizons* 24 (1997): 230–47.
Mitchell, Lionel L. "The Thanksgiving over the Water in the Baptismal Rite of the Western Church." In *The Sacrifice of Praise: Studies on the Themes of*

Thanksgiving and Redemption in the Central Prayers of the Eucharistic and Baptismal Liturgies, edited by Bryan Spinks, 229–44. Rome: C.L.V.-Edizioni Liturgiche, 1981.

Mitchell, Nathan D. "Conversion and Reconciliation in the New Testament." In *The Rite of Penance: Commentaries: Background and Directions*, vol. 3, edited by Nathan D. Mitchell, 104–22. Washington, DC: Liturgical Conference, 1978.

———. *The Eucharist as a Sacrament of Initiation.* Forum Essays, vol. 2. Chicago: Liturgy Training Publications, 1994.

———. "God at Every Gate." *Worship* 68, no. 3 (1994): 250–56.

———. *Liturgy and the Social Sciences.* Collegeville, MN: Liturgical Press, 1999.

———. "Lyrical Liturgy." *Worship* 67, no. 5 (1993): 460–69.

———. *Meeting Mystery.* Theology in Global Perspective. Maryknoll, NY: Orbis, 2006.

———. "The Once and Future Child: Towards a Theology of Childhood." *Living Light* 12 (1975): 428–30.

———. "That Really Long Prayer." *Worship* 74, no. 5 (2000): 468–77.

———. "The Weight of the Word." *Worship* 77, no. 4 (2003): 356–69.

Montagu, Ashley. *Touching.* New York: Harper Paperbacks, 1986.

Moorhead, John. "The Spirit and the World." *Greek Orthodox Theological Review* 26 (1981): 113–17.

Morice-Brubaker, Sarah. "Place of the Spirit: A Trinitarian Theology of Location." PhD diss., University of Notre Dame, in progress.

Nattiez, Jean-Jacques. *Music and Discourse.* Translated by Carolyn Abbate. Princeton, NJ: Princeton University Press, 1976.

Neunheuser, Burkhard. *Baptism and Confirmation.* Freiburg: Herder, 1964.

———. "Die Liturgie der Kindertaufe: ihre Problematik in der Geschichte." In *Zeichen des Glaubens*, 319–34. Zurich: Benziger Verlag, 1972.

Panicker, Gheevargese. "The Liturgy of St James and Theology of the Trinity." *Studia Liturgica* 30, no. 1 (2000): 112–28.

Pelikan, Jaroslav. *The Emergence of the Catholic Tradition (100–600).* The Christian Tradition, vol. 1. Chicago: University of Chicago Press, 1971.

Pickstock, Catherine. *After Writing: On the Liturgical Consummation of Philosophy.* Malden, MA: Blackwell Publishers, 1998.

Power, David N. "Postmodern Approaches." *Theological Studies* 55 (1994): 684–93.

———. *Sacrament: The Language of God's Giving.* New York: Crossroad, 1999.

Quinn, Frank C. "Made, Not Born: The Church as Baptismal Community." In *Christian Initiation*, 1–30. Valparaiso: Institute of Liturgical Studies.

Raes, Alphonse, ed. "Anaphora of John Chrysostom." In *Prex Eucharistica: Textus e Variis Liturgiis Antiquioribus Selecti*, Spicilegium Fribrugense, vol. 12, 224ff. Fribourg: Editions Universitaires Fribourg Suisse, 1968.

Rahner, Karl. "The Concept of Mystery in Catholic Theology." In *More Recent Writings*, Theological Investigations, vol. IV, 36–73. Baltimore: Helicon Press, 1966.

―――. "The Theology of the Symbol." In *More Recent Writings*, Theological Investigations, vol. IV, 221–52. Baltimore: Helicon Press, 1966.

―――. "Poet and Priest." In *The Theology of the Spiritual Life*, Theological Investigations, vol. III. Baltimore: Helicon Press, 1967.

―――. *The Trinity.* New York: Crossroad Publishing Company, 1999.

Ramsey, Ian. *Religious Language.* New York: Macmillan, 1963.

Redmond, Richard. "Infant Baptism: History and Pastoral Problems." *Theological Studies* 30 (1969): 79–89.

Reedy, William J. *Becoming a Catholic Christian.* New York: William H. Sadlier, 1979.

Riley, Hugh. *Christian Initiation: A Comparative Study of the Interpretation of the Baptismal Liturgy in the Mystagogical Writings of Cyril of Jerusalem, John Chrysostom, Theodore of Mopsuestia, and Ambrose of Milan.* Washington, DC: Catholic University of America, 1974.

Roman Catholic Church. *Ordo Baptismi Parvulorum.* E Civitate Vaticana: Typis Polyglottis Vaticanis, 1973.

―――. *The Rites of the Catholic Church.* Collegeville, MN: Liturgical Press, 1990.

―――. *Rite of Baptism for Children.* Collegeville, MN: Liturgical Press, 2002.

Ross, Susan. *Extravagant Affections: A Feminist Sacramental Theology.* New York: Continuum, 1998.

Rousseau, Olivier. *The Progress of the Liturgy.* Westminster, MD: Newman, 1951.

Rubin, Miri. Corpus Christi: *The Eucharist in Late Medieval Culture.* New York: Cambridge University Press, 1992.

Sawicki, Marianne. *Seeing the Lord: Resurrection and Early Christian Practices.* Minneapolis: Fortress Press, 1994.

Schillebeeckx, Edward. *Christ the Sacrament of the Encounter with God.* Franklin, WI: Sheed and Ward, 1999.

Schrijver, Georges de. "Postmodernity and the Withdrawal of the Divine: A Challenge for Theology." In *Sacramental Presence in a Postmodern Context*, edited by Lieven Boeve and Lambert Leijssen, 39–64. Sterling, VA: Leuven University Press, 2001.

Schwöbel, Christoph. "Editorial Introduction." In *Persons, Divine and Human*, edited by Christoph Schwöbel and Colin E. Gunton, 1–13. Edinburgh: T&T Clark, 1991.

Searle, Mark. "Infant Baptism Reconsidered." In *Living Water, Sealing Spirit*, edited by Maxwell E. Johnson, 365–409. Collegeville, MN: Liturgical Press, 1990.

―――. "Semiotic Analysis of Roman Eucharistic Prayer II." In *Gratias Agamus: Studien Zum Eucharistischen Hochgebet fur Balthasar Fischer*, edited by Andreas Heinz and Heinrich Rennings, 469–87. Freiburg: Herder, 1992.

Seasoltz, Kevin. "Anthropology and Liturgical Theology: Searching for a Compatible Methodology." In *Liturgy and Human Passage*, edited by David Power and Luis Maldonado, 3–13. New York: Seabury Press, 1979.

———. "Another Look at Sacrifice." *Worship* 74, no. 5 (2000): 386–413.

Second Vatican Council. "The Constitution on the Sacred Liturgy." In *Vatican Council II: Volume 1, The Conciliar and Post Conciliar Documents*, edited by Austin Flannery, OP, 1–36. Northport, NY: Costello Publishing Company, 1996.

Seeman, Don. "Otherwise Than Meaning: On the Generosity of Ritual." In *Ritual in Its Own Right: Exploring the Dynamics of Transformation*, edited by Don Handelman and Galina Lindquist, 55–71. New York: Berghahn Books, 2005.

Sperber, Dan. *Rethinking Symbolism*. Translated by Alice Morton. New York: Cambridge University Press, 1975.

Speyr, Adrienne von. *The World of Prayer*. Translated by Graham Harrison. San Francisco: Ignatius Press, 1985.

———. *John: The Farewell Discourses*. San Francisco: Ignatius Press, 1987.

———. *The Birth of the Church*. San Francisco: Ignatius Press, 1991.

———. *The Word Becomes Flesh*. San Francisco: Ignatius Press, 1994.

Staal, Fritz. *Ritual and Mantras: Rules without Meaning*. Delhi: Motilal Banarsidass, 1996.

Stosur, David. "Liturgy and (Post)Modernity: A Narrative Response to Guardini's Challenge." *Worship* 77, no. 1 (2003): 22–41.

Straus, Roger. "Religious Conversion as a Personal and Collective Accomplishment." *Sociological Analysis* 40 (1979): 158–65.

Taft, Robert. "'Eastern Presuppositions' and Western Liturgical Reform." *Antiphon* 5, no. 1 (2000): 10–22.

———. "Ecumenical Scholarship and the Orthodox-Catholic Epiclesis Dispute." *Ostkirchliche Studien* 45 (1996): 201–26.

———. "The Epiclesis Question in the Light of the Orthodox and Catholic Lex Orandi Traditions." In *New Perspectives on Historical Theology: Essays in Memory of John Meyerdorff*, edited by Bradley Nassif. Grand Rapids, MI: Eerdmans, 1996.

———. "Liturgy as Theology." In *Beyond East and West: Problems in Liturgical Understanding*, 233–38. Rome: Edizioni Orientalia Christiana, 2001.

———. "The Structural Analysis of Liturgical Units: An Essay in Methodology." In *Beyond East and West*, 187–202. Rome: Edizioni Orientalia Christiana, 2001.

———. "What Does Liturgy Do? Toward a Soteriology of Liturgical Celebration: Some Theses." In *Beyond East and West*, 239–58. Rome: Edizioni Orientalia Christiana, 2001.

TeSelle, Sallie McFague. *Speaking in Parables*. Philadelphia: Fortress Press, 1975.

Thomas Aquinas. *Summa Theologiae.* Blackfriars edition, edited by Thomas Gilby and T. C. O'Brien. New York: Cambridge, 2006.

———. *Summa Theologica.* Benziger Bros. edition, translated by the Fathers of the English Dominican Province. New York: Benziger Brothers, 1947. Available online at http://www.ccel.org/ccel/aquinas/summa.html. Accessed June 2008–May 2009.

Torrell, Jean-Pierre. *Aquinas's* Summa: *Background, Structure, and Reception.* Translated by Benedict M. Guevin, OSB. Washington, DC: Catholic University of America, 2005.

Turner, George Allen. "Infant Baptism in Biblical and Historical Context." *Wesleyan Theological Journal* 5 (1970): 11–21.

Turner, Victor. *The Forest of Symbols: Aspects of Ndembu Ritual.* Ithaca: Cornell University Press, 1967.

Van Gennep, Arnold. *The Rites of Passage.* New York: Routledge, 2004.

Vial, Theodore M. "Opposites Attract: The Body and Cognition in a Debate over Baptism." *Numen* 46, no. 2 (1999): 121–45.

Vincie, Catherine. *The Role of the Assembly in Christian Initiation.* Forum Essays, vol. 1. Chicago: Liturgy Training Publications, 1993.

Vogels, Walter. *Reading and Preaching the Bible.* Wilmington, DE: Michael Glazier, 1986.

Wainwright, Geoffrey. "Christian Initiation: Development, Dismemberment, Reintegration." In *Christian Initiation,* 31–57. Valparaiso: Institute of Liturgical Studies.

———. Doxology. New York: Oxford University, 1980.

———. "The Language of Worship." In *The Study of Liturgy,* edited by Cheslyn Jones et al., 519–28. New York: Oxford University Press, 1992.

Weil, Louis. "Reclaiming the Larger Trinitarian Framework of Baptism." In *Creation and Liturgy,* edited by Ralph N. McMichael Jr., 129–43. Washington, DC: Pastoral Press, 1993.

Westphal, Merold. "Onto-theo-logical Straw: Reflections on Presence and Absence." In *Postmodernism and Christian Philosophy,* 258–67. Mishawaka, IN: American Maritain Association, 1997.

Winkler, Gabriele. "The Original Meaning of the Prebaptismal Anointing and Its Implications." In *Living Water, Sealing Spirit,* edited by Maxwell E. Johnson. Collegeville, MN: Liturgical Press, 1995.

Wright, David F. "One Baptism or Two: Reflections on the History of Christian Baptism." *Evangelical Review of Theology* 13 (1989): 325–43.

———. "At What Ages Were People Baptized in the Early Centuries?" *Studia Patristica* 30 (1997): 389–94.

———. "Infant Dedication in the Early Church." In *Baptism, the New Testament and the Church,* 352–78. Sheffield, Eng.: Sheffield Academic Press, 1999.

———. "Out, In, Out: Jesus' Blessing of the Children and Infant Baptism." In *Dimensions of Baptism*, edited by Stanley E. Porter and Anthony R. Cross, 188–206. New York: Sheffield Academic Press, 2002.

Zimmerman, Joyce Ann. *Liturgy as Language of Faith*. Lanham, MD: University Press of America, 1988.

Zizioulas, John. "On Being a Person: Towards an Ontology of Personhood." In *Persons, Divine and Human*, edited by Christoph Schwöbel and Colin E. Gunton, 33–46. Edinburgh: T&T Clark, 1991.

———. "The Doctrine of the Holy Trinity: The Significance of the Cappadocian Contribution." In *Trinitarian Theology Today*, 44–60. Edinburgh: T&T Clark, 1995.

Index of Names

Ambrose of Milan, 27, 65
Apostolic Tradition, 75
Aristotle, 168n
Asad, Talal, 47–52, 55, 58, 83–84,
 90–92, 112
Attridge, Harold, 75
Augustine of Hippo, 29–30, 37, 66–
 67, 73, 77, 79–80, 82–83, 101,
 111, 133, 135–38, 158, 164
Austin, J. L., 41–42

Bakke, Odd Magne, 75n
Balthasar, Hans Urs von, 14–19, 31,
 36, 129–34, 150–51, 178–80
Baumstark, Anton, 70n
Bell, Catherine, 56, 107
Bernard of Clairvaux, 50–51
Bradshaw, Paul, 70–71, 75
Brown, Raymond E., 4–10, 24–25,
 150
Bugnini, Annibale, 93–94, 111n

Caputo, John, 168–80
Chauvet, Jean Marie, x, 34–44, 59,
 66–67, 85, 87n, 95n, 96n, 105,
 132, 149, 155, 159–61, 170–71,
 175, 178
Csikszentmihalyi, Mihaly, 90, 102
Csordas, Thomas, 51n
Cyprian of Carthage, 140
Cyril of Jerusalem, 27–29, 74n

Daniélou, Jean, 26

Deflem, Mathieu, 56n
Derrida, Jacques, 40, 44, 96n,
 167–80
Douglas, Mary, 148n

Ferguson, Everett, 26
Foucault, Michel, 49–51, 84, 91–92,
 103
Frank, Georgia, 27–29

Handelman, Don, 47, 55–58,
 109–10
Harmless, William, 111, 133, 148n
Heidegger, Martin, 38–41, 44, 171
Hetherington, E. Mavis, 85–90, 105,
 108, 116
Holeton, David, 77n
Horner, Robyn, 151n, 170n, 172n
Hugh of St. Victor, 24

James, Anaphora of, 20–23
John, Gospel of, 4–10, 25, 29–30,
 36, 65–66, 72, 101, 133, 141–43,
 150, 172
John Chrysostom, 27–29
Johnson, Clare, 62–64, 80, 82, 94,
 108, 120, 145
Johnson, Maxwell, 25, 61, 64–65,
 69, 71–72, 74–80, 82, 145, 149n,
 150n
Julian of Norwich, 146n, 167

Kapferer, Bruce, 110n

Kavanagh, Aidan, 22n, 44, 60–66, 105
Kilmartin, Edward, 22, 126, 149
Klauser, Theodor, 67n
Kockelmans, Joseph, 40

LaCugna, Catherine Mowry, 19–20, 156
Levinas, Emmanuel, 44
Liddell, H. G., 141n

Marion, Jean-Luc, 44–45, 116, 145–46, 150–51, 155, 168–69, 171–80
Mauss, Marcel, 47–49, 91, 103
Merleau-Ponty, Maurice, 52–55, 85–86, 88
Mitchell, Nathan, 45–46, 53, 55n, 58n, 68, 71, 98, 134–35, 166
Montagu, Ashley, 118n
Morice-Brubaker, Sarah, 17

Origen, 26, 54n

Panicker, Gheevargese, 20–22
Pelikan, Jaroslav, 26

Peter Lombard, 157–58
Phillips, Edward, 75
Prosper of Aquitaine, 22

Rahner, Karl, 3, 10–14, 17–18, 20, 32–36, 38n, 131, 152, 162–67
Ross, Susan, 35, 170n
Rubin, Miri, 42

Sawicki, Marianne, 98n, 147
Schillebeeckx, Edward, 38, 152
Scott, Robert, 141n
Searle, Mark, 60–61, 64, 79, 82, 140
Skarsaune, Oskar, 5n
Staal, Fritz, 110n

Taft, Robert, 20, 128
Tertullian, 26, 67, 74, 78, 81–82
Thomas Aquinas, 1–3, 38n, 69, 111, 138, 148, 157–62, 167–68
Torrell, Jean-Pierre, 2

Van Gennep, Arnold, 56
Vygotsky, Lev, 88–90, 105

Winkler, Gabriele, 72–73

Index of Subjects

anamnesis, 18, 37n, 153–54, 177–78
anaphora, 20–22, 36–37, 67, 132, 138
anointing, 71–74, 76, 78–79, 99–100, 108, 110, 117–23, 125, 129, 131, 135, 139–41, 143–45, 149–50, 157
appropriation, 16n, 30, 35–37, 99, 119, 169
assembly, 37, 59, 93, 108–9, 129–33, 137–44, 148, 154–55, 172

baptism:
  and cultic obligation, 178–79
  and death, 24–25, 36, 64–65, 67n, 73, 74n, 76, 77, 79, 98, 124, 172, 178
  history of, 24–30, 70–80
  infant, 43–44, 60–68, 70–80, 81–85, 91–92, 93–127, 128–55, 173, 178
  language model of sacrament, 43–44, 66–68
  in the New Testament, 4, 24–25, 67, 71–72
  paradigm for sacramental theology, 2, 66, 158–62
  pneumatology of, 173
  revival of, 69
  Rite of Baptism for Children, 85, 95–98, 101, 108, 110, 116, 120, 122, 131, 133–34, 143–44, 146–47, 173

as ritual, 58–59, 93–127
and Trinity, 69, 127, 128–55
being-in-the-world, 39–40, 47–48, 51–52, 55, 84, 105, 119, 129, 139, 142
body, 4–10, 20, 27–30, 33–34, 36–37, 44–52, 54–55, 59, 67–68, 82–83, 87, 91, 97, 99, 101, 103–4, 106, 113–14, 117–22, 126–27, 129–55, 158–60, 164–66, 172, 174, 179–81
bread (*see also* Eucharist), 4, 9, 25, 34–35, 138
breastfeeding, 103–4
breath, breathing, 16, 103–4, 121, 139–40, 142, 149–50

catechesis, 26n, 27–29
catechumenate, 64, 74–82, 119
cause, causality, 1–4, 38, 42, 45, 61, 69, 149, 155, 158–62, 165–66, 173, 175
child, children, 36, 46, 55, 61–65, 70, 74, 75–80, 85–110, 113–27, 128–50, 154, 172–73, 177–78
chrism, chrismation (*see also* anointing; oil), 64, 74, 78
Christ, Christology, 2, 4–27, 29–31, 34–37, 42, 59, 64, 66, 69, 71–73, 96, 99, 121–22, 129–33, 135–36, 137–55, 157–61, 167, 172, 179–81

church (*see also* assembly), 1–4,
8–10, 14, 18, 19–27, 29–30, 32,
35, 37, 42, 45, 57, 60–63, 65–67,
72, 75–77, 80–84, 93, 95–101,
112, 115, 117, 128–33, 135–40,
142–43, 147–48, 152–55, 156–
58, 160–61, 164–65, 173, 179,
181
commercium (*see also* exchange), 19
communication, 10–13, 18, 20, 35,
41–42, 61, 66, 83, 95, 105, 121,
162–63, 180
Communion, 35, 37, 43, 49, 63–64,
66–68, 71, 75, 79–80, 108,
180–81
confession, 49, 75, 81
confirmation, 63–64, 74, 78, 80, 98,
108
creation, 6, 9, 11–15, 18, 28, 31, 33,
43, 54, 102, 122, 141–42, 148,
154, 166, 179
cross, 96–97, 110, 117–20, 122,
125, 132, 134–35, 137, 141, 144,
147, 155–56, 167
culture, cultural efficacy, 1, 3–4, 12,
19, 23, 27–31, 32, 35–36, 39–40,
42, 44–48, 51–52, 55–61, 63,
68–70, 80–88, 91–92, 93, 95, 98–
110, 113, 115–19, 125, 128–29,
142–44, 148, 149, 151–52, 154–
57, 160, 165–67, 173, 179–80

death, 24–25, 36, 64–65, 67n, 73,
74n, 76, 77, 79, 98, 124, 151,
172, 178
disappropriation, 35–37, 95–102,
110, 129–38, 178
discipline, 3, 9, 23, 28–29, 45, 47–
52, 67, 83–84, 90–92, 122, 136,
138, 140, 150, 169, 179
doctrine, 10, 26, 109n, 145
doxology, 156

Eastern, 20, 24n, 28, 72, 74–76, 91

economy, economic, 3–4, 10–26,
31, 35, 42, 57–58, 68–69, 85,
128–30, 147–55, 156, 166, 167,
169–72, 175–76
epiclesis, 20–22
ethics, ethical (*see also* obligation),
34–37, 132, 178
Eucharist, 2, 4, 21–23, 25–28, 33–
34, 36–37, 42–43, 67–71, 77n,
78–80, 132, 135, 138, 142, 157,
165n, 181
eucharistic prayer, 36–37, 43, 67,
70, 132
event, 12–15
ex opere operato, 42, 68, 109n, 133,
142, 151–52, 157
exchange, 19, 35–43, 66, 105, 134,
141, 155, 167–72, 176–77
exodus, 6–9, 26, 73
exorcism, 73–74, 146

feminist perspectives, 35, 170
first bath, 106–7

gift (*see also* givenness; return-gift),
3–5, 7, 9, 13, 16, 18, 21, 28, 35–
38, 40n, 44, 64, 68–69, 98, 100,
130–31, 133n, 143, 146, 148,
150–55, 156–57, 161, 167–81
givenness, 168–81
grace, 1–3, 10–18, 21–22, 33–39,
42–44, 46, 60, 68–70, 74, 79,
81, 98, 100, 105, 111, 123, 127,
128–37, 142, 151–52, 158–61,
165, 170–71

Holy Spirit. *See* Spirit

identity, 21–23, 27–31, 34–37, 41,
44–47, 49, 51–52, 56, 59, 61–62,
66, 68–72, 80–81, 84–85, 91–92,
93–99, 104–5, 107–9, 111–27,
128–54, 175, 179–80
incarnation, 11–14, 151, 172

infant, 25, 30, 43–44, 46, 59, 60–92, 93–127, 128–50, 154–55, 157, 162, 172–75, 177–79

Judaism, 4–10

kenosis, 37, 131–32, 146

language, 3, 10, 15–16, 19–22, 34, 36, 38–44, 46–47, 50, 54, 60, 67–68, 76, 85–86, 87n, 89, 91, 94, 104–5, 138, 142, 150, 154, 160–61, 166n, 170
lex orandi, 22
Liturgy of the Hours, 50–51
Logos (see also Word; Christ), 11–12, 33, 40, 129–30, 163
love, 3, 9–10, 12–18, 31, 34, 36–37, 42, 46, 84, 111, 129–32, 135, 143, 146, 148, 150, 153–54, 168–74, 177–78, 181

marginality, marginalization, 45–46, 58–59, 177
memorial (see also *anamnesis*), 20–22, 25
ministry, 14–15, 30–31, 69, 78, 93, 99, 147, 154
modern, 1, 4, 10–23, 29, 47, 49, 61, 64, 75, 80–83, 91, 99, 111, 162
music, 53, 86
mystagogy, 26–29, 76, 79

obligation, 34–38, 138, 167–80
offer, offering, 11–14, 16, 26, 30, 34–37, 54, 60, 68, 71, 93, 95–96, 101, 105, 113, 115–16, 118–19, 121–24, 132–33, 135–39, 170, 172–81
oikonomia (see also economy), 3, 155–56, 169, 171, 179
oil, 72–73, 99, 106, 108, 112, 117, 119–20, 122, 126, 139, 142, 150
original sin, 64, 73, 77, 79, 99, 145–46, 154–55

parable, 134
paschal, 64, 74, 78, 81, 149, 159
passion, 2, 18, 117, 130, 132, 136, 149–51, 153, 159–60, 180
passive, passivity, 15–16, 32, 47–48, 52, 62, 88, 95, 120, 131, 171
Passover, 6–9
plan. See *oikonomia*
poetry, 38–39, 141
postmodern, 1, 145, 166–69
presence, 5, 7, 14, 21–22, 29, 41, 98, 117, 119, 130–32, 153, 171–72, 175, 181
   in absence, 34–35
   eucharistic, 33, 69n, 165n, 181
   prophetic, 5, 121, 134–37, 146, 148

reconciliation, 154
return-gift, 35–38, 41, 43, 168n, 169–72, 175–76, 179
ritual play, 123–27
ritual process, 47, 49–52, 55–56, 59, 70, 83–85, 88–92, 95, 102, 105, 107, 112, 124, 128, 138–39, 179

Sabbath, 5–8
sacrament, 1–4, 9, 14, 16–31, 32–57, 50, 52, 57–62, 65–68, 74, 76–79, 93, 100, 105, 111, 128–29, 132, 133–42, 148–55, 156–67, 170–71, 178–79
sacrifice, 15, 132, 135–38, 179n
salvation (see also soteriology), 3–31, 35–36, 43, 58, 60, 69, 98–99, 123, 128, 131–34, 137, 146–54, 159–61, 166–67
self-communication. *See* communication
self-development, 44, 48, 59, 81, 89, 95, 102, 112, 114
self-gift, 4, 16, 18, 36, 175–80
sign and signification, 1–3, 5–9, 32, 38, 54–57, 67, 72–73, 78, 89, 96–97, 101, 110–12, 117–22,

124, 126, 135, 137, 139, 141–44,
149, 152, 156–67, 174
soteriology (*see also* salvation), 3
space, 17, 28–29, 58, 90, 101, 108,
120, 131, 133, 139, 151–52,
154–55, 172, 179–81
Spirit (*see also* Trinity), 2, 4–26, 28,
31, 37n, 38, 64–65, 69, 72–74,
78, 81, 99–100, 108, 128–33,
135, 137–43, 146–55, 156–81
suffering, 141–42, 145–46, 149,
154, 180

technique, 48–49, 51, 84, 88, 91–92,
103–6, 112–26, 140
technology of the self, technology
of the community (*see also* technique; ritual process), 49, 84,
91–92, 95, 138

temple, 5–9, 129, 131, 135, 137,
139, 148, 180
Trinity, 2–23, 27, 31, 32–33, 35–37,
59, 65, 69, 72–73, 76, 81, 93,
101, 127, 128–35, 137–39,
142–43, 146–50, 152, 154, 157,
161–64, 166–68, 172, 178–80

Vatican Council II, 37, 59–64,
69–71, 79, 81, 93–97, 110, 115,
128, 132

water, 4–9, 25, 28, 30, 65, 67–68,
70–74, 79, 101, 106–7, 109–10,
112, 117, 119, 120–23, 125–26,
139–42, 146, 150, 155, 158, 161,
174
Word (*see also* Christ; Trinity), 2, 5–9,
11–16, 18, 21, 30–31, 132, 136,
138, 142, 148–55, 162–64, 168